China's Quest for Liberty

China's Quest for Liberty

A Personal History of Freedom

Promise Hsu

Preface by Ellis Sandoz

St. Augustine's Press

South Bend, Indiana

Library of Congress Cataloging in Publication Data
Hsu, Promise.
China's quest for liberty: a personal history of freedom / Promise Hsu; foreword by Ellis Sandoz.
pages cm
ISBN 978-1-58731-109-3 (hardback)
1. Christianity – China. 2. Church and state – China. 3. Liberty – Religious aspects – Christianity. 4. Hsu, Promise – Religion. I. Title.
BR1288.H78 2014
275.1'083 – dc23   2014004578

St. Augustine's Press
www.staugustine.net

Table of Contents

Preface

I take great personal pleasure in seeing Promise Hsu's account of *China's Quest for Liberty* finally come to publication. There is a biographical dimension to the event that makes it so. Eight years ago the author and I had an email exchange as he worked to establish an Institute for Liberty in Beijing, as he said. Ultimately he asked me: Why do you have Liberty and we don't?

Good question. The whole history of our very different civilizations is the likely answer.

But I eventually replied succinctly: Because we believe in God and you don't. I thought of the national motto stamped on our coins and currency, the proclamation of God-given rights in the Declaration of Independence, the constitutional protections including especially freedom of conscience in the First Amendment.

How this answer reverberated through the consciousness of our author and at least partly served to energize his life and researches is the story so elegantly told in the extraordinary volume before you. It is a tale of an ongoing pilgrimage both intellectual and spiritual in its scope. It touches on the life and mind of person and society as the quest continues. It is a highly creative chronicle that enlightens our understanding of contemporary China and tells the story of one of its finest minds.

Ellis Sandoz
2014

Prologue

An Invitation

Thank you for spending your time opening this small book. In the following pages, you will find out how a fellow human inhabitant of the earth has been learning to look at himself and the world he has been living in.

It is about an unexpected journey a Chinese journalist has taken to pursue freedom. You will meet the people and their stories he has stumbled upon. Some of them are Chinese. Some are residents of other parts of the globe. Some are no longer in this world. Some are still around here. Their stories happened in such diverse fields or disciplines as politics, business, humanities, science and technology, government agencies and non-governmental organizations. Some took place as daily life and some occurred in detentions or disasters.

With these people and their stories, you will see some dimensions of the world that have been basically obscured not only in China but also in the global public square. With these dimensions, the journalist has been led, step by step, to find, paradoxically, the hope in the depth of hopelessness, the strength in acknowledging weakness, the change in substance by, among other things, keeping the form unchanged for at least a while, the youth in growing up despite growing old, the invisible in the visible, the imperishable in the perishable, the reality in the shadow of numerous fake realities, and the freedom gained not mainly through human efforts but as mercy and grace from the one who created humans and other beings.

As well as digging out the overlooked Christian background in the rise of the sanctity of human life, creative culture, constitutionalism, work as a vocation, modern management, servant leadership, and catchphrases like "the global village" and "The medium is the message," the author tells of insider observations about the rise of Christianity in China generally and about Shouwang Church in particular. Through sharing these findings, this book aims at learning to show how the one who made the universe rules the world and how this creator sets his creatures free by himself.

That said, it is only a very humble beginning of a perhaps much longer road than imagined. "Now we see but a poor reflection as in a mirror; then we shall see face to face. Now I know in part; then I shall know fully, even as I am fully known."[1]

1   Corinthians 13:12.

Chapter 1
Why Bother Having Me Here?

Any time could be the last moment of one's life in this world. When I was asked by Dr. Arne H. Fjeldstad, the CEO of The Media Project in late 2011, what can be put on my tombstone as a headline over my life, I pondered for a few days. Then, gradually, I got no clearer answer in my heart than this feeling: I have lived for 35 years; it is the tender mercy of the one who created me that sustains my life. It is also this mercy that enables me to become a testimony of it. I wish an epitaph could be like this one: He was a witness to his creator's love (in both bad and good ways).

I don't know what my legacy may be after I die. It might be better if there were no epitaph at all. But such a question about looking back on one's life really helps me to think over how to spend the rest of one's life no matter how long or short it will be. Everyday life could give the illusion that the sun would always rise again. Once one is born, death will be closer and certain to come. If there is any sure sign that all human beings are equal, it is at least the inevitability of death. The question I was asked came as a wake-up call that should have arisen more often.

Unable to breathe and thus without crying, I was brought back to life after being born on the morning of February 23, 1976 at a hospital where my father worked. I heard from my parents about this when I was a child. My mother said I was born at a time when the night shift was about to end and the morning shift had come so that there were enough hands available. Yet only years after I became an adult did I consciously reflect on what the rescue would mean in my life. Without it, I would have left this world just on my arrival. Long before I could know anything, efforts had been under way to ensure my survival.

But prior to being able to realize and appreciate how crucial those efforts were, I would question: why bother letting me come to this world at all, especially as I found it difficult or meaningless to do some things. I was and am not strong physically. I was and remain not good at mathematics. I would easily get shy and nervous, though I am better off now after getting to know more about this world I have lived in for more than three decades. I had no patience and thus did not have real faith before I met some people who helped me to know about faith, which is "being sure of what we hope for and certain of what we do not see."[2] Even now, faith and patience are still qualities I lack on many occasions. Thus it is no surprise that hopelessness has been an underlying theme I was unable to shake off.

Another act of mercy I came to be ever more thankful for was that learning English has been my favorite part of life since I was an 11-year-old middle school student. That was in 1987 when my parents and sister helped me enroll at a local school that has been the best in a small county of China's eastern province of Jiangsu where I was born and spent the first 14 years of my life. I do not know why I grew fond of English. I did not do very well on school exams when I started learning this foreign language, which was compulsory in most of China's middle and high school education. I had a couple of English audio cassettes and I found the reading musical. Then in 1988 or 1989 at the latest, I began to tune in to short-wave radio programs from BBC (British Broadcasting Corporation), VOA (Voice of America), RFI (Radio France Internationale), CBC (Canadian Broadcasting Corporation) and some other international broadcasters. That was the first time I got to hear how the native speakers spoke English. I also had glimpses of the photocopy editions of some of the world's leading medical journals like *The Lancet* and *The American Journal of Cardiology*. It was my father who advised the hospital where he worked then to subscribe to these magazines. My mother, who originally was a traditional Chinese opera actress, was a librarian at the hospital in the 1980s. And this unexpectedly turned out to be the starting point of my learning experience of international journalism.

However, to survive the grade-centered educational system seemed an inevitably major concern, at least for someone like me who could not

2   Hebrews 11:1.

easily deal with numerous tests and exams throughout the school years. It was not until attending university that my somewhat independent life began. Being able to study English and International Journalism at Beijing Broadcasting Institute, China's leading institution of higher learning in broadcast journalism, was far beyond my expectations. I expected that enrolling in any local college would be my good fortune. I myself did not sign up for the Institute. It was my father who suggested doing so. Over the next five years, I had much more freedom to develop my interest-motivated study. History, philosophy, politics, sociology, literature, natural sciences—these were the subjects I wanted to read.

Despite this, hopelessness remained a part of my life. Enjoying much more freedom also meant I was much more exposed to exploring the meaning of my existence. Any possible relationship between nature and mind or body and soul, the place of an individual being in the universe, the origin of the universe, why love exists, will love also die, why bother having me here ... questions like these were not easy to address. It was in my third year in college that I began to read some articles and books that helped me embark on a spiritual journey that has taken me through different stages until today. A major breakthrough for me was getting to know something about God in the Christian context. Jesus on the cross showed me a unique image of the creator of the universe. Despair and hope, weakness and strength, death and life, body and soul, creator and creation, were paradoxically linked. Such an image of God gave me unprecedented comfort and consolation. However, since I only had a rather dim awareness of this image, hope remained elusive.

I wondered why time, my time at least, kept passing without an end. After finishing five years of undergraduate study, I spent almost six years working at the English news service that later turned into the English news channel of China's state-run broadcaster, China Central Television, or CCTV. It was a place I was reluctant to join, mainly due to the fact that it has been a government-controlled news organization. I tried other options but found them unfit for me. With the wisdom of hindsight, I benefited a lot from learning the basic practice of reporting on largely domestic and global politics despite evident censorship. The working environment was international with colleagues coming from Europe, North America, Oceania, and Asia. But in 2005, I finally decided to leave there and begin a personal research project. This project was to explore how an individual person, an organization, a society, could be free. Besides translating two books concerning the general history of freedom, I contacted the two authors, both professors in American universities, and hundreds of other experts from different continents in fields as various as politics, economics, sociology, philosophy, theology, history, journalism, and natural sciences. This helped me form a preliminary picture of what the human condition was like, and laid a conscious foundation for making sense of the complicated world.

In a sense, this research was a follow-up to my college study. With years of working experience, I found it necessary to return to the fundamentals. Throughout the process, the image of God I encountered on campus resurfaced. It seemed because of his beckoning that I was setting out on this journey. A personal Exodus, I supposed. The examples were not only the Israelites going out of Egypt and slavery but the Christian church's surprise rise in the first century and afterwards. To me, the faith in this God made a unique contribution to the partial realization of human freedom, first in the Israelites and then in the Roman Empire and later in Europe, North America and some other parts of the globe. Because of this faith, idolatry—the worship of great people or anyone other than the creator of the universe himself—lost its mass appeal. Human beings were reminded of their own limitations and even more serious character flaws—a sinful nature or rebellion against their maker. Problems like self-centeredness, authoritarianism, totalitarianism, materialism, nihilism and nationalism were but symptoms of idolatry. The exodus, in essence, was from idolatry and my sinful nature that included hopelessness.

The quest for freedom was hard. I did not think of trying to emigrate to other countries and I did not think I wanted to do that. For a year after quitting my state-run broadcaster job, I did not find a suitable place to work, and could only continue my personal research. The choice I made understandably disappointed the expectations of my superiors who were very kind to me, and more severely, my parents. My fiancée was not fully against my decision but we eventually parted company in early 2009 partly owing to the different paths we followed. Three years later, I have not yet recovered from this breakup. My parents gradually became sympathetic to my choice after coming to stay with me in Beijing in 2009 and knowing more about my life. The exodus affected not just myself but had implications for my loved ones. I feel very sorry for the harm brought to them by what I have done.

At times, I myself would worry about what kind of future lay ahead. Pressure came from my family. It also came from my own concern about my livelihood and my place in society. I am grateful that when basically finishing the first-stage research in 2006, I had a chance to join a team launching a new business magazine where I began tentatively sharing the gains of my research by learning to write articles. In the following five years, more chances came and I was able to write more articles for a number of magazines. The experience helped me comprehend the situation of privately-held but still state-controlled media companies. At the same time, it opened my mind to the business world, where I unexpectedly found some large and yet under-appreciated footprints of the Christian faith in shaping the field of management. Compared with politics and economics, management was a newer discipline and more concerned with the building up of a person or an organization rather than institutions and numbers. This worldview helped me learn to break down barriers between different fields and disciplines and to come straight to the common issues facing common people.

Hope was growing in my life, and not just because I survived the departure by being given the opportunities to share my research gains as a journalist. More importantly, I was given a surprise opportunity to meet a group of people who bore a striking resemblance to some early churches that I got to know in my research. A professor of political science in the southern American state of Louisiana whom I contacted during my research in mid-February 2006 introduced me a month later to a book editor in Shanghai who brought me to see this group of people in early September when he visited Beijing. Interestingly, neither the American professor nor the Shanghai editor knew them. After arriving in Beijing, the editor got a text message from his friend in a southern Chinese city about a place where those people met. On a Sunday morning in early September that year, we went to a room of a high-rise office building at Zhongguancun in northwest Beijing, known as "China's Silicon Valley." It was the first time I had gone to a house church, an unregistered Christian church. I had heard about these churches, mainly through Western media reports. But that visit, and regular attendance on almost every Sunday later on, gave me a feeling that was very different from most of those reports. I was baptized there with more than 50 other people including my fiancée in the afternoon of December 16.

The five years since then were a transformative period of time when I was no longer just studying the history of freedom, but getting to understand freedom itself in a light that was different from the conventional wisdom I had been familiar with. Sunday worships, weekly Bible studies, camp meetings, learning to pray, communication with other people in the church, facing the authorities' crackdown, all these things helped me gradually realize and feel ever more deeply that real freedom was not gained through human efforts, including my personal exodus, though they were not unimportant, but by the mercy and grace of the one who created me and saved me from the bondage of my rebellion against him and all other rebel powers by himself dying with my rebel self and being resurrected with his own eternal self in me. The search for liberty, and the mere fact that there could be a living being which is me, were out of his love.

Yet, such a transformation did not mean hopelessness in me was gone. At this stage, I found despair a paradoxically hopeful thing. For a limited being and sinner, the absence of hope seemed inevitable. For years, I had not known how to be freed from hopelessness. Now, I knew it was hopelessly impossible for me to get out of my despair on my own or by any human effort. I came to understand why the apostle Paul acknowledged he would boast all the more gladly about his weaknesses. I had lived long in a world where the autonomy of human beings was encouraged or even already taken for granted. But now, freedom would not mean being autonomous but being reliant on my creator who had the real power to set me free by giving faith, hope and love. However, such a transformation did not—and does not—redeem me from experiencing the pain and agony of my weaknesses. Sometimes, I would still be an autonomous man as if I were alone without the presence of God. To both my shame and relief, I felt the compassion and forgiveness of God had not forsaken me in the wake of my wandering from him.

In 2011, my journey seemed to enter into a further stage. I basically wrapped up the life of working at privately-held business or news and general-interest magazines. A major reason was that censorship and self-censorship, which remain prevalent in both state and privately-run media, would continue to prevent a journalist with more than 10 years of working experience in such an environment from any new growth. Besides the long-standing tradition of political censorship, the increasing profit-oriented media mindset and seemingly ever more fragmented life-style have made censorship a more complex and broader phenomenon. A plan of book writing was conceived early in the year. It would be a continuation of my research project about freedom. One aim was to give an unabridged account of the more important part of what I had learned over those years in both holistic and specific ways. I had never had a serious and bold idea of writing a book before. Yet it might be a new learning experience that would help me overcome the problem of self-censorship and grow into a more complete witness to the truth. Almost a year from then, the writing continues.

Compared with the initial stage of my odyssey, 2011 was a year that turned out to be both easier and more difficult. This time, my parents have supported my choice. They have known much more of my life after staying with me for most of the time since early 2009. My mother is the first member of my family who believes in the Christian God. That was as early as in 1985 when her brother, who was a naval officer and had not been a Christian, told her about Genesis. But she was not baptized until 2007. And in 2009 she began attending the Sunday worship of the house church where I was baptized. My father, though not yet baptized, also visited our church and read the church magazine where I have been an editorial member since 2008. In late November 2011, we moved to our new home in the far southwest of the city ending my 12 years of life renting numerous places after leaving the college. [The place is at the foot of a mountain where the ruins of The Temple of the Cross, which was built in as early as Tang Dynasty (A.D. 618-907) and is one of the earliest Christian churches ever found in China, are situated. I did not become aware of this fact until August 2010 when the editorial team of the church magazine had a day of retreat visiting the ruins and a Christian family who helps look after the ruins and maintains an orchard nearby. It is also close to a sub-company of one of the world's largest corporations and a cave site where fossil remains of Homo erectus, known as Peking Man, have been discovered.] It would help reduce the living costs. My parents and I bought the new home in 2008 for the planned wedding. Among the places we had seen in Beijing, that was the only one we could afford. One reason for a lower price here is that the flats, which were constructed by a local property developer, do not have a property right recognized by the state—a phenomenon more common in China since the property market was partially opened in the late 1990s. My parents offered to pay for the cost of "zhuangxiu," a Chinese expression without an English equivalent, which means changing an empty space with slabs of concrete in an apartment building into a livable home. In China, new flats would be mostly sold as concrete shells furnished with only such basic facilities as electrical wires and water pipes.

A difficulty that I did not have in 2005 is that now the church I attend has been facing an unprecedented crisis. I will not go into detail about the crisis for it has received extensive media coverage worldwide. I wrote an article in April and part of it appeared in *Christianity Today*, a US-based international Christian periodical. The crisis was ranked fifth among the magazine's top ten news stories in 2011.[3] The church has been unable to use its purchased venue or rent any indoor space for worship since April 2011 because of the continued intervention of the authorities. Major church co-workers including pastors, elders and deacons have been under house arrest. Every Sunday, congregants who attended the outdoor worship would be detained for between a few hours and two days. It is still unclear when the situation will change. As a member of the church, I have been facing a challenge. I supported the decision of the church governing committee, which is comprised of two pastors and three elders, to hold the outdoor service and remain so. My mother and I attended the two outdoor worships in November 2009 after our church was forced to move out of its earlier leased space. This time, my mother joined the first one on April 10. Along with many other parishioners, she was detained and taken to a police station. She was released in the

3   For details, see http://www.christianitytoday.com/ct/2012/january/top-news-2011.html .

evening after my father went to bring her home. At that time, I was in America participating in a seminar for Chinese Christian journalists co-sponsored by The Media Project and The Center on Religion and Chinese Society at Purdue University. People at the seminar were concerned about and praying for what was happening in Beijing. After coming back the next week, I learned from my parents that a police officer threatened to confiscate my mother's mobile phone and handbag. My mother refused and told the police officer that she would jump from the police station building if he insisted. She later told the police officer that she had been a deputy of the People's Congress in the city she came from and showed him the certificate. She said it was lawful to be a Christian in China and the People's Congress had the power to supervise the work of the government. After this, the police officer softened his attitude and freed my mother later in the day.

My parents and I discussed what to do next. We decided not to go to the planned place for outdoor worship, because our home would be guarded by police officers or people they sent if my mother and I were detained. That would block me from doing a thing that just started. It was not only about my book writing but also about a new fellowship or a small group that was just formed to explore and study the church and the broader society across China. But I still cannot avoid thinking about my decision to go to the police station to wait for the release of the detained congregants. One point that I see from the Bible is that as a member of the church, which is the body of Christ, I am not alone or autonomous but belong to the body. The church is under persecution and I am a part of the body being persecuted. Yet, not all the parts of the body have the same function. I have been thinking that I would continue doing my part as a witness to God by mainly writing articles and perhaps books for the general public about God and his deeds in the fields I have been led to be familiar with. But that does not mean I would not be willing to be detained because of my faith. I suppose the time has not arrived for me if it is the way I am called by God to go. Having written so, I do not think my choice is just what God wills. Weakness has been within me. I do not want myself to be followed by police officers or plainclothes police wherever I go. I do not want my family members to be treated likewise. I do not want my parents and I to be put under house arrest. I do not want us to be forcibly sent back to our home town. But I do want God to help me follow him regardless of what I personally want.

The first Sunday, or the Lord's Day, in 2012 fell on New Year's day. My mother and I got up at about 5:30 in the morning and spent nearly two hours on a bus and subway before reaching the outdoor worship place at Zhongguancun. We still chose not to be detained although we were ready for any possible detention. We did not bring any official documents like the identity cards, and we agreed not to tell them our names or where our home was if we were taken to a police station. We thought we might not be able to go to the top of the platform. But we did. We went there through a side entrance. We were not told by a police officer to leave the place until we had been standing there for a few minutes, during which time I prayed in my heart and took a photo of the square in the morning sunlight of the New Year's day. We went down to the ground floor of the square from where we saw the main entrance had been closed off. We did not see any of our fellow churchgoers that we knew. It was at about 8:30, just the starting time for the worship. That day, at least 49 people were taken to 13 police stations. The last two were not freed from the Zhongguancun Street police station until the small hours of January 3.

That I write at some length about the church's outdoor worship in my personal reflection on my personal pilgrimage is that the church and its situation mean something vital to my life. It is from the church that I have seen a promising dimension of the world that would otherwise have kept me worse than pessimistic. It has helped me to know more and more about the creator of the world that includes both the seen and unseen. The situation of the church indicates a deeper reality where the spiritual warfare is notable. On the surface, the persecution is from the authorities and it is an issue of human rights and religious freedom. But in the context of the Bible, it is a wrestling against "the spiritual forces of evil in the heavenly realms" rather than "flesh and blood,"[4] And it is not the people or the created beings but the creator who will solve the problem. Jesus Christ, the head of the church and the real ruler of the world, has shown us how he set his people free. Without knowing him and his way,

4   Ephesians 6:12.

humans would have no choice but to resort to the way of "flesh and blood." In the country where I was born and have lived until now, the way of Jesus is still quite unfamiliar to many people. And I am one of them. I myself have known him and his way for just a few years, and I know I still wander from him and his way. What the authorities do to the church is, in essence, only what anyone who does not know Jesus would do or what anyone who does know him might still do. What the church experiences is, in essence, only what any other church in the world experiences, however different the form of persecution may be.

The January 10 deadline for this personal reflection is approaching fast. I do not know to what extent I have answered the questions from Arne. As I look back on what has happened in my life so far, I find more and more of my past that followed the way of "flesh and blood" and I can't help bowing my head in shame. It happened in the relationship with my creator, myself, my family members, friends, colleagues, all the living beings I have met. When I arrived here, I think of a key question from Arne that I have not yet answered: where will I be ten years from now? That will be when I am 45 if I remain alive here on the earth. I pray my Lord may not forsake me as he has not ever before and enable me to be with him and follow him as much as he wants so that I could be a witness to his love much more faithfully and in much less bad way before his ever closer coming.

After I sent the above to Arne, he encouraged me to answer his follow-ups. Regarding the specific issues of censorship, one prominent thing is that once it is related to China, an article or a program will face much tougher examination from the authorities of various levels. In 2008 and 2009, I wrote a column at *Global Entrepreneur*, a leading Chinese business magazine, exploring the spiritual and intellectual foundations of a free and responsible society. I tried to write some stories about what is happening in China, for example, the rise of spiritual entrepreneurs, the people who established independent churches or faith-based non-profit organizations. The executive editor of the magazine did not object to publishing them but the authorities did not approve. It is the same at other magazines or other forms of media organizations in China I worked with. For a few years after leaving the state-run television, I wanted to try different privately-held media companies to minimize censorship and self-censorship. They proved to have somewhat less control but as long as the content is about China, the situation remains almost the same. But a benefit was that I was able to become friends with colleagues of different working places.

I consciously did not accept any formal leadership positions during my years in journalism. A major reason was that I wanted to focus on keeping an independent life as much as possible so that I would be less influenced by the ruling party-centered ideological circumstances. In my boyhood and later years, I consistently managed not to join the Youth League of the Communist Party or the party itself. Since early 2011, I have been taking part in leading an independent research fellowship aimed at writing about China and the wider world without censorship. Along with learning to lead the Bible study and attend or help organize some international meetings, the independent thinking and the gains from it over the past years evidently helped me in witnessing the start-up and growth of the independent group. But a lack of rich leadership experience is apparently my weakness.

The key people who have helped influence and shape me into the person I am today? In fact, I have mentioned most of them in the earlier part of this chapter. There are many and not just a single person. My parents and sister and school teachers led me to learn the basics of life. Besides bringing me up and making me a largely healthy (not strong though) person, my mother and father helped me to develop hobbies like learning to write ancient Chinese calligraphy and enjoying seeing chickens and other small animals. The inventors and producers of short-wave radios provided me an unforgettable opportunity in my childhood to hear the voice of BBC in my small and poor hometown. My father helped me choose the university and the major I would study. The college teachers from at home and abroad and the international colleagues I have met thereafter helped me enlarge the foundation of international journalism. The experts of various disciplines and fields in different continents I contacted helped enrich my understanding of the world. The church in which I was baptized helped me see a hopeful living reality I had not seen in China before. The Media Project and some other sponsors of international seminars and symposiums further broadened my horizons and mind. And in both negative and positive ways, my fiancée I parted company with and the break-up itself helped me reflect on the issue of marriage and unexpectedly helped guide me to make sense of what the Bible says about this perennial topic.

Chapter 2
God and the Essence of Liberty

A Preliminary Inquiry into the History of Freedom

Thanks to the internet, I have been able to contact hundreds of scholars in America and Europe and Asia about the history of freedom since August 2005, a little over a month before I formally quit my job at China's state broadcaster China Central Television to start up the liberty project.[5] It was during the course of this inquiry that I got to know Professor Ellis Sandoz and many other friends. They are political philosophers, historians, theologians, legal experts, journalists, economists and even natural scientists, some of whom are Nobel laureates. Not only did they send me their thoughts by hundreds of emails, they sent me scores of books and articles. I have really learned a lot from them and I am so grateful to them.

Then the question is, what on earth have I learned so far? There are certainly many important things concerning the specific aspects of liberty. Two years are no doubt far too short for me to figure out all these points. But for now, the single most important thing I would like to share is this: Faith in God as the Lord is the beginning of freedom.

When I began my project, the main question I asked myself was how and why freedom both as a value and as an institution figured prominently only in the Western society and even now still largely remains

5 This chapter was originally written as a paper delivered at the annual international conference of the American Political Science Association, August 30-September 2, 2007. The meeting was held in Chicago, Illinois. This presentation was made at Eric Voegelin Society's Panel 3: Scientism, Westernization, and Liberty in Chinese Politics at 4:15 p.m. September 1, 2007.

confined to this part of the world? The motive for this query is simple. I was very much curious and eager to know the elements that might have led to the institutionalization of liberty in the West with the hope that similar conditions might be established in China and elsewhere in the world.

The more I knew about the growth of freedom in the West, the more I was captivated by the role of faith in God as the Lord in the making of a free and responsible civilization. There may have been various reasons why liberty largely failed in the non-Western world. For me, a major reason for the stillbirth of freedom in the non-Western societies is that the bedrock for the building of liberty was missing in these cultures. That is, faith in God as the Lord did not become the vital part of the non-Western consciousness. One cannot say that individuals in those parts of the world did not want freedom. Yet in societies like China, with which I am relatively familiar, freedom could not stand a realistic chance of becoming a positive value or a viable institution because the rule by men instead of the rule of law was the constant pattern. For these societies, law was virtually the will of men in power so that it is meaningless to call for the rule of law. Without faith in God as the Lord, freedom with the popular (mis)conception of doing anything one wants could only be perceived by anyone in power as a threat to the established order. However for societies where faith in God as the Lord figures prominently, law is independent of the will of humans. It is the will of God, the Lord. The only truly right thing one can do is to do the divine will. As Ronald Reagan once put it, "the freedom to choose a Godly path is the essence of liberty."[6] For me, that freedom could basically survive in the West is not by accident, nor mainly by the Western individuals' extraordinarily persistent struggle for liberty, but by their prominent obedience to the will of God compared to the rest of the world. And may I put it in another way: a free West is simply a by-product of its continued faith in God as the Lord in spite of the rise and fall of various forms of idolatry.

6   Ronald Reagan, *Proclamation 4826 National Day of Prayer, 1981, March 19, 1981*, http://www.reagan.utexas.edu/archives/speeches/1981/31981b.htm .

Then, how and why was there such exceptional obedience to God in the West? What is the will of God? What is God like? And, does God exist at all?

I am not sure if I have got the answers to all these questions. I will present them to you as clearly as I can. But before that, let me make it clear that the exploration into these questions has brought me more than insight into the historical facts of how freedom grew in the West. Perhaps far more importantly, it also has brought me insight into "the ultimate questions of human existence,"[7] including those of my existence. For the first time in my life, I began to become clearly conscious of the existence of God and of his personal relationship with me. This, to me, is the most important landmark in my life since I was born 31 years ago. Without it, my understanding of freedom would never be like what I'm sharing with you now. What exactly begot this "leap of being"?[8]

---

7   On the relationship between freedom and truth, see John 8:31–47, especially 31–32, "To the Jews who had believed him, Jesus said, 'If you hold to my teaching, you are really my disciples. Then you will know the truth, and the truth will set you free,'" and Professor John W. Danford's analysis in his *Roots of Freedom: A Primer on Modern Liberty*, (ISI Books, 2000), especially Chapter 2, also Professor Sandoz's insight: "In a time when liberal democracy appears to be the only practicable alternative to authoritarianism or worse, it is precisely requisite that the ultimate questions of human existence be explored and, so far as possible, that the truth of reality be recovered as a living possession. Only thus can it be woven into the fabric of representative free government as the texture of political order, civic consciousness, and institutionalized statecraft in service of the good life. This, it appears to me at least, is the world-historic task of an authentic politics of truth – if a plunge into the abyss is to be avoided." Ellis Sandoz, *The Politics of Truth and Other Untimely Essays: The Crisis of Civic Consciousness*, (University of Missouri Press, 1999), 42.

8   "The leap in being, the experience of divine being as world-transcendent, is inseparable from the understanding of man as human. The personal soul as the sensorium of transcendence must develop parallel with the understanding of a transcendent God. Now, wherever the leap in being occurs experientially, the articulation of the experience has to grapple with the mystery of death and immortality. Men are mortal; and what is immortal is divine. This holds true for both Greeks and Israelites." in Eric Voegelin, *Israel and Revelation* (Louisiana State University Press, 1994), 235, and

Well, I have been deeply impressed by law, truth and transcendent being in both politics and philosophy of ancient Greeks.[9] But there has

Ellis Sandoz, *The Voegelinian Revolution: A Biographical Introduction* (Transaction Publishers, 2000), 117. "The term *leap in being*, though not invented by Voegelin, is given new amplitude. It is taken from Kierkegaard, and he was indebted to Hegel for the expression."

9   At least two instances regarding the idea of divine being and the rule of law in ancient Greece may be worth mentioning here. Apart from Sophocles' *Antigone*, Socrates, Plato and Aristotle, during my reading of the Hellenic history, I found these earlier passages being repeatedly quoted in the works devoted to Greek politics and philosophy. One is the words of Athena from Aeschylus' *Eumenides* (translated by E. D. A. Morshead, https://sourcebooks.fordham.edu/ancient/aeschylus-eumendid.txt).

O men of Athens, ye who first do judge
The law of bloodshed, hear me now ordain.
Here to all time for Aegeus' Attic host
Shall stand this council-court of judges sworn,
Here the tribunal, set on Ares' Hill
Where camped of old the tented Amazons,
What time in hate of Theseus they assailed
Athens, and set against her citadel
A counterwork of new sky-pointing towers,
And there to Ares held their sacrifice,
Where now the rock hath name, even Ares' Hill.
And hence shall Reverence and her kinsman Fear
Pass to each free man's heart, by day and night
Enjoining, Thou shalt do no unjust thing,
So long as law stands as it stood of old
Unmarred by civic change. Look you, the spring
Is pure; but foul it once with influx vile
And muddy clay, and none can drink thereof.
Therefore, O citizens, I bid ye bow
In awe to this command, Let no man live,
Uncurbed by law nor curbed by tyranny;
Nor banish ye the monarchy of Awe
Beyond the walls; untouched by fear divine,
No man doth justice in the world of men.
Therefore in purity and holy dread
Stand and revere; so shall ye have and hold

been a much bigger factor: Christianity. In retrospect, it is the most important phenomenon I have encountered since the beginning of my liberty project. To me, it's Christianity that mainly has kept the West's obedience to God for much of the past two thousand years.

For quite a while, I was amazed how and why an originally obscure Jesus movement with the Jewish background in the Middle East came to grow into such a worldwide phenomenon that shaped the heart and mind of the globe's most influential civilization in recent centuries. I read some works that try to give reasonable explanation. And I also began to read the Holy Bible in a more serious way than before.

The question did not become easy to answer until I was baptized late in 2006 at a house church in Beijing. Before that, I had already known from

A saving bulwark of the state and land,
Such as no man hath ever elsewhere known,
Nor in far Scythia, nor in Pelops' realm.
Thus I ordain it now, a council-court
Pure and unsullied by the lust of gain,
Sacred and swift to vengeance, wakeful ever
To champion men who sleep, the country's guard.
Thus have I spoken, thus to mine own clan
Commended it for ever. Ye who judge,
Arise, take each his vote, mete out the right,
Your oath revering. Lo, my word is said.

The other originates from Demaratus' reply to Xerxes in Herodotus' *Histories* (translated by George Rawlinson, https://sourcebooks.fordham.edu/ancient/herodotus-history.txt).

> *But, if need appeared, or if there were any great cause urging me on, I would contend with right good will against one of those persons who boast themselves a match for any three Greeks. So likewise the Lacedaemonians, when they fight singly, are as good men as any in the world, and when they fight in a body, are the bravest of all. For though they be freemen, they are not in all respects free; Law is the master whom they own; and this master they fear more than thy subjects fear thee. Whatever he commands they do; and his commandment is always the same: it forbids them to flee in battle, whatever the number of their foes, and requires them to stand firm, and either to conquer or die.*

the works on Western history the role of biblical faith and the Christian church in the making of freedom such as absolute truth, human dignity, moral values, the rule of law and separation of powers. But the house church Daniel Hsu, a book editor and independent scholar based in Shanghai with whom Professor Sandoz put me in contact in March 2006, helped me find in early September 2006 gave me the first taste of it in the social reality in which I live. Previously, either in Beijing or in my home town, I had gone to some government-sanctioned churches since I was a high-school student. My mother had begun believing in Christianity and often gone to church since 1985. She was not baptized until 2007. The high school I attended is an ex-Catholic church school where the church remains one of the largest in the region today. I liked both the style of the church architecture and its solemn atmosphere. Yet I did not go there very often partly because of the heavy burden of my school study—I never was a bright student—and partly because I did not think the church would necessarily have anything to do with the true God. It remained so after I went to college in Beijing where I spent much of the five-year undergraduate life reading what I would like to read with politics, philosophy, and sociology topping the agenda. A major question I began to ask then was whether what I held dearest such as truth and love and righteousness would turn out to be meaningless to me after I die. In other words, I wanted to pursue something eternally good but did not know yet how it was eternal and what its place was in the universe. It was part of a larger question I asked myself about the ultimate meaning of life and the world. In the third year at college, I started to become interested in the history of freedom in the West, especially after getting to know Chen Guiwen, then a boss of a small bookstore near the campus. I learned a lot from numerous discussions with him. Chen never went to college but when I first met him in his bookshop, he had pondered for years over the role of liberty in the making of Western civilization.[10] And I also came upon the books by Dr. Liu Xiaofeng, now

10   It was during this period of time that I came to know and became seriously interested in such subjects and personalities as Hellenic freedom, Roman liberty, Englishmen's tradition of "ancient freedom," Magna Carta, John Locke, Montesquieu, David Hume, Adam Smith, America's founding, Alexis de Tocqueville, Lord Acton and Friedrich von Hayek.

professor at China's southern Sun Yat-sen University. It turned out that Dr. Liu was a friend of Daniel's, one of the Chinese scholars who first suggested the Chinese translation of Eric Voegelin and the editor of the Chinese edition of *Modernity Without Restraint*. Against the backdrop of still widespread atheism and China's continued introduction of Western secular values, Dr. Liu's books on the Christian faiths, especially those of modern Russian and German philosophers and theologians, served as a stimulus to both my college study regarding the roots of Western civilization and my personal quest for the ultimate meaning of life and the world. From then on, my general feelings about life and the world have begun to evolve into a belief that it is God our creator that makes truth and love and righteousness eternal and that God is truth and love and righteousness. Later on, there has been a growing belief in my mind that the most important thing one should do before one dies is to do God's will. Yet as for what is the will of God exactly and in detail, up to then I still did not believe the Holy Bible was the answer. At that time, God remained aloof from me, or rather, I remained aloof from him, though my belief was stronger than ever that he did exist and that he was righteous. I gather such a situation was not mine alone. Many people in many societies might have been like this. You can't say the idea of God or the faith in God is absolutely absent from their consciousness. Yet in this case it seems God is elusive and the faith in God might be a personal matter at best or virtually extinct at worst: hence it is impossible for faith in God to figure prominently in social consciousness, let alone for society's obedience to the divine will to take hold.

As I went on with my study of Western history, I found what made it genuinely different was mainly its adoption of the Holy Bible as the founda-tion of its worldview. For many people in the Western world over the past two thousand years, the Holy Bible, as the apostle Paul says in his second epistle to Timothy, "is given by inspiration of God, and is profitable for doc-trine, for reproof, for correction, for instruction in righteousness, That the man of God may be complete, thoroughly equipped for every good work."[11] But how and why did this adoption happen? On the surface, it is incredible that people in the Roman and Hellenistic worlds and later those of Europe were converted to biblical faith that culturally came from the alien

11　2 Timothy 3:16,

Mesopotamia and Palestine. For many people in today's China, Christianity is still an alien religion. As my quest moved along, though, I found that the Bible itself, the New Testament more directly, revealed why this would happen. The Gospel according to John: "the Word was God ... and the Word became flesh and dwelt among us ... For God so loved the world that he gave his only begotten Son, that whoever believes in him shall not perish but have eternal life."[12] The Gospel according to Matthew: "Jesus came to them (his eleven disciples) and said, 'All authority in heaven and on earth has been given to me. Therefore go and make disciples of all nations, baptizing them in the name of the Father and of the Son and of the Holy Spirit, and teaching them to obey everything I have commanded you. And surely I am with you always, to the very end of the age.'"[13] In short, it is God himself who made it happen.[14] Humans' part was just whether to do God's will or not.

For unbelievers, all this would sound unbelievable. But the centuries that ensued indicate that ever more men and women became the followers of Jesus and many of them did try to do what Jesus told his disciples to do. The Acts of the Apostles is the beginning of the dramatic conversion to Christianity of the Roman and Hellenistic world and later of Europe, which became the global center of Christianity with generations of Europeans traveling to other continents to spread their faith mainly by establishing churches and schools and hospitals. I have been very much impressed by what the apostles had done, especially Peter and Paul. I could not imagine what the fisherman of Galilee and the Pharisee who once persecuted Christians would do to spend the rest of their lives if Jesus did not come to them and if Jesus was not Christ? For me who did not know what God was really like and often felt God was distant, both the Old and New Testaments are quite the eye-opener that shows how God communicated with his people. To believe them to be true, though, never came easy. I was especially annoyed with the passages of animal sacrifice and tribal bloodshed in the Old Testament. For quite a while, the Bible reading was on-again, off-again. Despite this, I very much appreciated the themes of both testaments: "The fear of the

12 John 1:1–14, 3:16.
13 Matthew 28:18–20.
14 2 Corinthians 3:6–9.

LORD is the beginning of knowledge,"[15] "It is better to trust in the LORD than to put confidence in man,"[16] "Man shall not live on bread alone, but on every word that comes from the mouth of God,"[17] and "Love your enemies and pray for those who persecute you, that you may be sons of your Father in heaven."[18] And, "We love because he first loved us."[19] All these were more than a great comfort to me, who had been wondering for years how the fate of truth and love and righteousness would be. From them, I sensed the source of comfort. It is the will of a loving God. It is he who decides the fate of truth and love and righteousness that I hold dearest and everything else. With this affirmation and assurance, I came to remind myself that I shall be as humble as possible when meeting anything I did not like or understand.[20] Either personally or publicly, pride or conceitedness seems always to have constituted the biggest obstacle to liberty. As Jesus after resurrection answered the apostles who asked if he was at that time to restore the kingdom of Israel, "It is not for you to know the times or dates the Father has set by his own authority."[21] Then, what is for me to know? As Jesus told a Pharisee expert in the law who asked which the greatest commandment was in the Law, "'Love the LORD your God with all your heart and with all your soul and with all your mind.' This is the first and greatest commandment. And the second is like it: 'Love your neighbor as yourself.' All the Law and the Prophets hang on these two commandments."[22] Personally, I found no reason not to heed this advice. Publicly, I found it just the foundation upon which a truly free society could be built.

15 Proverbs 1:7.
16 Psalms 118:8.
17 Matthew 4:4.
18 Matthew 5:44–45.
19 1 John 4:19.
20 "Obedience unlocks understanding." Rick Warren, *The Purpose-driven Life: What on Earth Am I Here For* (Zondervan, 2002), 72. Also see Professor Orlando Patterson's *Freedom in the Making of Western Culture* (BasicBooks, 1991), especially Part Four "Christianity and the Institutionalization of Freedom."
21 Acts 1:6–7.
22 Matthew 22:34–40.

After years of searching that I later believed stemmed from the drawing by my creator, the moment of truth came on December 16, 2006, when my fiancée and I were baptized along with more than fifty other people at the house church I mentioned earlier. That was three months after Daniel helped me go to the church during his short visit to Beijing. I had never been to churches other than government-sanctioned ones before then, chiefly because I had never thought house churches would necessarily be different from government-sanctioned ones and therefore I had never intentionally looked for them, and partly because house churches were underground and no one had ever invited me to these churches prior to Daniel's Beijing visit. As we had already heard of international media reports about the Chinese government's harassment of house churches across China, we were prepared for anything that might happen ahead. But we went there almost every Sunday morning without meeting any harassment except late last year when the church was prevented by the authorities from holding its Christmas service at a planned university auditorium. The church has several fixed worship places in Beijing. The one we go to is a rented downtown office building room where two Sunday services usually draw two hundred worshippers at least, mainly young people especially college students and professors. It's on the office building's 11th floor while the 8th floor also has a worship place with smaller size and older worshipers. The most crucial and direct reason why my fiancée and I decided to get baptized at this church is that we just felt at home with the church including its pastors, preachers, choir and congregation. In fact back in late 2004, my fiancée and I had begun attending a baptismal class at a government-sanctioned Catholic church in Beijing. It came after we had met at the church a devout and kind couple in their sixties who were poor senior citizens themselves but adopted an abandoned baby girl. Nevertheless, we dropped the class halfway for we did not think we had already found the permanent home we belonged to. For us, the government-sanctioned church remained distant from God. And perhaps more importantly, we ourselves remained distant from God too. I just felt that I had already been part of the world of atheism and agnosticism and materialism and nihilism despite my unwillingness to get involved.

It was shown not only by my experience with state-authorized churches. When I was completing my five-year undergraduate study in International Journalism at Beijing Broadcasting Institute, now the Communication University of China, I almost had no other choice but to work at state-controlled media. I once inquired about the possibility of working for Young Men's Christian Association of Beijing, which also has been government-controlled since the Communist takeover of power in 1949. But I received no reply from them for reasons I still do not know, perhaps because I was not a Christian. I worked at China Central Television for six years altogether. Yet long before my resignation in October 2005, I had already quit my job once for a while. That came only a little more than a year after I joined CCTV. However, I returned after finding no other job that could fit in with my major of International Journalism and my quest for liberty. Since then, I tried to focus my attention on improving the English news writing and the further understanding of international political affairs instead of looking for other jobs and the quest for freedom. To some degree, I was not that restless for about three years, in some sense because from 2001 to 2003 there was a somewhat relaxed environment for news reporting especially when it comes to international affairs. Yet after all, as Augustine of Hippo's *Confessions* shows, restless is our heart until it comes to rest in God.[23] That is why I quit again in October 2005, once and for all this time, to embark upon my liberty project. To me, it constitutes my personal Exodus, to borrow an expression from Eric Voegelin, "from bondage under Pharaoh to freedom under God."[24]

No doubt there was a big loss of income and I was under pressure from a variety of sides including I myself, yet one immediate big reward is that I got to know a number of people in China who had already been on the road to the Promised Land. So I became surer than ever that it was not simply someone's particular interest, nor a personal Exodus alone. Among them are the major co-workers of the church where my fiancée and I got baptized. One is the church's founding pastor, Jin

---

23 *The Confessions of Saint Augustine*, Book 1, Chapter 1, translated and edited by Albert C. Outler, http://ccat.sas.upenn.edu/jod/augustine/conf.pdf .

24 Eric Voegelin, *Israel and Revelation* (Louisiana State University Press, 1994), 112.

Tianming. Pastor Tianming was a graduate from Tsinghua University, a leading institution of higher learning in the Chinese mainland. When he graduated in 1991, two years after the 1989 Tiananmen Square democracy movement crackdown, unlike most of his schoolmates, Jin did not go to work nor pursue graduate study at home or abroad. Newly baptized, he and his future wife served at a house church. Later, Jin became a leader of Beijing's several house church fellowships, which have gradually merged into the current one in recent years. It is perhaps one of the biggest house churches in the Chinese capital. I once asked Pastor Tianming how he had managed not only to survive economic and political and psychological pressure over the past years but also to make the church grow into such a size. "With the spirit of faith," was his brief answer. He later elaborated on it during a sermon earlier in 2006 with Paul's second epistle to the church in Corinth: "We are hard pressed on every side, but not crushed; perplexed, but not in despair; persecuted, but not abandoned; struck down, but not destroyed ... It is written: 'I believed; therefore I have spoken.' With that same spirit of faith we also believe and therefore speak, because we know that the one who raised the Lord Jesus from the dead will also raise us with Jesus and present us with you in his presence ... so that the grace that is reaching more and more people may cause thanksgiving to overflow to the glory of God. Therefore we do not lose heart. Though outwardly we are wasting away, yet inwardly we are being renewed day by day. For our light and momentary troubles are achieving for us an eternal glory that far outweighs them all. So we fix our eyes not on what is seen, but on what is unseen. For what is seen is temporary, but what is unseen is eternal."[25]

Here, I will not go into the detail about what specific difficulties Pastor Tianming and his ministry managed to overcome. That may be part of what I am beginning to explore in the next step of my liberty project concerning how faith in God as the Lord can be cultivated in today's world.[26] For now, what I would like to highlight is this. Pastor

---

25 2 Corinthians 4:8–18.
26 How to build a free and responsible society is a topic that has begun attracting ever more public attention in China. A number of serious articles and books in this regard have been published. Some of them highlight the

Tianming is never alone. His church is continuing to grow despite many difficulties. And his church is only one of perhaps hundreds of house churches and non-government-sanctioned faith-based organizations in Beijing. Across China, the spirit of faith that descended from Abraham to Moses to Job to Paul to Augustine to American founders to Robert Morrison[27] might have been spreading far beyond what we could imagine. After centuries of vicissitudes and setbacks, in China, again to borrow from Voegelin a description of Egypt in the wake of the Amarna Revolution, "Man, in his desire for a new freedom, seemed on the verge of opening his soul toward a transcendent God."[28]

> role of classical philosophy and biblical faith in the making of the American and the wider Western culture. For now, few concern the church. From the social point of view, it looks like house churches and other non-government-sanctioned faith-based organizations including orphanages in China are gradually becoming genuinely robust social institutions [cf. Alexis de Tocqueville's *Democracy in America*, and Robert D. Putnam, *Bowling Alone: The Collapse and Revival of American Community* (Simon & Schuster, 2001), Robert D. Putnam and Lewis Feldstein with Don Cohen, *Better Together: Restoring the American Community* (Simon & Schuster, 2003)], which I believe will make biblical worldview known to the ever broader society and provide an important incubator for civic consciousness, civic engagement, civic norms and skills and civic recruitment especially among the country's younger generation. But there seems a long way ahead. Among other things, the legality of house churches and other non-government-sanctioned faith-based organizations is an important issue. Currently, despite continued reports of arrests and harassment, the government acquiesces in the growth of many urban and rural house churches. But it always turns down their registration requests. However in the end, a far more crucial issue may turn out to be how the church does God's will in any social circumstances.

27 Exactly 200 years ago this month, Robert Morrison arrived in Canton (Guangzhou), becoming the first Protestant missionary in China. Morrison also made history by producing and publishing the first ever Chinese translation of the Holy Bible, the first ever English-Chinese dictionary, the first ever Chinese-language magazine, and establishing the first ever modern school in Chinese history. The most immediate source about Morrison may be http://en.wikipedia.org/wiki/Robert_Morrison_(missionary) .

28 Eric Voegelin, *Israel and Revelation* (Louisiana State University Press, 1994), 111.

Yet how long will China eventually "break the bonds of Pharaonic order" to become "a new community under God"?[29] This is perhaps not for me to know. Whenever, faith in God as the Lord is for me the beginning of freedom. "Blessed are those who hear the word of God and obey it."[30] "Blessed is the nation whose God is the LORD"![31] I couldn't agree more. For as Zechariah writes, "This is what the LORD Almighty says: 'Return to me, and I will return to you.'"[32] I sincerely believe so.

29   *Ibid.*
30   Luke 11:28.
31   Psalm 33:12.
32   Zechariah 1:3.

Chapter 3
Origins of Individual Freedom
under the Rule of Law

Dear Professor Zank,

I am a common reader in China. First of all, please forgive me for taking the liberty of writing you directly to seek your help on a subject concerning the history of law and liberty.[33]

The question is about the origins of law and liberty: how and why was individual liberty under the rule of law first institutionalized in the West and why has it survived there as nowhere else?

Recently, I have asked at least three experts in ancient Greek law for opinions on the part of ancient Greece. They are Professor Edward Harris of Durham University, Professor Martin Ostwald of Swarthmore College, and Professor Michael Gagarin of the University of Texas at Austin. All gave me kind and swift replies. Professor Harris says that he believes the ideal of the rule of law was closely linked to the Greek opposition to tyranny, that is, the rule of one person who was not accountable to the people and ignored the will of the gods.

[This seems to me an insufficient answer. Where, then, is liberty enshrined in Greek law? What is the term and what is its philosophical legitimization? Liberty is rooted either in the will—a faculty of choice

---

33   This chapter includes a letter I wrote in May 2006 during an earlier phase of my liberty project and a response (in italic type and in square brackets) from Michael Zank, a professor of religion at Boston University. The letter summarized some of the major points I had learnt from various experts by then. Professor Zank's comments were among the most detailed replies I had received.

whose motivation is driven either by desire (the animal soul) or by knowl-edge (the rational soul); I am speaking in Greek terms, as you will imme-diately have noticed. In the academic tradition (i.e., Platonism from Plato himself down to, say, Cicero) is ultimately skeptical as to the ability of human beings to act from insight into the true nature or causes of things; in other words, it is elitist and certainly has no concept of universal human rights. It is interested in the freedom of philosophers to think without co-ercion; but Platonists (including Cicero) realize that a certain measure of concealment of their true opinions is necessary in order to maintain public order or, more precisely, in order to escape the fate of Socrates who un-abashedly undermined public order and was executed by the Athenian state for doing so. All public order, acc. to the Platonic order is tyrannical in the sense that it wants to maintain itself at all costs, even at the expense of truth. The only true freedom is that exerted by the philosophers who need to conceal their freedom under a mantle of conformity with whatever myth sustains the public order. If this sounds familiar from the situation of dissidents under modern forms of tyranny, that's because it is. What I am describing to you is more or less the analysis present in the political writings of Leo Strauss, esp. in On Tyranny.]

Professor Ostwald says he thinks the problem of "the rule of law" was first raised and discovered by the Greeks in their struggle with the Persian Empire from the late fifth century B.C. on. But both stopped short of pinpointing exactly what made ancient Greeks do so. Professor Gagarin's view is that Professor Harris's answer is in the right direction. But he goes on to point out that he would broaden it out to a broader view of Greek society, which from the very beginning (long before the tyrants) relied on some sort of larger advisory group (like a Council) even when there may have been a single ruler. He notes that when laws were first written in ancient Greece, they were not written by one ruler, but by a larger group, and many of the earliest Greek laws regulate and even punish magistrates. Professor Gagarin also quotes the view of Pro-fessor Geoffrey Lloyd that the reason the Greeks developed their unusual ideas and methods in science and philosophy is related to their system of open political debate. He holds that this led to open intellectual debate where people regularly criticized and questioned past thinkers rather than always following traditional views.

[*Neither of these views are unassailable. I don't know why rule by committee should be less tyrannical than rule by a monarch or single ruler. — As to debate, this is indeed what lead to the rise of rhetoric (and hence the art of persuasion) and sophism which is the point of departure for Socrates and hence Platonism. Sophism is the art of persuading by argument without regard to truth, which raises the question whether argument by means of language can ever be more than sophistry. Hence Plato seeks refuge in mathematics as a form of true representation beyond language, an intuition retrieved by modern science oriented philosophers in the Kantian tradition.*]

In reading these views on the origins of the rule of law in ancient Greece, I couldn't help asking again why the world's other ancient societies were not able to develop the legal and political cultures like ancient Greeks.

[*This seems to be based on a lack of awareness for the antiquity and variety of legal cultures in the Ancient Near East. Ancient Babylonians, Assyrians, and neo-Babylonians had elaborate law traditions (note the famous Code of Hammurabi) that precede the biblical law by many centuries. Egyptian society was based on lawful conduct based on Ma'at, a term that comes close to the Latin iustitia (justice) but also entails wisdom (as in the biblical "hokhmah," see Proverbs 8 and passim). Law and wisdom, justice and righteousness, good measure and conformity with the advice of the elders, you name it, they all have it. It is the common property of all ancient civilizations, because without it there could not be any civilization. Tyranny, corruption, greed, and all the other vices are part of the ancient wisdom and law traditions and excluded by them. In other words, in terms of contents, there are few variations among ancient societies (which, given the antiquity of the human species, is not all that ancient; what are a few millennia in comparison to the long pre-historical development of human rules of conduct?).*]

Absolute monarchs appear inevitable in these societies where the authoritarian or totalitarian rule has always been the only effective way possible to maintain peace and order however unsuccessful it was in many occasions.

[*The difference between ancient and modern societies is that ancient expected their rulers to conform to the generally accepted rules of conduct and enforce them, and they possessed the right to bring their complaints directly to the rulers; there is much Egyptian literature on this. In other words, because there were gods watching over the order of human beings; because the foundation of the state was such that the maintenance of order on earth was supposed to be done in uninterrupted continuity with the gods' maintenance of cosmic order—which was so important to the agriculturists of the ancient near east—that tyranny in the modern sense did not exist. —Modern tyranny or totalitarianism etc. are the direct result of the demise of religion—at least in the West — where fear of God and life as a preparation for reward and punishment in the hereafter was replaced by the desire to be free of violence that was turned into a natural right; the right of the pursuit of happiness. The modern tyrant is the one who violates this individual right in the interest of the collective. Hence any ancient theocratic regime appears to us as tyrannical because in ancient times individual rights did not exist. There were only duties toward the gods and fellow-human beings, and the possibility of acquiring a good name and avoiding shame, by means of generally accepted standards of virtuous conduct. —In modernity, with its radical elimination of all transcendence, even of the afterlife in form of the memory we pass on through our children and grandchildren, and the displacement of transcendence by means of instantaneous gratification, all power that is not conducive to our pursuit of happiness seems tyrannical.]*

Yet it does not mean they had no political debate at all. At least in traditional China, with which I am relatively familiar, some sorts of political debate were recorded in history. But all these had no chance to create a political environment as open as in ancient Greece. For me, the reason may be this. In whatever dynasties, the mainstream of the ancient Chinese way of thinking does not hold belief that there exist some rules that are free from the existence of human beings. What it believes in is everything about the human existence itself such as human wisdom and brute force. Even in aspects concerning the natural world, what it cares about most is how humans get used to these complex and mysterious surroundings. So, ancient China is not short of rough science. But it fails to generate a kind of scientific way of thinking, which is about the nature of the world and is independent of the human existence. What it generates instead is an idea that rough science itself is but another piece of evidence that humans are the pride of the world. And according to this way of logic, the ablest one in humans will be the most superior, or a superman. When this idea is added to the not-so-confident attitude toward the human relations as well as the natural world, a superman is likely to turn out to be a god, or the son of God. In other words, he has the favor of the most powerful being of the whole universe, although people can't be sure of its existence. But the superman's ability is real. Thus, the superman's offspring is the child of the divine, too. In the world full of uncertainties, it's naturally enough for people to accept such a family to assume the leadership and protect them, which will be reinforced by his growing supporters if he is able enough to continue to win hearts and minds of more people. Then, the laws will be gradually made in order to maintain the rule of the god-like man. But as the time goes by, his next generation may not be as able as him. And the most fatally important thing is the fact that the son of God proves to be a mortal one. Therefore, the divinity of the ruler is not absolute at all. And so is the ruler's law. In the end, some who may be like today's intellectuals conclude from these hard facts that the law has always been changed with the changeover of power. No one has been able to rule forever. The law is no more than the will or sometime rather the whim of the rulers. In this context, there's no reason for people to hold any belief in something called the rule of law. For them, what matters the most is, sadly, the inevitable rule of the power itself. People are born either to rule or to be ruled. Accordingly, there's no space for any alternative like the pattern of law and liberty to survive. People may have become skeptical about the legitimacy of the elite. However, the result is often that not only they are accustomed to this skepticism but also the elite themselves. It comes as no surprise that a usual extreme of such an attitude is no more than cynicism. Then it is not surprising either that even early ancient Chinese literature did not write much about the divine or the relationship between man and god. Rather, it was mainly about humans, their views, feelings and experiences. By comparison with this, the gods figured prominently in ancient Greek tragedy. Even with the rise of Sophists, it seems that the man-gods dimension was not removed entirely from ancient Greeks' consciousness.

In my view, the existence of this dimension itself offers a certain tension or room for people to struggle between what is man-made and what is natural or rather what is mortal and what is immortal. Under these circumstances, it is possible for the idea of the rule of law to survive. People may have lost confidence in the law of a particular ruler or a ruling class. But this would not necessarily lead to the loss of the law itself. People could challenge the ruler's man-made law with what they claim to be the divine law. I assume this way of thinking goes in the direction for the idea of the rule of law, which perhaps involves the conception that the world is not a product of human existence; on the contrary, human existence is a product of the world. In this regard, I suppose the ancient Greek example has some parallels in the medieval Europe where monarchs were mostly unable to grow powerful enough as their Chinese counterparts given the fact that there were the continuing tensions between church and state, which paves the way for the modern constitutional government. Of course, the two are largely different in other aspects.

[*Well said. What you describe about China is very interesting to me. And your thoughts about the mutual limitation of church and state as the precursor to modern constitutional government seems interesting to me, too. You know, perhaps, the important work by Augustine of Hippo, a profound churchman of the late 4th century CE, who wrote De civitate dei, a work distinguishing between the kingdom of god and the kingdom of men, making an identification of the two a heresy. In this work, the Latin church turned away from the principle of caesaropapism, embodied by Emperor Constantine ("the Great") and theorized by his successors, whereby the emperor was truly the vicar of Christ (i.e., God's representative on earth) and the state was the kingdom of God on earth. The Latin church and hence the Western middle ages divided between the secular and the spiritual, recognizing a certain measure of independence (yet also interdependence) between the two. So, in short, what you say makes a lot of sense to me.*]

Those are but my crude hypotheses that I have been developing so far in my mind as a result of reading and translating. At the beginning, I had felt reluctant to write them down. But on second thoughts, perhaps it is high time for me to "cast a piece of brick to elicit a piece of jade" (a Chinese idiom, meaning to offer a few preliminary thoughts in hoping to elicit more refined and profound ideas).

Currently, I am translating Orlando Patterson's *Freedom in the Making of Western Culture* into Chinese. More than a half is done. In August last year, I completed the translation of *Roots of Freedom: A Primer on Modern Liberty* written by John W. Danford. I chose these as the starting point for my quest for the origins of law and liberty.

For now, my ambition is simply to satisfy my curiosity about the complex and mysterious human condition. But if by any chance such self-interest is good for other individuals as well, then it will be a more worthy quest. For me, doing translation is a way of intensive reading that I believe could help one develop further insights into human condition through "reflection and choice." And I presume that this may also be a way to help introduce more perspectives on ways of living and thinking to some individuals in China, where individual liberty under the rule of law as an idea, a value and an institution have rarely been dealt with in an open, reasonable and serious manner.

Many scholars have long traced the origins of the idea of individual liberty under the rule of law to the Hebraic concept of living in accordance with a covenant with God, the source of creation. The question is—just what gave rise to such an unusual idea and what kind of factors may have been essential for the survival and maintenance of the idea?

[*This is, to me, an important question. I described some answers to this question, as given by the German-Jewish neo-Kantian philosopher Hermann Cohen (1842-1918) in a book with the title "The Idea of Atonement in the Philosophy of Hermann Cohen." Perhaps it is available in China? If not I'd be happy to send you a copy if you give me a mailing address. —In brief, Cohen begins his career by thinking that the modern idea of moral autonomy, i.e., the core of Kant's moral philosophy, has its religious roots in the Christian tradition of faith and that the Jewish element in Western culture is the belief in the transcendent God, the creator, who is the ultimate other of being and hence the source of our moral ideals. In later years, Cohen begins to relocate the origins of the modern ethical self. He believes that the individual self is discovered in Ezekiel 18, a chapter that quite clearly takes issue with preceding, collective notions of sin. Ezekiel quotes a saying popular among the Jews who have been exiled to Babylonia, which says: "the fathers have eaten sour grapes and the children's teeth are set on edge." In other words, they challenge the justice of their suffering for the sins (i.e., the idolatry) of their fathers. Ezekiel painstakingly (and almost pedantically) elaborates a new concept of sin; here it is the individual who sins who dies for his/her sin; but even this is further transcended when Ezekiel, in the name of YHWH, the God of Israel, says that the deity has no pleasure in the death of the sinner but in his/her repentance. I.e., it is all about the ability of human beings (as Cohen interprets) to deny the power of the empirical character (i.e., of the past) and to learn to consider themselves as open to change, to a reversal from evil to good, etc. This is a strong point of departure that Cohen traces further down to the later rabbinic tradition. For Cohen, and for many other modern Jews, social ethics, the progressive elimi-nation of injustice and poverty, is the principal obligation of Jewish law and liturgy and of Jewish belief in God. Human beings are empowered not only to live by divine law but by divine standards, which involves the power to modify the law where it fails to be helpful or just or uplifting. —The corresponding principle in the Greek tradition would be the "nomos agraphos," or "unwritten law," which points to the principles of the laws that guide human beings as they rewrite the laws in order to make them conform to the principles that the laws embody. —To be sure, legal scholarship and the philosophy of law are two different things, but if you want to read a modern law theorist who developed this idea further, you may want to look at the works of Hans Kelsen, an important theorist of the Weimar Republic in Germany, and a democrat. Both fascism and bolshevism opposed this theory, incidentally. Fascism—very much as you describe above—preferred to take recourse to nature (Nietzschean nature and the pseudo-Darwinian theory of the survival of the fittest) whereas bolshevism turned the promise of Marxism and revolution and universal justice into a tool of tyranny.]*

Apart from ancient Israelites and Greeks, the complicated situation surrounding medieval Europe is fascinating indeed as well. It is just when I was translating *Roots of Freedom* in 2004 that I first came to take a serious look at liberty in medieval Europe. Professor Danford quoted David Hume's *History of England* for explaining Europe's emergence from the feudalism: "perhaps there was no event, which tended farther to the improvement of the age, than one, which has not been much remarked, the accidental finding of a copy of Justinian's Pandects, about the year 1130, in the town of Amalfi in Italy." Later, I intended to find out the source of Hume's assertion. But I failed. What I have found, instead, are many versions of the story about the return of the Pandects. Among others, Montesquieu mentioned it in his *The Spirit of Laws*. The French writer, though, cited a completely different date, which was in 1137. In his *The Renaissance of the Twelfth Century*, Charles Homer Haskins observed that the Digest's rediscovery in Amalfi was an "ancient legend" and he gave another date—the year 1135. Professor Harold Berman suggested in *Law and Revolution: The Formation of the Western Legal Tradition* that it was in 1080. In his *The Revival of Jurisprudence* (in *Renaissance and Renewal in the Twelfth Century*, first published in 1982 by Harvard University Press, reprinted in 1999 by University of Toronto Press), Stephan Kuttner wrote: "But it is unthinkable that a science of law could have taken shape in the medieval West without the rediscovery of Justinian's Digest, about 1070 A.D." Yet despite different stories, all these have one thing in common: none has bothered to list any immediate source of their stories and none ever elaborated on theirs. Professor Peter Landau's "*The development of law*" (in the *New Cambridge Medieval History*, Volume IV, Part 1) is perhaps an exception. Professor Landau provided a somewhat detailed account of the process in which the Digest came to be discovered: "The sole manuscript of the Pandects which has come down from antiquity is the Codex Florentinus, now in the Biblioteca Laurenziana. Research has thrown some light on the adventures of this manuscript since it was written in Constantinople in the sixth century. It soon found its way into Byzantine southern Italy , and by about 1070 it was probably in Monte Cassino, where it was compared with another excerpt from the Digest, now no longer extant, which belonged to another tradition ..." However, Professor Landau failed to point out what his report was based on. And finally, thanks to Dr. Otto Vervaart of the Netherlands, I was able to get to know Dr. Wolfgang Müeller's monograph *The Recovery of Justinian's Digest in the Middle Ages*. Then in early November last year, Dr. Müeller generously sent me a copy of his essay from Fordham University. According to him, all those versions of date are purely conjectural. Authors placed it around 1070–80 simply based on a charter document from Marturi in Northern Italy , dated 1076, which contains the first Western citation from the Digest since the days of Pope Gregory I in 603. And the assertion that the Codex Florentinus was brought during the 1130s from Amalfi to Pisa (hence known from the 1150s as the "Pisanus," until it was brought to Florence in 1406), is based on the observation that the Florentinus contains marginal notes in Beneventan (*i.e.*, South Italian) script and that the Pisanus was something of a novelty at Pisa in the 1150s. Dr. Müeller goes on to point out that what has been ascertained is that the Florentinus was in Pisa during the 1150s, where the first generation of doctors (known as "The four doctors": Martinus, Bulgarus, Jacobus, and Hugolinus) teaching Roman Law at Bologna consulted the text on occasion. But he notes that there is no proof of continuing teaching activities in Roman Law at Bologna between the legendary founders of the school, Pepo and Irenius (both dead by 1125), and the Four Doctors (1150s). Dr. Müeller highlights that this observation is significant because it questions the old assertion that the recovery of the Digest was indispensable for Western legal culture. He says it surely was with regard to terminology and many technicalities, but the main thrust of Western legal development during the later Middle Ages came from the canon law schools, resulting, among other things, in a heavily "canonized" interpretation of Roman Law. And following these arguments, I raised some follow-up questions: Why did generations of historians continue to base their understanding of the origins of the modern Western legal culture on pure conjecture? Why has such pure conjecture invariably been centered on the recovery of the Digest? Until when did scholars begin to seriously question the assertion that the recovery of the Digest was indispensable for the Western legal culture? Why is it reasonable to believe that "the main thrust of Western legal development during the later Middle Ages came from the canon law schools"? Why are the canon law schools unique? What motivated the canon law schools for the pursuit of law? And how did such an unusual development not only survive but also thrive? In his kind response, Dr. Müeller says given the questions' complexity, he will need more time to answer them than he can currently afford.

[*It is very endearing to read the above. You clearly asked a philosophical-historical question of a medieval historian of law, and me-dievalists are notorious for getting lost in details of manuscript recovery and debates on the influence of manuscripts on later developments, but they often fail to consider the big picture. Your questions are excellent ones but you asked the wrong people. —I don't have the answer to this either. To me your question would warrant a dissertation.*]

I have also received kind replies from professors James Buchanan, Harold Berman and Rodney Stark. Professor Buchanan thinks that as concerns the origins of the idea of liberty, neither the Greeks nor the early Christians had an idea of individual autonomy. He believes that the 17th century is critical in this respect, when Hobbes and Spinoza really invented the notion of autonomous man, as an entity, a consciousness if you will, independent of any tribe, city-state, church or God. Professor Stark also thinks ancient Greeks left far less of the liberal tradition than classicists presume in that it was only freedom for a very tiny elite—even in Athens. In his view, the first more substantial democracies arose in the northern Italian city-states from about 1000 A.D. onward, and they increasingly included a larger proportion of the population in the decision-making and electoral processes, largely as a result of industrial development spreading both wealth and power—the rise of capitalism. And he goes on to point out that all of this was rooted in Christian theology which by about 700 AD had eliminated slavery from Europe and which fostered beliefs in equality. [*I like the preceding a lot. I think it's basically on the mark.*] This explanation is different from that of Professor Brian Tierney, who believes it was the continuing tensions between church and state that created a persistent tendency toward the emergence of constitutional forms of government. And it is not the same as that of Professor Harold Berman, who asserts it was the bringing together in Western Europe of ancient Greek philosophy, ancient Roman law and ancient Hebrew theology—in the late eleventh and twelfth centuries—that provided the philosophical, the legal, and the religious support for freedom. But whatever the differences, the rise of Christianity itself and its spread across the European cultures over the centuries since the Roman times are remarkable indeed. The question is: how did such an originally obscure regional religion in ancient Palestine come to grow into an institution that was able to pose a lasting challenge to the state in Western European nations? It seems that all the religions elsewhere in the ancient world simply turned out to be either the tool of the powerful state or the state itself.

[*Again, an excellent set of observations. The rise of Christianity is crucial. And the fact that Christianity inherits many of its ideas from Judaism but then amalgamates them successfully with, or penetrates them from, pagan ideas, is also crucial. —You ask why was Christianity successful. This is such an important question and yet it is such an elusive one to answer. What was so compelling about it that it was adopted by the Roman state? And why was it strong enough to overcome this state and its ideological co-option of Christianity from the inside and eventually produce revolutionary movements, such as the monastic movement (I think of St. Bernard), the reform popes (e.g., Gregory VII), the Lutheran reformation and the Calvinist states, the peasants revolts, and the revolution in England. What works itself out in the history of the west is the inherently revolutionary character of the prophetic monotheism of the ancient Israelites and Judahites, which values morality higher than the king and justice higher than riches and which, above all, considers history itself the field wherein truth and justice are enacted. The Israelite tradition which focuses on history rather than on the afterlife has imbued human action with redemptive qualities concerning not just oneself but primarily the other, the poor, the orphan, the widow, and hence: society and humanity at large. In this it is equally profound if not more lasting in impact to Socrates' turning away from speculations about the cosmos and making ordinary human pursuits the object of methodical inquiries. Jewish messianism has become the driving force of Western politics (for good and for ill). —To be sure, since there is more than one type of messianism, what drives the West is the ultimately undecidable struggle for dominance between two fundamentally different visions of the future, namely, what one might call the millenarian type (which aims at continuity, progress, the establishment of a kingdom of God on earth), and the apocalyptic type (which envisions a great cataclysm and a new heaven and earth and recommends for the believers to stay out of politics and wait for God to act). Here you have the origin of the division of all Western societies into the Left and the Right wing: activism vs. quietism; optimism vs. pessimism; readiness to change and experiment vs. conservatism and anti-government attitudes.*]

And there are also many experts at legal, political and economic history who have singled out the Anglo-American tradition of constitutionalism as the unique source against absolutism and totalitarianism. Again, the questions are how and why.

For me, the exploration into the history of law and liberty is part of a wider examination of a more perennial issue concerning the place of human beings as well as everything about human beings in the cosmos. Topping the list of concerns may be the identity and nature of human beings, the relations among humans, and humans' relationship with what is called nature, universe, the devil and the divinity or the divinities, perhaps in particular—the place of love and truth in the cosmos. For now, my focus is more on the living condition of any individual in the context of human society. It is the issue of any human being's dignity and the possibility of the pursuit of happiness. In other words, it is about human rights and the nature of the rule of law [which may be close to this idea: there must be a set of basic principles that constitutes a consistent and unchangeable standard by which government of any form is held accountable, regardless of whether it is exercised by an individual (tyrant, monarch, autocrat), by a restricted group of people (the rich, the military, the priesthood, etc.), or even by the masses, if they ride roughshod over the claims of minorities]. What I am concerned about is every single step human beings have taken towards the living condition wherein each individual has her or his due and leads a dignified life and dies a dignified death. I would like to trace these steps including both conscious and unconscious in human history. The history of the Western individuals is part of it. So is that of the Chinese individuals. A vital part of this exploration is to find out how powers have come to be checked and how personal freedom under the rule of law has come to take root. Given the hard facts of the world, I am not seeking the best at all, but the least bad.

Lastly, I wonder if I may present my long-term plan for the exploration into the history of law and liberty. In the end, I would like to see a research institute established for this project so that more people with different backgrounds from across the globe could contribute their insights and work in close collaboration. That I got this idea was partly inspired by Lord Acton and Joseph Needham. The latter is the late British historian who had dedicated himself to investigating the scientific and technical contribution that the Chinese people have made to human culture. His research was chiefly to answer this question: why was it that despite the immense achievements of traditional China it had been in Europe and not in China that the scientific and industrial revolutions occurred? Over the past fifty years this has grown into the *Science and Civilisation in China* project, which to date has resulted in twenty-three substantial published works written by Joseph Needham and his collaborators. The project has been characterized as "perhaps the greatest single act of historical synthesis and intercultural communication ever attempted ..." Needham passed away ten years ago at the age of 95. But his research institute remains. A group of scholars from around the world are continuing with the project that has been expanded to cover the history of science, technology and medicine in East Asia. A research institute for the history of law and liberty may be decades away or even longer. But it is worth a try. In this regard, I wonder if there is any possibility to have your counsel and assistance.

Forgive me for such a long email, and for my amateurishness. I would be much obliged to receive instructions from you.

Best regards,
Sincerely yours,
Promise Hsu

[*Dear Promise, I hope my comments above make some sense and are of some use. Your project sounds very interesting and I hope you will be successful in establishing such an institute. Please let me know if I can be of further assistance.*

Sincerely,
Michael Zank]

Chapter 4

How Fishermen Turned into Fishers of Men

It would have been impossible for the disciples of Jesus to be associated with the great undertaking of changing the world.[34] They were not well-educated nor self-taught. They were mostly fishermen in the countryside who would at times worry about their livelihood. They were called to join a mission. And yet, they mostly once fled in panic.

Nevertheless, very few other groups of people helped usher in an era like them. Since their lives were changed, many other lives have been changed and this change continues until now. After their lives were changed, they got out of the predicament. What they later did would shock not only those who had known them but also themselves.

They lived in the east Mediterranean coast of West Asia. But later generations in many countries would name themselves and their children for these people, such as John, Peter, Paul, Mary, Martha, Matthew, Mark, James, Philip, Andrew, Thomas, Stephen.

They were Jews. But unlike the fame their modern descendants achieved in as diverse fields as natural sciences, the humanities, politics and business, the Jews at that time were notable for losing independence of their country for hundreds of years. Since the Assyrian destruction of Israel in the early eighth century B.C. and the Babylonian conquest of Judah less than two hundred years later, the Jews have been in diaspora or exile.

34 A Chinese version of this chapter originally appeared in the March 20, 2009, issue of *Global Entrepreneur*, a leading business magazine in China. It was one of my columns about the spiritual and intellectual foundations of a free and responsible civilization. In the Chinese public square, still little is known concerning to what extent and how the tree of liberty has been shaped by the continued growth of the Christian church across the globe.

In the days of Peter, John and Paul, their home country was part of the Roman Empire and would remain so in the next few centuries. As they were born, Augustus was the first Roman emperor. It was not yet in the empire's heyday. The Roman Empire, one of the longest in human history, would not completely collapse until the fifteenth century.

However, it was just during this period of time that a more far-reaching history was in the making. And it all began with this group of people—"unschooled, ordinary"[35] in the eyes of the contemporary Jewish elites. According to their own record, it was because of the emergence of a very unusual man.

One day, Peter and his brother Andrew were casting a net into Lake Tiberias or the Sea of Galilee. The lake is situated in what is now Israel and Palestine. Just north of the more famous salt lake, the Dead Sea, it is the lowest freshwater lake in the world.

"Come, follow me," a man said to them, "and I will make you fishers of men."[36] They knew the man. He was named Jesus, the son of Joseph, a carpenter in a nearby town called Nazareth. From John the Baptist, Andrew had heard that Jesus was the Messiah, the one the Jews expected to come and be their savior and king. Andrew had been a disciple of John the Baptist, who was Jesus' cousin and about six months older than Jesus.

Andrew and Peter immediately left their net and followed Jesus. Shortly after that, Jesus met James and his brother John. Both were also fishermen and were preparing their nets. Jesus called them. They followed him at once leaving their boat and their father.

Later, eight more people joined in. Many more also heard and saw what Jesus had said and done. All this might arouse suspicion. After all, too many people have followed one or another in history. Would this man be a charlatan or even worse?

Indeed, the story of Jesus and his followers seemed bound to be in vain. On the one hand, Jesus went through the neighboring towns and villages preaching "Repent, for the kingdom of heaven is near."[37] He

---

35   Acts 4:13.
36   Matthew 4:19.
37   Matthew 4:17.

helped heal disease and sickness, including leprosy, paralysis, and what would be odd-sounding to modern people, the demon-possessed. He could let the blind see, the mute speak, the lame walk, even the dead rise. But on the other hand, he himself was killed on the cross just three years after he began his work at about 30 years old. By then, most of his followers were not with him.

Even before Jesus was crucified, his followers had not been following him wholeheartedly. It has long been well-known that one of his disciples, Judas, betrayed Jesus to the hands of the Jewish chief priests for 30 silver coins. Even Peter, who acknowledged Jesus as the Christ and the Son of God and promised to go with him to prison and to death, disowned him three times. That was despite Jesus having helped his mother-in-law recover from suffering a high fever. Peter and other followers were exhausted from sorrow before Jesus was arrested.

Far beyond their expectation, the man whom Peter and other people followed had told them repeatedly that he would and must be killed and would rise from the dead on the third day. For them, it would be understandable not to believe in such a prediction. Would this be the fate of the savior they and their ancestors had been waiting for?

Peter once took Jesus aside and even rebuked him, "Never, Lord! This shall never happen to you!"[38] In response, Jesus rebuked his follower, "Get behind me, Satan! You are a stumbling block to me; you do not have in mind the things of God, but the things of men."[39]

All this appears to have bordered on the absurd. What looks even more absurd is that the followers of Jesus, including Peter and John, would write that their Lord indeed was alive again on the third day after he was crucified and it was his resurrection that changed their lives.

After Jesus' resurrection, his eleven disciples except Judas, who hanged himself after betraying Jesus, went to Galilee to see him as Jesus had told them to do. He asked them to do this: "Go and make disciples of all nations, baptizing them in the name of the Father and of the Son and of the Holy Spirit, and teaching them to obey everything I have

38 Matthew 16:22.
39 Matthew 16:23.

commanded you. And surely I am with you always, to the very end of the age."[40]

From then on, the followers of Jesus set out on a long journey they had not expected. A group of "unschooled, ordinary" people would surprisingly turn into educators for generations of people worldwide.

Another unexpectedly faithful follower was a man called Paul. Originally named Saul, he was trained under Gamaliel, a leading authority of Jewish law in the first century, and persecuted those who followed Jesus. As a young man, he gave approval to the death of Stephen when the disciple of Jesus was killed by stoning.

But after conversion, Paul became a man who would spread the word of Jesus all across the Mediterranean region, from West Asia, Greece to as far as Rome, the capital and the heart of the Roman Empire. By his own accounts on different occasions, Paul's change did not come from that of his mind but rather an experience he could never imagine.

He once went to Damascus, a city more than two hundred kilometers northeast of Jerusalem, to arrest more of Jesus' followers. About noon as he neared Damascus, Paul saw a bright light from heaven flashing around him. He fell to the ground and heard a voice, "Saul! Saul! Why do you persecute me?"[41] He asked who was speaking to him. The answer was that it was Jesus of Nazareth whom he was persecuting. The voice asked Paul to go into Damascus where he would be told what he must do. From Damascus, Paul was to preach the word of Jesus among other peoples as well as the Jews. Paul would have to tell this story numerous times because anyone who had known or heard of him couldn't help asking why he had changed so much.

Along with much of what Paul recorded, a number of writings from Peter, John, Matthew, Mark, Luke and some other of Jesus' followers would form a considerable portion of the Bible, the New Testament. A verse John wrote down in his account of Jesus would be viewed as the Bible in a nutshell: "For God so loved the world that he gave his one and only Son, that whoever believes in him shall not perish but have eternal life."[42]

40   Matthew 28:19–20.
41   Acts 22:7.
42   John 3:16.

Yet, it might be difficult to believe these people have eternal life simply because they had faith in Jesus. Most of the eleven apostles lost their lives just because of their faith in Jesus. Many more perished for the same reason. Facing hardships, they appeared not to have any special course to follow except that they would ask the God they believed in for help. In their accounts, Jesus taught them not to worry but to seek first the kingdom of the heavenly Father and his righteousness and all things needed would be given to them. And when Jesus sent his disciples out before his crucifixion, he told them that whoever lost one's life for his sake would find the new life.

If the faith in Jesus was to be passed down only within a few generations after Peter and Paul, this group of people would be no different from any religious belief or social movement that enjoyed popularity for a time. Even when the faith in Jesus gained official recognition in the early fourth century, it only had a history of nearly three hundred years. Approximately ten percent of the Roman Empire population then were followers of Jesus.

However, this was still far removed from what Jesus told his disciples to do—"go and make disciples of all nations" and "to the very end of the age." Large though it was, the Roman Empire was made up of just a small part of the entire globe. And "all nations" would not only mean the whole world geographically and ethnically but also to all the hearts and minds.

In the late fifth century, the Western Roman Empire fell. The faith of Peter and Paul kept going. The fruits it bore after centuries of growth constituted the foundation of a working society. They included what the followers of Jesus built: churches, schools, hospitals, libraries, and orphanages. From these institutions, Europe began its life.

It wasn't until the mid-fifteenth century that the Eastern Roman Empire took its final breath. The followers of Jesus seemed not to stop there. But how could a faith continue to grow after spreading for more than a thousand years?

For those who wanted to bring back the spirit of the word of Jesus, it was merely the beginning. Since then, more and more Europeans have begun to see the Bible—both the Old and New Testaments—in their local languages translated from the original Hebrew and Greek texts.

Before that, the Latin translation of the Bible had been the only version available. Some people were killed simply because they ventured to do the translation.

Again, Europe was still only a part of the world. Thanks to the progress in transportation, the successors of Peter and Paul were able to take the word of Jesus elsewhere. North America would replace Europe as the main springboard for the further spread of the faith in Jesus.

It has been nearly twenty centuries since Peter and John left their boats and nets on the shores of the Sea of Galilee. Many more people became "fishers of men." East Asia might be the next Europe or North America. South Korea, roughly the size of the American state of Indiana, is sending the second-largest number of Jesus' followers abroad, after the United States. China, still officially an atheist country, has one of the largest Bible producers in the world.

When will the followers of Jesus make disciples of all nations? Or will they? Peter and ten other apostles asked a similar question before Jesus was taken up into heaven, "Lord, are you at this time going to restore the kingdom to Israel?"[43] Jesus said to them, "It is not for you to know the times or dates the Father has set by his own authority. But you will receive power when the Holy Spirit comes on you; and you will be my witnesses in Jerusalem, and in all Judea and Samaria, and to the ends of the earth."[44]

43   Acts 1: 6.
44   Acts 1: 7–8.

Chapter 5
The Politics of Jesus?

In China, politics is a matter of old, big and difficult concern.[45] Facing politics, one would become frustrated, fearful, angry, depressed or indifferent. One would complain that the political reform was still nowhere in sight. Some others would seem more pessimistic, sighing that even if there was political reform the change would be in form rather than in substance. Of course, there might be some people who think otherwise. They try their best to bring about an improvement no matter how slight it would be.

However different the attitudes are, they would inevitably be shaped more or less by the society in which they live. If there is no feasibly new idea, politics will remain a matter of old, big and difficult concern. The question is, would there be any feasibly new idea? From time immemorial, numerous people have tried what they considered new ideas and yet all seems to have disappointed people's expectations. Could there be any feasibly new idea?

Who Is In Charge?

In 1972, a book called *The Politics of Jesus* was published in America. Its author is John Howard Yoder, then a 45-year-old professor of Christian theology. History has been full of books of politics in various versions. This one may have been simply one of them.

In 2000, *The Politics of Jesus* was ranked by evangelical magazine *Christianity Today* as the fifth most important Christian book of the twentieth century. Unlike *The Politics of Jesus*, other books on the Top

---

45   This chapter was originally published in Chinese in the 2010 winter issue of *Almond Flowers*, a quarterly of Shouwang Church.

10 list, such as C. S. Lewis' *Mere Christianity*, Dietrich Bonhoeffer's *The Cost of Discipleship* and Oswald Chambers' *My Utmost for His Highest*, did not address themselves to the issue of politics.

In 2010, which was nearly forty years after *The Politics of Jesus* came out, Yoder's newest book was published. *Nonviolence: A Brief History* is a collection of lectures Yoder presented in 1983 in Warsaw, Poland. It is their first publication together, almost thirteen years after Yoder died in 1997.

To Chinese readers, both John Howard Yoder and his books might sound unfamiliar. Even if one has read his books, it is still possible that neither the social background the author was in nor the content of his books looks familiar. Despite this, what Yoder did through his books could serve to help people in China make sense of politics anew.

On December 29, 1927, Yoder was born in Smithville, a village of northern Ohio, the United States. His parents and ancestors were Mennonites. Like Lutherans and Calvinists, Mennonites owe their origin to the sixteenth-century Protestant Reformation named after Menno Simons, a Dutch theologian. Though Mennonites have different denominations, they share a common characteristic of commitment to nonviolence.

Mennonites also have their own schools. Yoder was educated at Goshen College in Indiana. According to the Bible, Goshen is a place where ancient Israelites once lived in Egypt. In 1949, Yoder went to Europe where he took part in the Mennonite relief program in France and North Africa.

Apart from work, Yoder studied at the University of Basel in Switzerland. He earned a Doctor of Theology in 1962. His teachers included theologian Karl Barth and philosopher Karl Jaspers. Since then, Yoder spent the most of his life teaching theology at American universities, first at his alma mater Goshen College and then at the University of Notre Dame.

The Politics of Jesus and Nonviolence: A Brief History are not the only books Yoder wrote. But they are representative of Yoder's thoughts. Generally, he wanted to clarify what the Christian faith really taught about the hope and the way of politics by restoring the truth of the Bible and the world history.

Yoder found that there were often divisions in the faith-life relationship among Christians. For many believers, what Jesus Christ has said and done seems of relevance to only some part of life. Yoder focused on the relationship between faith and politics. Even in Europe and North America where the Christian faith has played a critical role, what many Christians think and do about politics has in fact almost nothing to do with the words and deeds of Jesus Christ.

One reason is perhaps that the time Jesus lived is considered to be very different from contemporary society, and therefore some of his teachings don't apply to today's life. Another reason might be that many Christians believe that what Jesus Christ cares about is the eternal kingdom of God instead of this world, and thus the Christian faith does not have any direct connection with the politics of this world, and that the Christian church is not a political organization, nor should Jesus Christ, the Christian faith, the Christian church, Christians be used by politics.

For Yoder, just because of such isolation, many Christians and Christian churches in history resorted to non-Christian ideas when it came to politics. Particularly, Yoder was concerned with the issue of violence. He pointed out that behind what was called "just war" doctrine there was human calculation. Some use of force appears to defend justice and the use of force is viewed as the "last resort." But the threshold of "last resort" might have been lowered for one's convenience.

Against this background, Yoder appealed to his fellow Christians to return to the Bible and see how on earth Jesus Christ faces politics. This, first of all, may have been relating to who Jesus Christ is. In the Bible, Jesus is Christ (Anointed One, Messiah), God's one and only Son and only "whoever believes in him shall not perish but have eternal life."[46] But the place of Jesus in the lives of many Christians seems not as high as this.

In the life concerning politics of any form, power is an issue that cannot be ignored. All the Christians may have believed that Jesus Christ is King of Kings and Lord of Lords who rules over everything. Yet in daily life, people would fail to see the existence, place and

---

46   John 3:16.

deeds of this only Sovereign and Lord. What they see is the visible ruler.

Yoder reminded his readers that the Old Testament text most frequently quoted in the New Testament was none other than Psalm 110:1, "The LORD says to my Lord: Sit at my right hand until I make your enemies a footstool for your feet."[47] Throughout the Bible, the New Testament in particular, it is easy to find a verse claiming the sovereignty of Jesus Christ. Jesus is not only the Redeemer but also the Creator and the Governor.

The question is, why is it that even the followers of Christ would fail to see the sovereignty of Jesus? And how to make sense of what the apostle Paul wrote to the church in Colosse, "… by him all things were created: things in heaven and on earth, visible and invisible, whether thrones or powers or rulers or authorities; all things were created by him and for him"?[48]

To those who have experienced the redemption by Jesus Christ, the answer is perhaps evident. The sin of human beings has alienated them from him. In this situation, human beings are his enemy. Those who have been saved by him remain human beings who would continue to sin and would still run into difficulties where human beings are separated from God.

What human beings need to do is to keep trusting in God and growing up in his word, as what Paul prayed for the people at the church of Colosse, "we have not stopped praying for you and asking God to fill you with the knowledge of his will through all spiritual wisdom and understanding. And we pray this in order that you may live a life worthy of the Lord and may please him in every way: bearing fruit in every good work, growing in the knowledge of God, being strengthened with all power according to his glorious might so that you may have great endurance and patience, and joyfully giving thanks to the Father, who has qualified you to share in the inheritance of the saints in the kingdom of light."[49]

47　Psalm 110:1.
48　Colossians 1:16.
49　Colossians 1:9–12.

How Does Christ Govern the World?

What Yoder did is to return to God's word even when it comes to politics despite living in a world that is seemingly very different from that of Jesus. From what Yoder shared, one could see how Jesus Christ governs the world is completely different from how human beings govern the world.

Briefly, the politics of Jesus may be like this: Apart from being the Creator and the Redeemer, Jesus Christ is also the Governor. But he governs not by himself but by obeying the Father. On the one hand, he and the Father are one. On the other hand, he has been sent by the Father to do what the Father wants. As the Son of the trinitarian true God; as the Word through whom the Father created all things; as the radiance of God's glory; as the exact representation of God's being; as the Word becoming flesh and humbling as a human being sent by the Father in heaven; as the Son of Man betrayed and crucified; Jesus always obeys the Father despite that both are one.

After seeing how God governs the world, one could fully understand why human beings have been unsatisfied with all kinds of governments with human beings governing the world. When human beings govern, it is not new that they claim to be the servant of the public. Yet they fail to be the servant. Others may replace them as the new public servant. Yet again, they fail to be the servant as well. The heart of the problem is, as they fail to see the real Governor, human beings would almost inevitably think of themselves as the Governor; then in this case, how could human beings become the servant of their own?

History is not short of human beings who assert themselves to be a God-sent ruler. But what they do and how they do it show they have not exactly represented God's being. They inevitably are self-centered. From the Bible, which claims itself what is "God-breathed,"[50] one could see God knows the situation of human beings to the full. And God's solution to solving the self-centered problem of human beings is to show how he humbles himself through Jesus Christ.

Just in this process of what is called "The Word became flesh,"[51]

50   2 Timothy 3:16.
51   John 1:14.

the world's greatest ever political tragedy happened. God was accused of blaspheming God by the human beings he created. God was handed over to the governing authority God has established. The governing authority found no basis for a charge against him. But the people would prefer the governing authority to pass a death sentence on him and to release a man who had committed murder. The people's petition prevailed. The governing authority granted their demand. God was crucified.

It was a government that appeared to have cared very much about popular opinion. It did not use force to crack down on the people's peaceful petition. It even went all out to appeal to the people to set free the man they charged, after a careful investigation that found in the alleged criminal no grounds for the death penalty. What's more, this was a group of people who seemed to have earnestly pursued justice. They worshipped God. They would not allow anyone to pass oneself off as God. They believed it would be far more serious a crime to commit blasphemy than to commit murder.

What on earth led up to this political tragedy? Is it because both the government and the people were not good enough? Would it not happen if it was the best government and the best people today? Sadly, all this looks inevitable. It is God who took the initiative to complete the tragedy. And God has long known this. He has said through his chosen prophet: "he was led like a lamb to the slaughter, and as a sheep before her shearers is silent, so he did not open his mouth."[52]

All this sounds quite incredible. If it were not for God's inspiration, one would hardly understand how it came to be. It is like the seemingly common relationship between light and darkness. Unless the light shines, the darkness will remain dark and will never understand what the light is. Wherever the light shines, the darkness disappears. This is just how God's sovereignty is shown to human beings through Jesus Christ on the cross.

For Yoder, the cross of Christ is the model of Jesus's politics. Yoder liked to quote a verse from Paul's letter to the Colossians to illustrate how the politics of Jesus triumphed over all other politics: "And having

---

52   Isaiah 53:7.

disarmed the powers and authorities, he made a public spectacle of them, triumphing over them by the cross."[53]

Indeed, the darkness does not understand the light. But the light determines to shine in the darkness. When it comes to showing his almighty power, God is not only like the light but also like a lamb indeed. But how could God be killed if he was God? How could God be killed like a lamb if he was God Almighty as he called himself?

In fact, long before he was crucified, Jesus had told his followers three times that he would be killed. Even though he also said each time that he would be raised to life on the third day after death, his followers would unsurprisingly feel weak. When he was truly crucified and after that, most of his followers were not present.

Even after the resurrection of Jesus, such weakness continued. How would a group of "unschooled, ordinary men" in the eyes of their contemporaries[54] feel when their resurrected Lord told them that he would return to the Father and asked them to "go and make disciples of all nations, baptizing them in the name of the Father and of the Son and of the Holy Spirit, and teaching them to obey everything I have commanded you"?[55] How could they stay loyal to their Lord given the fact that even Peter, one of the best-known apostles, once disowned Jesus three times?

Aside from promising his death and resurrection before he was crucified, Jesus also said to his followers that they would not be as helpless as orphans because the Spirit of truth would come to them and would guide his followers into all truth. And in the interim period between rising from death and going back to the Father, Jesus reassured them that they would receive power when the Holy Spirit came on them.

Yoder held that the weakness of Jesus's disciples was "a logical unfolding of the meaning" of Jesus's work on the cross. It is perhaps in what Jesus told Paul later in the Bible that the significance of weakness is fully shown: "My grace is sufficient for you, for my power is made perfect in weakness."[56] This echoes what God Almighty said to his

---

53   Colossians 2:15.
54   Acts 4:13.
55   Matthew 28:19–20.
56   2 Corinthians 12:9.

prophet Zechariah in the Old Testament: "'Not by might nor by power, but by my Spirit,' says the LORD Almighty."[57]

All this shows that what makes the weakness of Jesus and that of his disciples significant is God's spirit and grace. It is on weakness that God's strength is manifested. Indeed, this is a recurrent theme throughout the Bible. As Paul's first letter to the Corinthians indicates, "For the foolishness of God is wiser than man's wisdom, and the weakness of God is stronger than man's strength."[58]

Regarding the Holy Spirit, Jesus once explained to his disciples about his relationship with the Father and the Son: "It is for your good that I am going away. Unless I go away, the Counselor will not come to you; but if I go, I will send him to you ... He will not speak on his own; he will speak only what he hears, and he will tell you what is yet to come. He will bring glory to me by taking from what is mine and making it known to you. All that belongs to the Father is mine. That is why I said the Spirit will take from what is mine and make it known to you."[59]

Like the Son, the Spirit is not on his own authority either but on the Father's. Both the Son and the Spirit are Counselors (or the Helpers, the Comforters, the Advocates in some other English Bible translations) sent from the Father to humanity. From this, one could see the governing order within the trinitarian God. This is exactly what Jesus wants the community of his followers to be likewise, which would stand in stark contrast to the rule of human beings: "You know that the rulers of the Gentiles lord it over them, and their high officials exercise authority over them. Not so with you. Instead, whoever wants to become great among you must be your servant, and whoever wants to be first must be your slave—just as the Son of Man did not come to be served, but to serve, and to give his life as a ransom for many."[60]

Nearly two thousand years on, the followers of Jesus have grown from a group of "unschooled, ordinary men" in the eyes of their contemporaries into a worldwide community. It was perhaps far beyond the

---

57 Zechariah 4:6.
58 1 Corinthians 1:25.
59 John 16:7–15.
60 Matthew 20:25–28.

imagination of most people in their generation. However given the promise of Jesus, this came as no surprise at all. But even by today's standards in much of the world, the top ruler of this community is still very different from those of others. For the residents of this community, their leader is not only theirs but that of the entire cosmos. Yet, he is a leader "Who, being in very nature God, did not consider equality with God something to be grasped, but made himself nothing, taking the very nature of a servant, being made in human likeness."[61]

The Ministry of Reconciliation

This community is the church, or the body of Jesus Christ as the apostle Paul calls it. [62] Politically speaking, the existence of the church is a witness of the governing order of Jesus Christ. In a world where the sovereignty of Jesus Christ could be seen, the church respects the governing authorities Jesus Christ has established. Facing any authority and the society it is in, the church must do as Jesus Christ does.

The environment the church faces is not completely different from that Jesus did two thousand years ago. A perennial character is that this still is a world of sinners. It means this world is still not short of alienation from God and humanity remains God's enemy. It is just against such background that God continues to reconcile human beings to himself through Jesus Christ and give the church and its members the ministry of reconciliation.

In this sense, any solution to the political problems in today's world still lies in Jesus Christ. Though many people in the world have long recognized the crucial importance of peaceful dialogue in solving various disputes, it is simply impossible to create a bridge for genuine dialogue all on humanity's own. The estrangement and even hostility between human beings turns out to be the manifestation of those between humanity and God. No matter if it is the relationship between human beings or that between humanity and God, Jesus Christ is the bridge or the interface where true reconciliation can be achieved.

61 Philippians 2:6–7.
62 Colossians 1:24.

The reason why Jesus Christ is the bridge of reconciliation is that he is the one who has been sent by the Father to redeem humanity from sin, and he is the example of the one who does not sin by always obeying the Father. Since the Bible has made it clear that God created human beings in his image,[63] it is proper for human beings to exactly reflect God's image. If each human being can live in Jesus Christ who is the exact representation of God's being,[64] then the estrangement and hostility between human beings and those between humanity and God will cease to exist.

Before he was crucified, Jesus had prayed repeatedly to the Father for the reconciliation: "Holy Father, protect them by the power of your name—the name you gave me—so that they may be one as we are one … My prayer is not for them alone. I pray also for those who will believe in me through their message, that all of them may be one, Father, just as you are in me and I am in you. May they also be in us so that the world may believe that you have sent me. I have given them the glory that you gave me, that they may be one as we are one: I in them and you in me. May they be brought to complete unity to let the world know that you sent me and have loved them even as you have loved me."[65]

The more one who has been redeemed through Christ by God read this prayer, the more he or she could be touched by the amazing relationship between the Son and the Father! One could also be reminded of a moment when Jesus was baptized and the Spirit descended on him and the Father said, "This is my Son, whom I love; with him I am well pleased."[66] It is a moment when the governing order of the trinitarian God was remarkably displayed.

But that is also a moment when numerous people did not see God's rule. For anyone who has seen it since then, the reality of the world is not only about this world. The full reality is found in Christ.[67] Of course, that includes the reality of politics. In Christ, one could see any political

63 Genesis 1:26–27.
64 Hebrews 1:3.
65 John 17:11, 20–23.
66 Matthew 3:16–17.
67 Colossians 2:17.

conundrum was not so special. Even in China where politics is a matter of old, big and difficult concern, everything remains within the sovereignty of Jesus Christ. Because of his mercy, the body of Jesus Christ has also been growing in this country, which has had an ancient name "God's Land."

In China where hostility to God remains widespread, the church and its members have also been given the ministry of reconciliation. Again like elsewhere in the world, Jesus Christ is the bridge or the interface where true reconciliation can be achieved: "For God was pleased to have all his fullness dwell in him, and through him to reconcile to himself all things, whether things on earth or things in heaven, by making peace through his blood, shed on the cross."[68]

68   Colossians 1:19–20.

Chapter 6
Change the Herbs, Keep the Water

As long as you live in this world, it seems inevitable not to be perfectly content with your lot: hence the need for a change.[69] However, any genuine change will not come easy. The form may change, but the substance will remain the same.

Is it possible to keep the form and change the substance? For Charles Handy, the answer is "yes." The Irish management thinker has shared this discovery with us.

In today's world, Handy is arguably the most eminent management thinker of European origins. Since Peter Drucker, widely viewed as the father of modern management, died in 2005, Handy is the best-known management thinker alive today with views close to Drucker's. However, very few people seem to have appreciated the importance of this prominent author's revelation about form and substance.

On July 25, 1932, Charles Handy was born in Clane, a small town which is about 30 kilometers west of the Irish capital of Dublin. His father was the rector of two country parishes in a nearby town, Sallins.

Handy was educated at Oxford. After graduation, he worked at Royal Dutch Shell, a global oil and gas company, for nearly 10 years. Then Handy went to America where he earned an MBA at MIT's Sloan School of Management. When back in Britain, he helped found the London Business School and began teaching management there.

In 1977, Handy left the School to become Warden of St George's House in Windsor Castle, where he stayed until 1981. St George's House had been founded in 1966 by the Duke of Edinburgh, the husband of

69 This chapter first appeared in Chinese in the 2011 summer issue of *Almond Flowers* magazine.

Queen Elizabeth II, and the then Dean of Windsor, Robin Woods. It claims to have two main objectives: "to organise and host consultations on matters of national and international concern and to run conferences for clergy of all denominations who, having had some ministerial experience, come to the House to reflect theologically on the Church and the world."

Handy both worked and lived in Windsor Castle. He would ask those who participated in the gatherings of St George's House to look around. He told them that the castle had a history of nearly one thousand years and that almost from the beginning, it has been a residence of the British monarchy. On the surface, there have been no changes. The castle is still here and the British royal household remains its owner. However, the substance of the British monarchy has changed much. It still provides the head of state and yet its power has been greatly limited.

From this discovery, Handy went on to suggest: "Change was often easier if you kept the form but changed the substance when the world around you changed."[70]

For those who get used to changes in form rather than substance, the change that Handy saw in Windsor Castle may sound strange. The past ten centuries have witnessed a variety of alterations in the form of governance in many countries. Not only have monarchies been overthrown but the republics which replaced them have undergone transformation. And yet, the substance of governance remains the same.

To take an example, China experienced at least three different forms of governance in the twentieth century alone. The name changed first from the Empire of the Great Qing to the Republic of China, and then to the People's Republic of China. The year 2011 marks the 100th anniversary of the 1911 Revolution, which converted China from a monarchy into a republic. Despite these changes, China has not seen a genuine change in the substance of governance so far.

Interestingly, the Chinese language has an idiom that vividly illustrates this phenomenon: The water has been changed but the herbs have

70   Charles Handy, "The Unintended Consequences of a Good Idea":
      http://www.druckersociety.at/files/charles-handy_where-next-for-capital-ism.pdf

not been changed yet. In traditional Chinese medicine, the prescribed herbs are first placed in water, then boiled and simmered. This creates a soup for a patient to drink. Generally speaking, different herbs rather than a change of the water is crucial in targeting different diseases. So, it is the change of herbs that makes the difference.

How did Britain realize the need to change the substance while keeping the form? The answer, according to Handy, is to be found in the history of Windsor Castle. One day in 1215 King John, the then monarch of England, rode out from the courtyard of Windsor to sign with the leaders of the church and the barons a document limiting the power of the monarchy.

The document was later called Magna Carta in Latin or Great Charter in English. Before it was signed, England had been at war with France. King John of England wanted to raise more taxes from the public to finance his campaign. The leaders of the church and the barons objected to the policy. They forced King John to accept their demands on June 15, 1215.

Magna Carta required the king to raise taxes through "the common counsel of our realm." It also provided that, except by the lawful judgment of his peers or by the law of the land, no free man should be taken or imprisoned, no free man's property should be confiscated, no free man should be declared to be deprived of legal protection and no free man should be put to death or tortured.

During the rest of King John's rule and the centuries that followed, these clauses were not fully put into practice. But Magna Carta has been influential, inspiring later constitutional documents like the Bill of Rights in seventeenth-century England and the US Constitution in the eighteenth century. All these have contributed greatly to a social order in today's world that is favorable to the development of both individuals and a wider society.

Since Magna Carta, a major characteristic of the British politics has been to keep the form and change the substance. Of course, King Charles I was beheaded in 1649 and there was a republic which lasted from 1649 to 1660. However, Britain remains a kingdom, although not a tyrannical state.

Britain was not alone when it came to keeping the form and

changing the substance. During the time of King John, his counterparts in the European continent had to sign their own Magna Cartas, the late twelfth and the early fourteenth centuries seeing similar changes in what is now Italy, France, Germany, Spain and Hungary.

Of all the European charters, England's Magna Carta is by far the best-known. England became much less chaotic than continental Europe since it was signed. After the Glorious Revolution of 1688, Britain largely established constitutional monarchy. Ever since, the use of force has been ruled out in the transfer of power at home.

However, in comparison with the rest of the world, Europe in general would go in the direction of keeping the form and changing the substance. This, in turn, was a by-product of the social atmosphere. And the life of Charles Handy as a European gives a good illustration of how the atmosphere has shaped a somewhat unique European culture in this respect.

Handy's father played a critical role in his life, in both negative and positive ways. He was a rector in rural Ireland. Such a quiet, poor and unambitious life did not appeal to the young Charles. "By the time I was eighteen, I had resolved never to be poor, never to go to church again," recalled Handy years later.

Handy wanted to change. He wanted to make a difference. So he went to study at the famous Oxford where he achieved a first-class honors in Greats, that is, classics (including ancient Greek and Latin), history and philosophy. He worked at the famous oil giant, Shell. After studying management at another famous place, MIT, he co-founded the London Business School, Britain's first graduate business program.

By the time he was in his 40s, Handy seemed already very successful in realizing his boyhood ambition. A real change, though, was yet to come.

One day in Paris, when Handy was attending a business conference, he heard that his father was dying. He went back to Ireland. His father died after he reached home. Then came the funeral on the third day.

In the church his father served for more than forty years, at least hundreds of people showed up. Many were local residents with others coming from all across Ireland. The local police volunteered to clear a way for the people going to the church. Handy wondered how it was that they came together from various places at such a short notice. That was the late 1970s when even in Europe there was no faster forms of communication than landline phones.

Standing by his father's grave, Handy saw the tears in the eyes of many people. They had received help from his father who baptized them or their children, administered at their weddings, and visited them like a shepherd.

Who will attend my funeral with tears in their eyes? What is success? Who will be successful, me or my father? What is one's life for? Handy could not help asking himself these questions. Quiet as his father was, he made a great deal of difference to hundreds of souls. He turned down urban parishes and dedicated his life to this country backwater.

At about 45, Handy began his life anew. He wanted to live a life like his father's. He thought of studying theology and becoming a priest. But friends in the church suggested that if he wanted to serve God, it would be much better for him to remain as an expert in management than put on a dog collar. They encouraged Handy to apply for the position of Warden of St George's House in Windsor Castle.

St George's House was in a courtyard behind St George's Chapel. It was named after a Roman soldier called George in the third century. He was killed for refusing to disown his Christian belief. Almost every day for four years, Handy worked and lived at St George's House. He attended regular services in the chapel. This went against his boyhood vow that he would never go to church again.

The life at St George's House paved the way for the next stage of Handy's career. In 1981 when he was 49, Handy became a freelance writer and consultant. He began earning his living by writing books and articles, consulting companies and training executives.

This means Handy's life would not be as stable as that at Shell or London Business School or Windsor Castle. He would no longer bear the title of professor or warden. He told his friends, "I shall just be Charles Handy." His wife was very supportive of his choice. As a freelance photographer, Mrs. Handy has been his partner in both life and work. At that time, both their daughter and son were of school age.

On average, Handy would spend half of each year on his work. The other half would see him helping his wife with her work and housework.

Since 1981, Handy has completed nearly twenty books. *The Future of Work, The Age of Unreason, The Hungry Spirit, The Elephant and the Flea* are among the best-known.

The ideas these books try to get across to the audiences have perhaps gone beyond what an ordinary management expert cares about. The rural pastoral life of his father made a significant impact on Handy's management thinking. In his eyes, "A company ought to be a community, a community that you belong to, like a village."

For Handy, the future of business and the broader world of human organizations would not lie in the familiar form of a shareholder company that only seeks profit-making. He suggests that no one should claim to be the owner of a company, as nobody should own a village. He says that each member of a company should be a citizen with civil rights and shareholders would become financiers getting rewarded according to the risk they assume.

As a consultant, Handy would invite his clients to visit his home and tell him all about their organizations. Handy says he does not like prowling around companies like a consultant. Instead, he likes to know what the people in an organization think and feel. In his own words, "I want to see the organization through their eyes."

In a sense, the later life of Handy resembles what his father did in his country parish. He helps people in the business world find his or her purpose. The acclaimed US management magazine *strategy+business* once described Handy as a "vicar and visionary" in modern management.

Handy sees himself as a prophet, not in the sense of telling us about future events but more like an Old Testament prophet who reminded people to beware, repent and change their ways. He asks people in today's commercial society not to submerge themselves in social sentiment or the organizations they work with. People ought to live out the rich dimensions of their lives.

From Handy's life hitherto, you may have seen how a human being who was not content with one's life changed oneself. Contrary to his expectations, it was the humdrum pastoral career of his father in the sight of the young Charles that became an example for the mature Charles. The point is that Handy still remains in his field of management but his ideas about management have witnessed a sea change.

Different as the size and the scope of these things may appear, the change in Handy himself and the change he saw at Windsor Castle are cut from the same cloth. Those who would like to abolish the monarchy and create something completely new resemble the young Charles. Those who would like to keep the monarchy but limit its power seem like the mature Charles.

What makes a person or a society become mature (which here means, they are able to change for the better in substance rather than just the skin-deep)? In the story of Handy, it is the father's soul-touching and the son's soul-searching that make all the difference. In the history of Europe, the story of Handy is far from unique. For more than ten centuries, numerous parishes[71] have been set up all over Europe where generations of fathers and sons like the Handys lived. They include where the kings and queens reside.

In 1215 when King John was forced to accept Magna Carta, a church could be found in every major community of the British isles. St George's Chapel is one of the places where the British monarch attends church services. There, people like Handy's father shepherd the parish, no matter who the sheep are. That means all the sheep have the same Great Shepherd, *i.e.*, God, and even the king has his King.

Within such a framework, Stephen Langton, Archbishop of Canterbury during the reign of King John, was able to become a key mediator between the monarch and his opponents. Langton was also known in ecclesiastical history for dividing the books of the Bible into chapters. He studied at the University of Paris—a center of higher learning in medieval Europe—and was teaching theology there as late as about the age of 57 when he was elected as Archbishop of Canterbury. Because of King John's opposition, Langton was not able to return to England until July 1213 at 63.

Within such a framework, it is not hard to understand why European monarchs could humble themselves to accept the charters forwarded by the church and baron leaders. For the church and baron leaders, they were but sheep under the same Great Shepherd so that it was not very

---

71 The word "parish" comes from ancient Greek παροικία (paroikia) meaning "sojourning in a foreign land."

easy for them to overthrow the incumbent monarch who was also the sheep of the same Great Shepherd.

Even though King Charles I was beheaded, the monarchy might still be resumed after the sheep in general realized it was just the change in form. And with the continued soul-touching and soul-searching among the parishes, a mature society came into being. For them, as Handy discovered, "Change was often easier if you kept the form but changed the substance when the world around you changed."

Chapter 7
The Good News in China

It is the fourth time I am attending The Media Project workshops since May 2008 in Sydney.[72] In less than two years, many things have happened in China in both the church and the press.

My two main points are: first, religious freedom in China, and second, the freedom of the press. I would like to discuss the relationship between the Christian faith and the future of the press.

First of all, I would like to share several Bible verses which have already explained the two points. It's from Acts 1:4–8, "On one occasion, while he (Jesus) was eating with them (the disciples), he gave them this command: 'Do not leave Jerusalem, but wait for the gift my Father promised, which you have heard me speak about. For John baptized with water, but in a few days you will be baptized with the Holy Spirit.' So when they met together, they asked him, 'Lord, are you at this time going to restore the kingdom to Israel?' Jesus said to them: 'It is not for you to know the times or dates the Father has set by his own authority. But you will receive power when the Holy Spirit comes on you; and you will be my witnesses in Jerusalem, and in all Judea and Samaria, and to the ends of the earth.'"[73]

A few years ago, I did not expect Jesus had anything to do with my career, or my country or everything. But for now, these verses have everything to do with me and my church and my brothers and sisters and my friends in the broader society.

---

72   This chapter was originally a talk given at The Media Project's Philippine cruise workshop on February 11, 2010. It was transcribed by Baby Lyn Cacho Resulta. The Media Project (www.themediaproject.org) is a non-profit educational and research organization for journalists worldwide.

73   Acts 1:4–8.

The question is why Christianity is on an unprecedented rise in China today, rising in number, rising in spirit, and also going widespread across the society, in many professions, in cities, villages. Of course, the percentage of Christians is still small, perhaps still less than ten percent of the whole population. But when you look at big cities like Beijing, Shanghai, Guangzhou, more and more professionals have converted to Christianity in the last ten years.

Why now? If you would trace the history, just not very long after the time of the Acts of the Apostles, the gospel has already been spread as far as to China, perhaps as early as in Han Dynasty. Christianity has a long history in China.

A few hundred years later, about seventh or eighth century, there was another wave of spreading gospel in China. Then at another time of the sixteenth and seventeenth centuries, it was spread, but then it almost died out. Then in the late nineteenth and early twentieth centuries, the gospel was spread again in China. About that time, many missionaries from Europe, from America, from other parts of the world spread the gospel, in cities as well as in villages. They built churches, church schools, church universities, hospitals and many facilities for Chinese people. But all this ended in 1949 and later when the Communist rule began. Over the past sixty years, the basic situation in Chinese politics has not changed much.

As all of you may have known, the policy of reform and opening up over the recent thirty years has changed China so much, especially in the economy. This year, China is expected to overtake Japan as the second largest economy in the world, second only to the United States. Some experts believe that in ten or fifteen or twenty years, China will overtake America as the number one economy of the world. So, in terms of economy, China has become a major world power.

This situation is nothing new however, because in the history of China, for more than 5,000 years, I think for two or three thousand years, China had already been the number one economy of the world. Many inventions, many contributions in material wealth, as well as spiritual wealth to the whole humankind community. But what is special, what is unique, about this rise in economy of China is that it has opened itself to the whole world ... to the outside world. In the past, China considered itself the middle of the whole world. In Chinese, China as a country means Zhong Guo, the middle country ... the middle of the whole universe. So that means China was the focal point of the whole world. So, there's nothing new that China was and will be the biggest economy and already has the biggest population in the whole world.

This uniqueness is about the opening up to the whole world, especially to the West. A major incentive behind this is that Chinese intellectuals, the elite, over the past 100 years, just wanted China to be a superpower, especially in material wealth. They wanted China to be as rich as the West. For now, more and more Chinese people have become rich and some are among the richest of the world.

Against this backdrop, let us look at another picture, which is about politics, about spirituality, about education. In this, things are very complicated. Before I became a Christian, I was very pessimistic about China's future, because as more and more Chinese people become rich, they do not find happiness. To be rich does not mean happiness, it does not mean you have peaceful hearts. And in the poorer regions, there are many protests, although the official media do not report about these protests as often as they happen.

Two major historical periods since 1949 may have contributed to the rise of Christianity in today's China. First is the Cultural Revolution, which was between 1966 and 1976. It was one of the key founders of the People's Republic of China, Chairman Mao Zedong, who initiated the Cultural Revolution. He wanted China to be a new China. Chairman Mao was also an intellectual. He liked to read poems and books. He himself was a poet. He was also an artist, especially in calligraphy. He wanted China to be a new China, not only as a political entity but also as a spiritual entity. He wanted China to become a leader in the world. That's why the Cultural Revolution was initiated. But that turned out to be a disaster, maybe the biggest in the Chinese history.

After that, it was the second-generation Communist leader Deng Xiaoping who initiated another revolution, called Reform and Opening-up.

The second major historical period is the late 1980s, especially in 1989, when the Tiananmen Square democracy movement happened. Why the Tiananmen Square democracy movement? Because at that time

China had begun the Reform and Opening-up for ten years. But people, including intellectuals, found that there were too many corrupt officials. Corruption was widespread like an epidemic. So people, from the bottom of their hearts, thought things should be changed; effective measures should be effected against this widespread corruption.

And the government itself was also in a crisis. There were some problems in the policies between the conservatives and the reformists. Deng Xiaoping at that time was still alive. But based on some memoirs, especially that of the late Premier Zhao Ziyang, one of the key persons whom Deng Xiaoping appointed to move ahead with the reform and opening-up, Deng was in a struggle as to how to get ahead with the reform. At that time, the opening-up and the reform had proven to be a success to some extent. But regarding education and the wider spiritual condition, China was in a less successful situation. It is not just that the officials were bad, but that the spiritual condition was a major problem among people.

These two revolutions show that after China achieved its independence as a country, as a nation it had its own troubles, especially in terms of spirituality. The Cultural Revolution turned out to be a disaster and the second one, the Tiananmen Square democracy movement, turned out to be a failure.

After these two key historical periods, a spiritual vacuum was created among Chinese intellectuals, elites and the broader society. For some of them, all these experiments have proven to be failures. What was next? How to help China become a great nation? So, at that time, some of them began their soul-searching process. Some of them later became the co-workers of house churches in China.

For example in our church, our founding pastor is a graduate of Tsinghua University, a leading institution of higher education in China. He would have become an excellent scientist or engineer in the 1990s. Then more and more Chinese intellectuals began their spiritual journey. To be rich is just one step to make China a great country.

In the beginning of 1990s, these house churches appeared. And after another twenty years, and until now, greater changes have happened in Chinese villages and cities. For example, the founding pastor of our church was born in a village in the northeast of China. But now, he and his wife and his two children live in Beijing. Their faith can be a kind of influence among his family members and relatives among villages.

What is unique about this spread of the gospel among Chinese intellectuals is that almost everything is home-grown. These house churches were not founded by foreign missionaries. They're founded by Chinese themselves; most of them never went abroad. One thing is very interesting. Many founding members of these house churches were baptized in the official Three-Self churches in China. At that time, other than the Three-Self official Chinese churches, you almost couldn't find any other major Christian groups; foreign missionaries were not allowed to spread the gospel in China, although some may have come in secret, and the members of the independent Chinese churches founded before 1949 were very small and their influence was limited to a very small population. Some university graduates in the early 1990s went to the church and the church was the official Three-Self church. After just about a couple of years, they went out to establish their own independent churches.

Now, our church has a history of seventeen years. Each Sunday, we have more than 1,000 worshippers in three services. The members are several hundred. To be a member means almost each Sunday you go to church and you commit to this church; you become a co-worker of the church and you lead a Bible study group, a small group, or some fellowships.

The first time I attended the Media Project seminar was back in May 2008 in Sydney. Our church then began to publish our own magazine. Up to now, we have continued to publish our quarterly magazine called *Almond Flowers*. We also have established our website. The website was closed by the government several times. But the latest one is still alive. Also, we have an online community. There are about 1,000 members of that community.

So, briefly, that is a long history of China, especially about spirituality. The major reason is because the spiritual vacuum has to be filled with something. And for unbelievers, maybe it is but an accident that Christianity is on the rise. But to Christians, this is not an accident but a promise/providence by God.

The second major point is the press. What is the situation of the press? The situation now is very volatile. For the last ten years, China has had its own independent, privately-owned magazines, newspapers. But it's hard to say which one is officially state-run or which one is privately owned. Generally speaking, many of the magazines and websites are already owned by individual business people. Of course, they have to gain government approval in terms of editorial policy. But to me, as a journalist who worked with the state-run television, there has been great improvement in the Chinese press.

For example, over the past couple of years, in some magazines and newspapers I have worked with, each week we would have editorial meetings but never, even in a single editorial meeting, had we ever received any direct order from the government publicity or propaganda authority about the content of the media. So, it's already very free among the independent press compared to the past. Yet in the last ten years, there also have been intense struggles because they have different views on how independent press should go. For example, one of the latest significant struggles took place in the *Caijing* or *Finance* magazine, a leading financial magazine in China. Partly because of the struggles, the team who originally had built the *Caijing* magazine has just recently left en masse from their former investors and established a new publication, the *New Century* weekly. From my own experience and from what I have seen, it's very hard to establish a long-lived news media in China. That is why among many colleagues I've met so far there's a kind of pessimism or hopelessness. That's why there's a kind of vacuum in spirituality. In recent months alone, I've met more and more Christian journalists although the numbers are still small.

Basically, that's what I'd like to share with you about Christianity and the press in China.

I will end with two expressions. The first, a major change among some Chinese intellectuals is about moving from saving a country to saving a soul. For the past hundred years, the goal was to save China from the domination of the Western powers. Independence has been the overwhelming faith among the Chinese elite. But since 1949, this has been already achieved. Now, saving the country is not a problem anymore, but saving a soul is still a problem.

The second expression is about the press. From my point of view, we are still in the news industry, but more than that, we are in the good news industry. There is a saying among the Western countries, only bad news is the news. But to me, the worthwhile news to spread is good news. Of course, you should show the bad side of news, but what's next? Because even if you show every dark side, then, what is your answer to that? The answer is even more important than to show the reality. As journalists, we need to show the truth. The truth is not only to show the bad. In the end, we want something good to be established. That is why we become Christian journalists. That is my attitude towards my profession. We need to be a good witness to the truth ... that is Jesus Christ, only through whom all the universe has been created by our Father in heaven and human beings are saved from sin. So, that's the secret. The only way we can be victorious in our profession is to be a good news witness, not only as a good journalist. Because that to me is the essence of a good news messenger.

Chapter 8
The Meaning of Shouwang

Towards the end of his lifetime in this world, Peter Drucker famously said more than once, "The most significant sociological phenomenon of the first half of the 20th century was the rise of the corporation. The most significant sociological phenomenon of the second half of the 20th century has been the development of the large pastoral church—of the mega-church. It is the only organization that is actually working in our society."[74]

When Drucker, often called "the father of the modern management," made the observation at the turn of the century, his eyes were largely on the United States. A little more than ten years later, the two most significant sociological phenomena Drucker highlighted are becoming increasingly—perhaps quite surprisingly—evident in the world's largest economy behind America.

Since the late 1970s when China initiated the reform and opening-up policy, companies have become one of the most significant parts of the Chinese society that touch plenty of people's lives. To a considerable extent, the rise of the corporation—both state-owned and privately held enterprises—contributed to the rise of China.

The private sector is even more notable. It has accounted for most of China's economy. However, in the early stage of the Reform and Opening-up era, private businesses were still not universally recognized. Before that, China's government had not allowed private firms to exist

---

74 Part of this chapter appeared in the April 26, 2011 web issue of *Christianity Today*: http://www.christianitytoday.com/ct/2011/aprilweb-only/beijinghousechurch.html. *World Magazine* published an updated part of it in the issue of July 30, 2011: http://www.worldmag.com/articles/18359.

at all for most of the time since the People's Republic of China was founded in 1949. One risked one's life if he or she did private enterprises.

If the spectacular growth of private companies in China was beyond the expectation of many people, the development of large pastoral churches came as a much bigger surprise. Private companies were once viewed by China's government officials as what belongs only to what they call "capitalism" or "the Western capitalist countries." Now, they have regarded the private economy as an "important component" of the socialist market economy. Compared to private businesses, large pastoral churches seem even more foreign to China. Are they really growing in popularity in China?

The answer is yes. Indeed, from early April 2011 on, Shouwang Church, a large pastoral church in the Chinese capital of Beijing, has begun dominating the international headlines. Almost all the major global media have been following what was unfolding concerning the church. Among them are *Reuters, The Associated Press, Agence France-Presse, BBC, CNN, NPR, The New York Times, Wall Street Journal, The Washington Post, Time, The Daily Telegraph, Guardian, Al Jazeera, South China Morning Post, The Economist,* and both the Chinese and English versions of the *Global Times,* a daily newspaper operating under the official Chinese ruling Communist Party newspaper, the *People's Daily.*

Over the past few years, there have already been various reports about the rise of Christianity in China. A classic is *Jesus in Beijing: How Christianity is Transforming China and Changing the Global Balance of Power.* It was first published in 2003 when David Aikman, its author and former Beijing Bureau Chief of *Time* magazine, wrote that "the number of Christian believers in China, both Catholic and Protestant, may be closer to 80 million than the official combined Catholic-Protestant figure of 21 million." In contrast, some estimates show that there were only about 800,000 Christians in China in 1949 and some two million in the late 1970s.

In 2011, it was still hard to know for sure how many Christians were in China. An official census published in 2010 reckoned the number was approximately 23 million. Other calculations have ranged from 40 million to 130 million. According to *God is Back: How the Global Revival of Faith is Changing the World,* China probably has close to 100 million Christians and will soon have the world's largest Christian population. The book, published in 2009, was written by John Micklethwait, Editor-in-Chief of *The Economist,* and his colleague, Adrian Wooldridge.

Yet, as Aikman pointed out in *Jesus in Beijing,* "in numerical terms they were still a small minority ... but they were being noticed, and they kept turning up in the most unexpected places." The Christians Aikman met across China were farmers, businesspeople, students, scholars, artists and even government officials.

Now, it is not only that Christians could be found from almost all walks of life in China but that like private companies, the non-state-owned churches—what is called "house churches"—many go to are beginning to grow into an "important component" of the Chinese society. According to Li Fan, Director of the World and China Institute, a Beijing-based non-governmental think tank, house churches have become the most powerful non-governmental organization in China. Li Fan reckoned that all over China, house churches had nearly one million worship and meeting places where the participants might account for one-third to one-half of China's NGO population.

Shouwang Church is only one of those numerous house churches scattered across China.

Since April 2011, more than thirty house churches in Beijing alone have declared to show their solidarity with Shouwang by holding prayer meetings. Some of them are also large pastoral churches. And on May 11, pastors or co-workers of nearly twenty house churches in six Chinese cities delivered their signed petitions to the National People's Congress, China's top legislature, to investigate the government's crackdown on Shouwang Church based on the country's Constitution that enshrines the liberty of faith. But the story of Shouwang may have shown how an originally obscure Bible study group could not only survive in a (seemingly) hostile environment, but also thrive and go on to make a great deal of difference to ever more individuals and the wider world.

The current global media spotlight centers around the worship or meeting place of Shouwang Church. Since April 10, 2011, the church has been forced to worship outdoors for more than forty consecutive Sundays. In early 2012, little sign was shown of an immediate end to the situation. Before that, the Shouwang congregation of about one thousand people had been gathering for more than a year in a conference hall of the Old Story Club in the northern urban area of Beijing. But according to Shouwang Church, the owner of the rented venue was under mounting pressure from the government. In March, Shouwang planned to rent a conference hall of a hotel northwest of the city. However, the church said some relevant government agencies again interfered and prevented it from renting the new premises.

Every Sunday since April 2011, numerous uniformed and plain-clothes police officers have been sent to a public square at Zhongguancun, known as "China's Silicon Valley," in Beijing's northwestern district of Haidian. That is where Shouwang worshippers were supposed to gather. Hundreds of people of the Shouwang congregation were detained. The time ranged from a few hours to 24 or 48 hours. They worshipped, including reading the Bible, singing hymns and praying, after being loaded on to buses or put into police stations. Some people who were free went to the local police stations to wait for the release of their fellow Shouwang congregants. Many others were put under house arrest for various periods of time. Almost all the church's main co-workers have been under house arrest for the whole or much of the time since the evening of April 9. Some church members have lost their jobs or rented homes or both. Some others were threatened to lose either one— or both. Many of them are young professionals in different fields, for example, in companies, NGOs and universities.

Easter Sunday April 24, 2011, was the third time the Shouwang parishioners held outdoor worship. More than thirty people were rounded up and herded onto buses or police cars after they worshiped in or near the square at Zhongguancun. Like the first two Sundays, they were then sent to local police stations. They were asked to leave their names and contact information and give a guarantee of not attending the outdoor worship again. Some declined to make any pledge and some others simply told the police that they would continue to worship outdoor the next Sunday. Some of them have been detained two or three times. More than half were released later in the day. But the rest, all in the eastern district of Chaoyang, gained their freedom after having to stay at the police stations for up to two days.

On May 1, over thirty people including two children and their mothers were detained when they were at Zhongguancun for outdoor worship or taken away from their homes. The children and their mothers were released later in the day and so were ten other people. Once again, the rest of them were freed after 24 or 48 hours.

On May 8, at least fifteen people were taken to about ten different police stations across Beijing. All except one were freed later in the day or by the early next afternoon. Hu Jian, a Shouwang church member, was not released after 48 hours in custody. The police station said he was sent back to his Hukou (household registration) place. They refused to say where he was. The Hubei provincial office in Beijing said they did not know this. The central Hubei Province is where Hu Jian's household is registered. After previous detentions, 26-year-old Hu Jian had already been forced to quit his job as an instructor at KindyROO, an international school for children under three years old. He also lost his place to stay because he lived at the school office.

Later on May 10, a roommate of an apartment Hu Jian stayed at for a couple of weeks before May 8 received a phone call from Hu Jian. He said he was sent to an office of Hubei's capital of Wuhan in Beijing from the police station earlier that day. The office was asked by the police officers to buy a train ticket for Hu Jian's return to Hubei. They said they could not get a ticket and would try and buy one the next day. The police officers confiscated Hu Jian's identity card and told him later that they could not find it. They asked Hu Jian to go to Hubei to apply for a new one. But by early 2012, Hu Jian still had not got a new ID card from the police authorities in his hometown. That made it difficult for him even to buy a train ticket for a family reunion during the traditional Chinese Spring Festival holiday. From day one of 2012, travelers were required to show identity documents when buying train tickets. To the surprise of Hu Jian, his new identity card was issued and sent to him from his home town a few days before the traditional Chinese New Year's day. He took a train on the day of Spring Festival and spent the holidays with his family. He then went back to attending the outdoor Sunday worship on January 29, 2012, when he was taken to a police car and was freed a short while later.

Back in May, 2011, Hu Jian told one of his English fellowship co-workers of Shouwang Church on the phone (a Wuhan office worker's) that he wanted to go and see his parents and his maternal grandmother and also wanted to get a rest after a month when he attended all the five Sunday outdoor worships and was detained four times. He, with an almost-60-year-old police officer who was a section chief of Wuchang(a district of Wuhan) Public Security Bureau based in Beijing's Wuhan office, took a train to Hankou Railway Station in Wuhan at about 9:10 in the evening of May 11. More than twenty Shouwang congregants were at Beijing West Railway Station to see Hu Jian off. They prayed hand in hand and sang a hymn at a waiting hall of the railway station. A Shouwang member took a photo of it, which was later published on the 2011 autumn issue of *Xing Hua* or *Almond Flowers*, the church's quarterly journal. Hu Jian and the police officer arrived in Wuhan the next morning. The Wuhan's Beijing office bought two hard-sleeper tickets for them. They later went to Jingzhou, Hu Jian's home town in Hubei. After having lunch, the police officer returned to Wuhan. Hu Jian said he might be back to Beijing and try to find a new job in about a month. It was the first time that the authorities sent a Shouwang congregant back to his home town because of attending outdoor worship. Two local police officers visited Hu Jian's home asking about the basic information of his family on May 16, four days after he returned home. He was back in Beijing in mid-June and was detained for a few hours after attending the June 12 outdoor worship.

On May 15, some thirteen Shouwang parishioners were taken to police stations. They were freed later in the day or the next day. On May 22, at least twenty-seven people, including an elderly woman in her eighties and a two-year-old child, were detained. Most were released on the same day except one who was not able to return home until the next afternoon. On May 29, twenty-two congregants were detained. Like the previous Sundays, most were freed later in the day and one got freedom on Monday. On June 5, twenty people were detained including two from other churches, and one from the Three-Self's Haidian Church. Sixteen were released later in the day and the other four were freed by the next noon. On June 12, seventeen people were arrested. Among them, three were taken to the basement at a Haidian police station where they wanted to visit a Shouwang member who was already detained. Police officers accused two of them of stealing. All were freed on the same day except one who wasn't released until the next afternoon. On June 19, thirteen Shouwang congregants and a member of New Tree Church were imprisoned, and all were freed before midnight. On June 26, fifteen people were detained and all were released on the same day.

On June 27, Wang Chuanliang, a Shouwang member, was sent back to his home town in the eastern province of Shandong by Haidian's Dongsheng Police Station and the Shandong provincial office in Beijing. It was the second repatriation since Shouwang began the outdoor worship on April 10. It was the same Dongsheng Police Station that sent back Hu Jian, another Shouwang parishioner, to his home town in the central Hubei Province in May. Hu Jian returned to Beijing almost a month later and continued to attend outdoor worships and thus was detained almost every Sunday since then.

At about 5 o'clock in the afternoon of June 27, three police officers from Dongsheng Police Station and Haidian Public Security Bureau detained Wang Chuanliang in a market where he was getting a mobile phone fixed. He was handed over to a Shandong office based in the capital and was sent back to his home town in the evening. The Shouwang parishioner was forbidden to use his mobile phone.

Only in the next morning was he able to send a text message to his fellow church members about his expulsion. He was sent to his parents' home at noon. His identity card was confiscated and he was warned not to return to Beijing before July 1, which was to be the 90th anniversary of the founding of China's ruling Communist Party. Local village officials were asked to watch over him.

In a weekly bulletin about outdoor worship issued on June 28, Shouwang Church lodged a protest against and condemnation of the eviction. It considered "the forced expatriation by Dongsheng Police Station and Haidian Public Security Bureau has constituted a complete contempt for and a flagrant violation of the law in effect depriving a citizen of any guarantee of the most basic of foundational existential rights."

On July 3, nineteen people were taken into custody. Most were freed later in the day, but a couple were held at Longyuan Police Station in the northern district of Changping until the early hours of the next day. Also in the early morning of July 4, two other Shouwang congregants were forced to move out of their newly-rented apartment rooms because of the mounting pressure on the landlord from Balizhuang Police Station in the eastern Chaoyang District. On July 10, at least twenty-six people were taken to fourteen police stations, including Minister Yan Xin'en and his wife Dai Jiexin, who had been studying theology at a theological seminary in America since 2008 and returned to Beijing for summer vacation. Two members of New Tree Church were also taken. All were released by two o'clock the next morning. Some other Shouwang parishioners were detained as well but were freed on the road before they were supposed to be taken to police stations. On July 17, twenty-two people were detained, including two from New Tree Church and one from a church outside Beijing. All were freed by midnight. On July 24, thirty-five people, including Pastor Wang Shuangyan and two other members of New Tree Church and two from Shanghai and Tianjin respectively, were taken to at least twenty-one police stations. Seventeen were released later in the day. The rest weren't freed until twenty-four hours later or even after forty-eight hours. On July 31, at least twenty-two people were imprisoned. Seven were released by midnight, and fifteen others walked free by August 2. On August 7, eleven people were detained and all were freed by the next noon. On August 14th, sixteen people were arrested. More than half were not freed until the next day. Pastor Wang Shuangyan of New Tree Church was released from Dongtiejiangying Police Station of Fengtai District at noon on August 16. During her detention, Pastor Shuangyan was on a hunger strike in protest against the act. The police station did not allow the visitors to send her food. On August 21, seven people were taken to seven police stations and two others were detained on Friday evening. All were freed by the next evening. On August 28, at least fifteen people were detained and all were released by noon on August 30. On September 4, twelve parishioners were taken to police stations and all were freed by the next night. On September 11, at least thirteen Shouwang congregants and two from other churches were detained. The last one was released in the morning of September 13. On September 18, at least six people were taken into custody. All were freed by the next morning. On September 25, fourteen people, including Elder You Guanhui who tried to go to the platform at Zhongguancun, were arrested and all were set free by midnight. On October 2, ten people were detained and all were freed by noon the next day. On October 9, Pastor Zhang Xiaofeng and seventeen other people were detained for attempting to worship at the supposed outdoor place. One Shouwang member was not released until late morning of October 11.

Over the Sundays since April 2011, many other Shouwang members were confined to their homes. On the Easter 2011, a young couple asked the police to drive them to the Zhongguancun square. The police agreed. They sang hymns, read the Bible and prayed in the police car. They also gave the police officers a copy of the Bible and an autobiography about how a Chinese biologist became a Christian and his views about Christianity and science. The police car moved around the square. After the young couple finished worship, the police officers drove them home. The young couple shared their experience with fellow Shouwang members through the church's online forum, which was shut down in mid-April but resumed later. The forum was closed again in the second week of June. Many Shouwang congregants resorted to Google buzz, a micro-blogging site, (from late 2011 on, Google+), for keeping informed.

Into the seventh week since the outdoor worship began, local police officers asked some church members not to attend Shouwang's evening prayer meetings, which had been held on weeknights at a rented place of New Tree Church at Zhongguancun. Pastors and other co-workers of New Tree Church and a number of other house churches in Beijing and some other cities in China shared their sermons in the evening prayer meetings. Into the ninth and tenth week, some Three-Self Church people were sent to police stations asking the detained parishioners to leave Shouwang Church and join them or put an end to the outdoor worship. In its weekly bulletin on outdoor worship issued on June 14, Shouwang's governing committee quoted the apostle Paul's letter to the Romans in the New Testament, "Who are you to judge someone else's servant? To his own master he stands or falls. And he will stand, for the Lord is able to make him stand."[75]

It was not the first time that Shouwang Church made global headlines. In November 2009 when the US President Barack Obama just

75   Romans 14:4.

wrapped up his first visit to China, *The Wall Street Journal* ran an opinion piece entitled "The China President Obama Didn't See." It was about Shouwang's first indoor worship after having to meet outdoors for two successive Sundays. That was the first time the Shouwang congregation held an open-air service. They were evicted from an office space in northwest Beijing's Huajie Mansion that the church had rented for three and a half years. On November 1, 2009, about five hundred people worshiped near the gate of a suburban park in northwest Beijing during a snowstorm, which was the earliest to hit the Chinese capital in more than two decades. A week later, some seven hundred worshipers met at the same place. But the chief pastor was prevented from going there to give a sermon.

The chief pastor is Jin Tianming. In 1993, he and his bride began a Bible study group in their small home. A year later, they rented a room of a house near the west gate of Tsinghua University in northwest Beijing. In 1991, Jin Tianming graduated from Tsinghua, a leading institution of higher learning in China. He became a Christian the previous year when he was invited to attend a worship meeting. That was a year after the 1989 Tian'anmen Square democracy movement crackdown, which turned out to be an unexpected help in Jin Tianming's spiritual journey where he eventually lost faith in any worldly wisdom. At that time, he was named Jin Yongkui who was born into an ethnic Korean peasant family in northeast China's Heilongjiang Province in 1968. His new given name of Tianming means "the coming of dawn."

In 2002, 34-year-old Jin Tianming was ordained as a pastor by Pastor Xie Moshan or Moses Xie, a Chinese house church leader who died on June 30, 2011, and had been imprisoned for more than twenty years between 1950s and 1970s because of refusing to join the government-owned Three-Self church. By the year 2005, Shouwang, which means "watching" or "to keep watch," had more than ten fellowships. At that time, the church decided to apply to register with the government. But in 2006 authorities rejected Shouwang's application, asking it to join the Three-Self instead.

Also in 2005, Shouwang Church began to rent office buildings for the Sunday worship. And a year later, Shouwang started forming an integrated church out of different fellowships across the city. According to an open letter issued by the church in mid-April 2011, "these were part of Shouwang's efforts to become a transparent and open church and also a mega-trend of the house church growth in China in a new era." In another letter to the congregation issued in late March 2011, the church's governing committee also made it clear that "under the leadership of the vision of 'a city on a hill,' Shouwang Church has gradually grown into a holistic Christian community that is open to the general public."

But by 2007, Shouwang remained almost unknown to the broader society. It was already arguably one of the largest house churches in Beijing. That year, it began publishing *Xing Hua* or *Almond Flowers*, a quarterly church magazine. One of its earliest issues had a special report on Shouwang's registration process publicizing all the major documents about it. That gained attention from other house churches and those who were following China's Christianity. The *Almond Flowers* magazine— "an almond tree" in Hebrew shares the same pronunciation of "watching" in Hebrew[76]—has gradually become well-known among house church readers.

It was the issue of worship or meeting place that has given rise to Shouwang Church being known in the general public. Like almost any other house church, the Shouwang congregation has faced the issue of survival from the moment it was established. The most serious direct crackdown came on May 11, 2008, when the armed forces broke into Shouwang's Sunday worship in a rented office space. The authorities ordered the church to put an end to the worship. But it continued. All the three services from morning to afternoon were held as usual. Many worshippers were asked to leave their names and contact information. It came in the run-up to the Beijing Olympics. It was a day before the massive earthquakes shook China's southwest province of Sichuan and many other parts of the country.

Amazingly, Shouwang survived the clampdown. Yet, the church realized that the pressure on the landlords of the facilities it rented was a weak point in both the survival and further growth of the congregation. It had been forced out of the previous rented venues. And in 2008, it faced another eviction. The church established a group in an effort to

76   Jeremiah 1:11–12.

solve the problem by purchasing a permanent place for worship. Then, the church's governing committee came up with a blueprint for purchasing a permanent worship site. After the church's main co-workers and the representatives of the church members approved the blueprint, Shouwang formally launched the purchasing project in March 2009.

In late October that year, Shouwang moved out of the Huajie Mansion. During the ensuing period of time when the two Sunday services were held outdoors, the church handed in a letter to Beijing's religious affairs authority. It made a proposal to solve the problem of a worship place by putting the premises officially on record. The authority once again asked Shouwang to turn to the Three-Self church.

By the end of 2009, Shouwang paid about 27 million yuan or some four million US dollars for the second floor of the Daheng Science and Technology Tower in northwest Beijing's Zhongguancun area. The fund was from the offering of the Shouwang congregation and other contributors to buy a permanent worship place. Authorities once again interfered and the property developer has refused to hand the key over to the church. In early December 2011, the church paid off all the money borrowed for the space.

Before that, Shouwang's governing committee agreed to the government representatives' promise to allow the church to return to indoor worship. In a further statement about outdoor worship issued in mid-April 2011, the governing committee explained that they "believed the wish that it would be good for the government to have more time in solving the problem of worship place." After that, Shouwang went through a number of difficulties having to change worship facilities. The change of premises came to a halt in early 2010 when Shouwang began to rent a conference hall at the Old Story Club, which is a part of the state-run broadcaster, China Central Television. Yet, authorities kept on interfering. In early April 2011, like before, Shouwang moved out of the leased venue. And the rest is history.

For now, it is not known when the outdoor worship will end. Shouwang stated that "as long as the church has a guaranteed worship space, the premises it has already purchased in particular, the church will immediately return to worshiping indoors just like it was in November 2009." In his pastoral letter sent on April 23 2011 that was Easter Eve,

Pastor Jin Tianming, who had been under house arrest, reaffirmed the stand on outdoor worship: "The 'outdoor' in the outdoor worship is not a means to an end but a stand: it is a stand when we face our Lord of glory and the authorities, I believe the stand itself is a kind of worship before the only true God who is the only head of the church, and in this particular period of time, it is a worship that is even more precious than any hymn or sermon and would much more please God."

2011's Easter Sunday also marked the 100th anniversary of Tsinghua University, Pastor Tianming's alma mater and also that of the Chinese President Hu Jintao. The pastor was supposed to attend the twentieth anniversary reunion with his Tsinghua classmates on Good Friday, which Christians remember as the day that Jesus Christ was crucified. But the police forbade him to go. A day before Good Friday, Pastor Tianming went to a hospital with an escort of four police officers. A less-than-two-year-old daughter of a young couple who were also Shouwang Church members fell from a high-rise early that day and died after being rushed to hospital. Another pastor, Zhang Xiaofeng, also asked to visit the couple but was refused.

In an article published on Google buzz, later that day, Elder Liu Guan wrote about his response to the unexpected death of the toddler. He said he once again choked with tears when he prayed with his son in the evening. He also recalled how a recent midnight prayer had helped him overcome his fear of leaving his wife, his children and his aged parents if he was put into prison. He came to believe more than ever that God would surely take good care of all his loved ones. He said in that night he finally keenly understood what it meant by "I have been crucified with Christ and I no longer live, but Christ lives in me."[77]

Elder Sun Yi also has been under house arrest. He is the chief editor of Shouwang's *Almond Flowers* magazine and a professor at Renmin or People's University, another leading institution of higher education in China. In an article sharing with his magazine co-workers, Sun Yi said three fellow church members came to see him on a mid-April Saturday afternoon. Since they were not allowed to enter Sun Yi's home, they met and chatted with the elder on a corridor.

---

77   Galatians 2:20.

Then, somewhat to the elder's surprise, the three visitors suggested praying together. Beside them were a police officer and three other men who were sent to stand guard over Sun Yi. They prayed for the church. And they prayed for the people who were just on the watch. When finishing the prayer, Elder Sun Yi opened his eyes and saw one of the four guards smiling at him and the three visitors. "Though three other people's eyes buried in the newspapers, I know their hearts have already been touched," wrote Sun Yi. Later that day, Pastor Jin Tianming and another pastor, Li Xiaobai, were taken to the police stations. Elder Sun Yi heard the news and sensed he might be taken away in the same night. But thanks to the afternoon prayer, he felt huge relief. After that prayer, he said he had emerged from the shadow of any potential threat. More police officers did not come that night. He remained under house arrest.

The two pastors were released later. Pastor Tianming returned home the next morning. Pastor Xiaobai and his wife were freed at midnight. Before becoming Christians, the couple were engineers working at some leading global IT companies. During the first outdoor worship in April, they were detained at a local police station and were not released until 48 hours later.

During the first three Sundays since the outdoor worship began, Pastor Xiaobai had sent his Sunday sermons to his fellow Shouwang members. The latest was on Easter. He continued with the Book of Esther in the Old Testament to illustrate God's unfailing salvation of his people. Towards the end of his Easter sermon, Pastor Xiaobai said the ground for faith and hope and love remained in the Lord Christians trusted in: "Jesus Christ is the same yesterday and today and forever. Do not be carried away by all kinds of strange teachings. It is good for our hearts to be strengthened by grace."[78]

The choice of Esther for the Sunday sermons in the period of outdoor worship is symbolic. Prior to being forced out of the previous rented premises in early April, Shouwang's Sunday sermons had been around the Acts of the Apostles for a few months. That is about the beginning and expansion of the Christian church. And Shouwang was planning to plant churches in other parts of the city or the country. The Book

---

78   Hebrew 13:8–9.

of Esther tells a story of how God delivered the Jewish people from a genocide in Persia plotted by the empire's highest official. The immediate reason for the plot was that a Jew in the Persian capital refused to kneel down and pay honor to the highest official.

In the case of Shouwang, the issue of worship place is a reflection of a deeper struggle over the legality of the non-state-owned church in China. The government under the atheist Communist rule of course does not want any independent religious organization to exist and expand. But more than thirty years after the Reform and Opening-up policy was put in place, it looks impossible for the authority to control everything. It has considerably shifted its ground on economy by having to allow the non-state-owned companies to exist and expand. Now, it is increasingly faced with the continued rise of the non-state-owned churches, which it has long considered only belong to "the Western culture."

Will there be an Esther who can help deliver Shouwang and other house churches from the crackdown? If history is any guide, the possibility is not unreal despite both who and how could be anyone's guess. Even more than a decade into the reform and opening-up era, the Chinese government was still chained to its ideology that market economy was restricted to "the Western capitalist countries." It was Deng Xiaoping, China's de facto leader in the 1980s-90s, who admonished his colleagues to halt splitting hairs over "whether it is surnamed socialist or capitalist." He said "the policy is okay if it works." His insistence on the economic reform paved the way for the further expansion of private enterprises and the official recognition of private property. In fact, this has gone on to help grow house churches making it possible for them to rent or even own places for worship.

If the current government leaders could carry on with this part of Deng Xiaoping's theory, they would probably help usher in the continued rise of China. They would see a newer China where some truly respected schools, universities, research institutes, hospitals and philanthropic foundations could grow out of house churches or those churchgoers, like it has been in the global church history. In fact, Shouwang Church has planned to open a theological seminary. Pastor Song Jun, who is a historian of the Christian church and ancient Chinese religions, was supposed to be responsible for the institution. Currently, Shouwang has already had a Sunday school. For many years, it has helped educate hundreds of children of Shouwang members. It's Li Enping, the wife of Pastor Tianming, who has been in charge of the school.

Apart from publishing the *Almond Flowers* magazine, Shouwang has its own library. Its director is Elder You Guanhui, who was in the same class with Elder Sun Yi when they pursued their PhD studies of Christianity in the late 1990s at Peking University, another top institution of higher learning in China. Elder You Guanhui leads a publishing company called Oak Tree that has helped introduce to the Chinese readers a series of Christian classics, including John Calvin's *Institutes of the Christian Religion*, Athanasius' *On the Incarnation of the Word*, Eusebius' *The Church History*, Gregory of Nazianzus' *Theological Orations*, Basil's Hexaemeron, Ambrose's *Exposition of the Christian Faith*, Augustine's *The Harmony of the Gospels*, John Foxe's *The Book of Martyrs*, and contemporary works like Alistair E. McGrath's *A Life of John Calvin: A Study in the Shaping of Western Culture*, Timothy George's *Theology of the Reformers, Roger Olsen's The Story of Christian Theology: Twenty Centuries of Tradition & Reform,* and Marilyn Dunn's *Emergence of Monasticism: From the Desert Fathers to the Early Middle Ages.* Even after the outdoor worship began in April, the company continued to help publish the Chinese translation of more books with G. K. Chesterton's *Heretics* and *Orthodoxy* and D. H. Williams' *Retrieving the Tradition and Renewing Evangelicalism: A Primer for Suspicious Protestants* coming out in May and June respectively. Later in 2011, Martin Luther's *A Commentary on St. Paul's Epistle to the Galatians* and a number of other books concerning the origin of the Bible, biblical interpretation and the spirit of early Christian thought were published in Chinese. More books like George Marsden's *Jonathan Edwards: A Life* and Millard J. Erickson's *Introducing Christian Doctrine* appeared in 2012, and Jonathan Edwards' *Religious Affections* and Richard Baxter's *Saints' Everlasting Rest* in early 2013.

If the rise of private companies means creating and producing ever richer material products and services without the interference from the government, the rise of house churches could mean creating and producing ever richer spiritual products and services without the interference from the government. For top management thinkers like the late Peter

Drucker who was also a Christian, the free enterprises and pastoral churches combined could help people find a fuller meaning as human beings whom, according to the Bible, God created in his own image. It seems hard for the Chinese government leaders to thoroughly ignore the fact that the growth of both private businesses and house churches in China had taken place long before it was known when they would gain official approval. This might indicate that the growth of both institutions came from a deep and universal longing for becoming free, creative, caring, connected, humble and responsible beings. Once their country starts opening up, they would keenly learn to do it, sometimes at any price.

For now, it seems crucial for the Chinese government to make more sense of what the church is. On the bright side, numerous detentions and arrests of the Shouwang Church congregants might have provided golden opportunities for the police officers and their leaders to know more about Christians and their faith at first hand. They might have found it strange when they read a Shouwang's Q&A fact sheet like this one: "What if the police arrest me because of my participation in outdoor worship? Do not resist, let them take us away, just like a lamb to the slaughter. In our hearts, we know that we gather here to worship; and for the sake of worship, we will pay the price. We believe in what the Lord has said: 'Blessed are those who are persecuted because of righteousness, for theirs is the kingdom of heaven.'"[79]

Once they detain or arrest those Christians, they would see and hear how those people behave and speak. A police told a Shouwang co-worker who visited a police station in the east Chaoyang District where a church member was detained for 48 hours that he and his colleagues were taught not to hit back when beaten and not to answer back when insulted. The church co-worker said that was what God asked his people to do. A deputy chief of the Olympic Village police station told a Shouwang parishioner who was detained on May 15, 2011 that he would believe in Christianity after he retired. The Shouwang member gave the police officer a copy of a booklet entitled "Why I Live" and was freed later in the day.

Another Shouwang member was a pianist of the choir before she began studying theology in Regent College, an international graduate

79   Matthew 5:10.

school of Christian studies based in Vancouver, Canada in autumn 2011. She was under house arrest after being detained many times. On a rainy night, a police officer knocked on her door asking if she could leave the door open so that he might hear the music. A little more than twenty minutes later, other listeners joined the police officer, including his wife, their son and daughter-in-law. The pianist and her mother sang hymns for them. After seeing them moved by the songs, they briefly told them how to read the Bible. Whenever the police officer was on duty, the pianist would give him and his family members some copies of the hymnal and sang hymns for them. One night, the police officer again knocked on her door. The pianist said the piano pedals did not work so that she could not play that night. "No playing?! Feel that something is lost …," said the police officer disappointedly outside. At times, the police officer and his family members would ask, "Is there God? Where is God?" The pianist responded, "But why is it that you felt the hymns very pleasant? Didn't you feel that your heart was moved? That's just what God placed in your heart!" They fell silent and seemed lost in thought.

Of course, it might be equally significant for the house church members to further figure out what the government officials think and do. After ever more communication, they might develop a better understanding of why the government was still so hostile to the house church and if possible, what could be done to help them change their views. Some Shouwang parishioners said the police officers knew almost nothing about the church. Some police officers did not say "Shouwang Church" but "Shouwang Religion or Shouwang Sect." Some claimed Jin Yongkui (Jin Tianming) was "the Founder of Shouwang Religion" and he wanted to own the place Shouwang had bought. On such occasions, Shouwang congregants would help the police officers correct the mistakes saying Shouwang was a Christian church and Jin Tianming (Jin Yongkui) was the founding pastor of Shouwang Church. For his part, Pastor Jin Tianming reaffirmed his stand in his May 22, 2011 sermon sent to Shouwang members by emails that the enemy of the church was not the government nor anyone else of "flesh and blood" but "the spiritual forces of evil in the heavenly realms."[80]

---

80   Ephesians 6:12.

A few weeks or months might be still too short to solve the decades-old problem. As a matter of fact, there have been different opinions even within the house church about the Shouwang governing committee's decision to worship outdoors. Some people held that the church could worship as separate groups indoors (since Shouwang currently has dozens of family Bible study groups and fellowships) and some others warned that it was too sensitive to hold outdoor services at present when what was called "Jasmine Revolution" was spreading from North Africa to Asia. On May 31, 2011, the Shouwang governing committee sent emails to church members announcing Pastor Song Jun, Minister Jiang Lijin, Deacons Ji Cheng and Yuan Yansong left Shouwang Church due to disagreements over outdoor worship. Shortly after that, Pastor Song Jun and Minister Jiang Lijin started up a new church. For more than once, the Shouwang governing committee has issued open messages explaining the outdoor worship decision. In a letter, they said, "we ask the Lord to preserve the unity of our church, that despite of our different viewpoints, we may still be able to submit to and bear with one another."

As for how long the outdoor worship will last, Shouwang Church said that if the problem of worship place could not be solved, they would continue to worship outdoors until Christmas 2011. They would reassess the situation and devise new plans for the coming year. That means Shouwang seems to have been prepared for a longer road ahead. In the history of the Christian church, a year or even a decade would not be a long time. But the next few months or even the next few weeks might witness another turning point for the church in a country whose ancient name is, surprisingly, "God's Land."

In December 2011, Shouwang Church pursued an end to the outdoor worship. It launched a new appeal to pray for a permanent indoor worship place. The church's governing committee issued an open letter to the congregants on December 16, 2011, eight months after they began worshiping outdoors. The church tried a number of times to lease an indoor venue for the first few Sundays in 2012 but it has been of no avail due to the continued intervention of the authorities. On January 13, 2012, the Shouwang governing committee issued a bulletin saying the outdoor service would continue until the church could return to the indoor service. According to this special report, the relevant governmental departments have made it clear that they would not allow the church to use any indoor premises for worshiping in its entirety.

When this book is to be published in 2014, the outdoor worship remains. Things seem to get worse in May 2014 when some Shouwang Church outdoor worshippers were sent to a Beijing detention center for at least five days. This came shortly after the authorities were demolishing many crosses or churches in China's southeast province of Zhejiang amid tougher nationwide campaigns against Christianity and anything deemed disobedient.

Chapter 9
Why Love Is Patient, and How It Can Be Done

As the world media keep following Shouwang Church—one of the largest house churches in Beijing—since it began outdoor worship in early April 2011, the growth of Christianity in China gets more international attention. Besides Shouwang, there are a great number of non-government-run churches in the globe's most populous country. Most of them remain unknown to the general public. In fact, before Shouwang was founded as a tiny Bible study group in 1993, many house churches had already existed with some in operation even during the most repressive Cultural Revolution between 1966 and 1976. Their stories of existence and development may not only shed new light on how people of faith could live in one of the darkest days of human history, but also help one make better sense of how a civilized community could be built.

Qiquanhu is perhaps one of the world's most unlikely places to build a church. It is a small town with a population of approximately 13,000, about forty kilometers northeast of Tulufan or Turpan, an eastern city in Xinjiang Uyghur Autonomous Region of northwest China. Turpan is renowned for its sweet fruits and raisins as well as ancient Silk Road civilizations. But it is also an oasis surrounded by the Gobi desert. It has one of the Earth's lowest points on land and is both the hottest and driest area in China. Yet, Qiquanhu is not a resort town. Though its name means "Seven Springs Lake," Qiquanhu now does not have such a lake as its name suggests. For the past decades, it has been home to a state-owned chemical plant, which went bankrupt and was bought by a private enterprise in about 2005. However, it was just during the period of the state-owned factory that a house church was established and gained approval from authorities. Qiquanhu Church is one of the few house churches in China that has been successfully registered with the government but does not belong to the state-run Three-Self Church. And if one takes into account the Uyghur and Hui ethnic groups that are largely Muslims and make up more than seventy percent of the whole population in Turpan, Qiquanhu Church sounds even more incredible. It is also in Turpan that the tallest minaret in China is situated.

If traveling on a train from the Xinjiang provincial capital of Urumqi to Qiquanhu, one could see the cross atop the church at the end of the 200-kilometer ride. The cross is just a couple of hundred meters south of the railway. To the north, one could see Tian Shan or Celestial Mountains capped with snow even in summer. Construction began in March 1989 and basically finished in June 1990. Outside the church's courtyard are mainly one-story brick-built houses and dirt roads in the Gobi desert. Inside the courtyard, different kinds of grapes are grown along with cacti, chrysanthemums, and vegetables such as tomatoes and green peppers. But before it was to open for holding services, the church was announced illegal by the officials of the state-owned chemical plant. Four times every month in the next three years, Pastor Li Daosheng and other church co-workers went to Urumqi petitioning authorities to redress the injustice. It was not until July 1993 that the church was recognized as a legal entity. Later on, more than two hundred people went to church every Sunday. According to Pastor Li's memoirs, *Walking on the Highway to Zion*, a top Xinjiang religious affairs official told him in Urumqi in May 1993 that the issue had been addressed in a national religious affairs meeting in Hangzhou, the capital of the eastern Zhejiang province. To Pastor Li, this outcome came as a big surprise, though he believes what the Bible says about authorities is true: "The king's heart is in the hand of the LORD; he directs it like a watercourse wherever he pleases."[81] He wrote in his memoirs, "Qiquanhu Church is a very small church without any big worldly standing or fame. Even some people within Christianity would not recognize it. Why could a church that is located in proximity of a minor railway station of Gobi desert trouble a nationwide religious affairs meeting to address its issue?" In an interview in July 2011, Pastor Li said it was Li Ruihuan, a top central government

81   Proverbs 21:1.

leader in the early 1990s, who gave instructions to solve the Qiquanhu Church issue.

An equally big, if not a bigger, surprise is that a church could appear in Qiquanhu. It all began with the arrival of Pastor Li in October 1981. At that time, he retired as a worker of the chemical plant and moved to live in Qiquanhu from Aydingkol Lake, which is about 50 kilometers southeast of urban Turpan and approximately 155 meters below sea level, the lowest land point in China. Li Daosheng had worked around Aydingkol Lake since the spring of 1971, when he was transferred from a mining area in a neighboring county called Shanshan. From 1950 to 1972, Li Daosheng was jailed for seven years and worked in labor camps for another 15 years because of spreading the gospel in Xinjiang. He and his wife Zhang Huirong came all the way to Xinjiang from the eastern Shandong province in 1947. Pastor Li was twenty-five years old and his wife twenty-seven. He studied theology at North China Theological Seminary in Tengxian, a county in southern Shandong. It was founded in 1919 by Watson McMillan Hayes, who came to China in 1882 as an American missionary and educator. Hayes once served as the president of Tengchow College, which Calvin Wilson Mateer, also an American missionary, helped found in Penglai of Shandong in 1882 and has been regarded as the first modern university in China. Mateer is also known as the chairman of a committee responsible for producing the widely circulated Chinese translation of the Bible, the Mandarin Union version, which was published in 1919 and one of the first translated works published in modern Chinese. For his part, Hayes is also viewed as a pioneer in Chinese journalism, who helped publish the first newspaper in Shandong. He even contributed to ushering in a new era of Chinese holidays by suggesting the Chinese government in the late Qing Dynasty grant a holiday on Sundays.

After studying at North China Theological Seminary in Tengxian, Li Daosheng and his wife went to Weihsian's Ledaoyuan, which means the Courtyard of the Happy Way or the Campus of Loving Truth. It was a missionary compound established by American Presbyterian Church and once had churches, schools, hospitals and dormitories. All were destroyed in 1900 when the Boxer Uprising or the Righteous Harmony Society Movement opposing foreign imperialism and Christianity erupted. The buildings were rebuilt in 1902 but were again much destroyed in the Cultural Revolution in the 1960s-70s. Weihsian or Weixian is now known as Weifang, a city in east Shandong. From late 1945 to early 1947, Li Daosheng and his wife were trained as missionaries at the Courtyard of the Happy Way. That came after the end of World War II and the Civil War. The invading Japanese military turned the missionary compound into an internment camp in 1942. Some two thousand people, mainly European and American expatriates, were held there until August 17, 1945. Many of them were missionaries, including Watson McMillan Hayes who died in the camp and Eric Liddell, an Olympic gold medalist who was born in China of Scottish missionary parents and died of a brain tumor in the camp on February 21, 1945. *Chariots of Fire*, a British film that won four Academy Awards in 1981, is partly based on Liddell's story. As the war ended, foreign missionaries left Weihsian. A group of Chinese Christians who once worked at the Courtyard of the Happy Way returned and reopened the missionary compound. Li Daosheng and his wife studied at a newly-established school, Lingxiuyuan, or the Court-yard of Spiritual Cultivation.

It was at this school that Li Daosheng and his schoolmates and teachers had a vision of bringing the gospel to Xinjiang, Central Asia and finally, Jerusalem. Pastor Li recalled that after Pentecost of 1946, a few of his schoolmates spoke in tongues about the vision. Pentecost is a day when Christians remember the descent of the Holy Spirit after the resurrection of Jesus, which Christians celebrate in Easter that is in March or April each year. In the autumn of 1946, Liu Shuyuan and Zhang Meiying, two of those who spoke in tongues, set forth to Xinji-ang. Then in the spring of 1947, Li Peizhen and Huang Deling, another two young ladies, also went to northwest China. They were followed by Li Daosheng and his wife. Seven months later, they reached Hami or Kumul, an eastern city in Xinjiang where they met their four school-mates who had arrived. They stayed at a church that could hold some two hundred people. Most of the worshippers were peasants from the eastern province of Henan. The six immigrants from Shandong became the church's co-workers. They were responsible for organizing Sunday worship and Sunday school, prayer meeting, choir, and visiting church members. More and more people came to the church, which was full to capacity a few months later.

In August 1948, Li Daosheng and his wife went to Zhenxi, a county now known as Balikun or Barkol that is more than one hundred kilometers northwest of Hami. Zhang Junting, another Hami church co-worker, was also with them. It was the first time for the missionaries from the Courtyard of Spiritual Cultivation in Weihsian to spread the gospel in Xinjiang besides Hami. They did not know anyone in Zhenxi. But when walking on a street in the county, they met a man who came from Hami and knew them because his wife went to their church in Hami. He helped them find a place to stay at a courtyard. From there, they began holding worship meetings. They earned their living by helping local peasants unearth potatoes. The daily wage was about ten kilograms of potatoes. After working for fifteen days, the potatoes they got were already enough for them to eat for the whole winter. By Christmas that year, more than twenty people worshipped with them each Sunday. Even some members of the local military came to their church. Zhang Huirong, the wife of Li Daosheng, also helped many children whose parents were poor to learn how to read, write and sing. When the traditional annual Chinese New Year or Spring Festival came, the church members shared gospel with peasants and herdsmen who attended the temple fair. They also sent booklets on Christian faith to local government agencies. By February 1949 when Li Daosheng and his wife were succeeded by other co-workers from Hami, more than thirty people had been baptized and a church building was planned.

Meanwhile in Hami, Li Daosheng's co-workers were preparing for a new church building. It was completed in June 1949 and could hold as many as three hundred people. A name inscribed on a board at the church's gate read, "The Christian Northwest Spiritual Work Mission." The name was suggested by Pastor Yang Shaotang, who graduated from North China Theological Seminary in 1925 and once worked with China Inland Mission, which was founded by British missionary James Hudson Taylor in 1865 and until 1953 was one of the largest evangelical agencies working in China. The inscription was written by Pastor Zhang Guquan, a major co-worker of Weihsian's northwest mission. He graduated from North China Theological Seminary in 1943 and became a teacher there. It was Pastor Zhang who led Daosheng and his schoolmates to join the Courtyard of Spiritual Cultivation in Weihsian. He was also responsible for launching the mission's magazine, *Northwest Spiritual Work*. Pastor Xie Moshan or Moses Xie, another alumnus of North China Theological Seminary, helped publish the journal in the coastal city of Shanghai. But it was banned in December 1950. Pastor Zhang was arrested in Hami in 1951 and died in a Urumuqi prison in 1956. Jia Yuming, who was a Tengchow College alumnus and once served as Vice-Principal at North China Theological Seminar, hailed the mission as a great undertaking.

Some missionaries sent to other areas in Xinjiang, including Li Daosheng and his wife, returned to Hami to attend the Pentecostal meeting in June 1949. Nearly thirty people came with them from various places and expressed their willingness to join the northwest mission on the seventh day of the meeting. A day later, forty-five people were baptized. After the Pentecostal meeting, the northwest mission continued sending out its missionaries. Some traveled to Fuyuan, a county now known as Jimsar in north Xinjiang. Some others headed for Turpan. Along with three other co-workers, Li Daosheng and his wife journeyed to Kashi or Kashgar, a city in southwest Xinjiang. It took them nearly two months to reach Kashgar, which is approximately two thousand kilometers from Hami. In September 1949, they arrived in Shule, a county near Kashgar. Zhao Maijia or Mecca Chao, who had arrived in Shule a year ago, helped them rent a place to stay. In the summer of 1948, Li Daosheng and his co-workers received Mecca Chao in Hami. Mecca Chao was a member of The Back to Jerusalem Evangelical Band, a missionary group founded in 1943 at Northwest Bible Institute in Fengxiang, a county in the northwestern province of Shaanxi. The institute was established by James Hudson Taylor II, the grandson of the founder of China Inland Mission. The name, Mecca, was adopted after Chao decided to devote himself to spreading the gospel in northwest China and the further west of Asia where many Muslims inhabited. He went to church with his family when he was a child. Later, he joined the army in the anti-Japanese war and studied in the Communist Party's Anti-Japanese Military and Political University in Yan'an of north Shaanxi. His Christian faith resumed after he was arrested by the Nationalist army. At the age of 24 he was released, and in Xi'an of Shaanxi he met Pastor Zhang Meng'en who helped him believe in Christ. Pastor Zhang, who graduated from North China Theological Seminary in 1936, suggested he go to Fengxiang and study theology at Northwest Bible Institute. The wife of Mecca Chao, He Enzheng, was a teacher at Northwest Bible Institute and continued ministering to the church in Kashgar even after her husband died in 2007.

On Christmas 1949, more than thirty new believers and seekers gathered at the church in Shule. They and the co-workers visited Christian families nearby. The hymns they sang could be heard on the streets. Quite a number of local residents were attracted to hear what the gospel was. For Li Daosheng, the scene was so impressive that more than sixty years later he could still remember what it looked like. And it would be the last Christmas Pastor Li and his friends could celebrate together freely for the next three decades. In August 1950, Li Daosheng was arrested by the local police officers. That came less than a year after the People's Republic of China was founded on October 1, 1949. More of Pastor Li's co-workers were sent to jail in the ensuing months. Despite this, Li Daosheng could still bring two copies of the Bible with him. One was a Uyghur translation of the New Testament and the other a Chinese version of the New Testament. He learned Uyghur with a Uyghur prisoner. One day when prisoners were allowed to go to the toilet, a group of Uyghur prisoners stood up showing Li Daosheng their respect. They knew Li Daosheng was a Christian minister and they called him "ahung" or imam, a prayer leader in Islam. Before he was arrested, the Islamic leaders Li Daosheng and his co-workers knew or heard of would generally regard Christianity as a religion of the Han ethnic group, the largest in China. Pastor Zhang Guquan made a number of visits to the Muslim leaders in Hami after a board of "The Christian Northwest Spiritual Work Mission" was set up at the church gate in June 1949.

On a summer afternoon sixty-one years later, Pastor Li read the first verse of the second chapter of *The Gospel According to Matthew* in Uyghur in his home, which is in the courtyard of Qiquanhu Church. The verse is about the birth of Jesus and the coming of Magi to Jerusalem from the east. Pastor Li said he was prepared to share the Christian faith with Uyghur people in Xinjiang. But he spent the next thirty years in various prisons, labor camps and factories in Xinjiang. He did not expect that he would contribute so much of his life to helping build Xinjiang's infrastructure such as mines, roads, railways and reservoirs. Besides being beaten, he could have been killed on numerous highly perilous occasions. For Li Daosheng, it is God he trusts in who has delivered him from all those dangers. In those days and nights of darkness, prayer became like breathing, for if there was no praying no fresh air would come in.

From the road Pastor Li and his colleagues have walked, one could see a fragment of history that has long been largely out of the public eye but in fact has been shaping the civilized world. The Christian missionaries from Europe and America played a critical role in laying the foundations for cultivating God-fearing people and God-centered communities in China. In Xinjiang, the earliest missionaries in the modern time were from France, Britain and Sweden in the late nineteenth century. They were among a long line of the followers of Christ since the first century when Jesus after resurrection told his disciples to "go and make disciples of all nations."[82] After they were forced to withdraw from China because of World War II and the rise of the Communists in the late 1940s, they left an enduring legacy through such institutions as North China Theological Seminary, the Courtyard of the Happy Way, and Northwest Bible Institute. They proved to be incubators for the unexpected growth of Christianity in China several decades later when those Chinese Christians they helped nurture survived all the persecutions and grew into maturity by not only holding fast to the Christian faith but also passing it on to the younger generation. Both the withdrawal of overseas missionaries and the rule of atheism also worked wonders in helping purify the church and expose the Chinese to the evils the human-centered wisdom has created. Without support from the state and the international community, Christians in China had nothing to rely on except the God they believed in. Such circumstances would also be a test whether Christianity was a religion just for foreigners or whether the God of Christianity was an alien and limited deity. And once their faith could live on in such difficult situations, its tenacity would be evident. The faith of Li Daosheng and his fellow Christians strongly indicates the life-long patience they have with both the belief itself and the world they live in no matter how it may change. Both tenacity and

82   Matthew 28:19.

patience are vital for any individual or group of people who want to make a truly healthy impact.

When Li Daosheng and his wife Zhang Huirong set foot in the Gobi desert from eastern Shandong in 1947, they could not have known how their church could be really built in Xinjiang at all. During their seven-month odyssey covering more than three thousand kilometers, they were given a hand by fellow Christians in every stop. This shows churches were already planted in almost all the major cities from Shandong to Xinjiang in the late 1940s. It is interesting that in a time when China was at war and ordinary people apparently lacked modern communications, Christians in different places were still able to keep in contact. In some places like Lanzhou, the capital of Gansu Province in west China, Li Daosheng and his wife stayed for weeks serving in the local churches. This experience and the one after the Lis arrived in Hami combined to help them re-establish a church once the opportunities arose. When Li Daosheng retired as a worker at the chemical plant in Qiquanhu in 1981, he and his wife finally had much more time reading the Bible, praying together and singing hymns. Soon after, more than twenty people joined them. In 1983, more than ten new believers were baptized in Pastor Li's home, which was built by the pastor based on a pigsty. That was how Qiquanhu Church was started. That was when Pastor Li was sixty years old, thirty-five years after he and his co-workers set up the first church from scratch in Zhenxi. But that was a time when beliefs other than atheism were still a kind of taboo, despite China's central government ending the Cultural Revolution and initiating the "Reform and Opening-up" policy in the late 1970s.

Local officials said the prayer meetings in Li Daosheng's place were of superstition. In 1984, twenty copies of the Bible Pastor Li ordered from Shanghai were confiscated by the chemical plant's security section after they reached Qiquanhu. Li Daosheng inquired of the local post office about the parcel's whereabouts. The post office recovered nineteen copies of the Bible from the plant's security section saying the confiscation was against the law. The one left was in the hands of the party secretary of the chemical plant. After this, several police officers from Turpan came and asked Pastor Li about his church. They acknowledged that the religious freedom was endowed by the Constitution as an inalienable right of a Chinese citizen. But they asked Pastor Li to register with the government's United Front Work Department because the agency was responsible for religious affairs. But the officials at United Front Work Department flatly denied the church's registration. They said Xinjiang was an Islamic region and Christianity was not allowed. They also said religion was forbidden at an industrial area like the chemical plant in Qiquanhu. In response, Li Daosheng said those reasons had no legal foundation and the Constitution did not stipulate that Christianity could not exist in either Xinjiang or a chemical plant. However, the United Front Work Department officials insisted on their decision. For Pastor Li and his co-workers, there was still no sign that they could see the light at the end of the tunnel even after so many years of waiting and wailing had passed. Walking out of the office of United Front Work Department in Turpan, Li Daosheng glanced at his watch and saw that he had talked with the department official for nearly five hours.

Returning to Qiquanhu, Pastor Li felt it was too hard to overcome the mounting pressure from both the environment and within the spirit. Just at that time, a few founding members of The Christian Northwest Spiritual Work Mission visited his church. They included Chen Lianxiu, the wife of Pastor Zhang Guquan. After her husband died at the age of thirty-six in prison in September 1956, Chen Lianxiu spent much time visiting many co-workers who were in prison or labor camp. She died on July 24, 2009 at the age of ninety-four. Pastor Moses Xie also prayed for the church in Qiquanhu. The church meetings continued. In the spring of 1986, two religious affairs officials in Turpan came to Pastor Li's church. After finding out about the church's basic information, they said that the church's religious faith and activities were legal and the church ought to report to the authorities for record. On June 16, 1986, Li Daosheng and two other major co-workers Zhao Ximen or Simon Chao and Guo Zhimao sent the chemical plant, which was of county-level in administration, a registration form for record. Seven days later, they received a reply from the security section of the chemical plant approving the application.

It is noteworthy that Qiquanhu Church was registered not as a state-run Three-Self Church. For Li Daosheng and the congregation, the head of the church should be Jesus Christ rather than any earthly or other spiritual powers. An unexpectedly big advantage for a church in Xinjiang to be registered as the church of Christ is that Xinjiang did not and does not have a region-wide Committee of Three-Self Patriotic Movement, despite the fact that there are local Three-Self Churches in two cities including Urumqi and neighboring Changji. Since then, the church in Qiquanhu has been open to the public. For Pastor Li, a church should be like a light shining in the darkness although the darkness has not understood the light, and it should be like a city built on a hill and cannot be hidden.

More people came to the church. Li Daosheng's home was becoming ever smaller for the growing congregation. That was despite the chemical plant giving him a small courtyard with a brick-built house of three rooms in 1985, and another room that could hold more than forty people was added later. After praying and discussion, the co-workers decided to apply to the chemical plant for a piece of land building a church. The leader of the chemical plant's security section, who led the efforts to persecute the church before, said they could choose a place as long as it would not get in the way of the chemical plant's overall plan. On July 30, 1987, an open space of 800 square meters was earmarked for building the church. With only 500 yuan or about 130 US dollars at that time, it looked impossible for the congregation to build a modern church. For Pastor Li, a building that could shelter the worshippers from bad weather would be good enough. Yet, all would go beyond his expectations. Christians in Urumqi and some other places in Xinjiang and some other provinces like Shandong and Jiangsu offered to help. Some came with a blueprint of the church building and steel bars. Some sent them the money. Some helped ship bricks. It took a year and a half to level the land and prepare the building materials. It took almost another year and a half to complete the building. And of course, it took another three years to solve the legality of the church. A year later, that was in 1994, the intermediate court in the western city of Kashgar acquitted Li Daosheng of the anti-revolution charges. Pastor Li was seventy then.

In 2011, Pastor Li was eighty-eight. That is fifteen years after his wife died in August 1996 of a cerebral hemorrhage, an illness that bleeding happens within the skull. Pastor Li intended to return to Shule in west Xinjiang and rebuild a church there after retirement in early 1980s.

But he stayed in Qiquanhu largely because of his wife's bad health. Pastor Li himself suffered from heart disease that hospitalized him several times. It is incredible that after going through numerous kinds of hardships Pastor Li was in good health and joyful. He was born into a Christian family in the northeastern city of Shenyang in November 1923. They moved to their hometown in Weihsian of Shandong in 1930. His parents earned their living by weaving cloth. He was baptized at age fourteen in a local Presbyterian church. He has four brothers and he is the second youngest among them. He almost died of a serious illness when he was a little child. Soon after getting married, he was beaten up by a group of Chinese soldiers loyal to the Japanese invaders because he protested against their looting of his house.

Looking back on those misfortunes, Li Daosheng said they made him give thanks to God for the salvation even when he was young. This might help explain why perseverance could become one of his most noteworthy characters. In him, it is also evident that he has led a life of "live and learn." He said that if one could give oneself up and learn with an open mind, most difficulties would be overcome. Pastor Li likes to use a verse of the apostle Paul's first letter to Corinthians to remind himself of this fact: "So neither he who plants nor he who waters is anything, but only God, who makes things grow."[83] He added that one should not rely on feelings or impressions, but on God's word through the Bible and the Holy Spirit. He warned that the guidance of the Holy Spirit would never go back on the principle of the truth throughout the Bible. In this way, Li Daosheng suggested, praying to God and paying attention to the world one lived in could help to make better sense of God's will and time. For him, God has always arranged various environments to fulfill God's word and spirit.

Pastor Li's reflections also include lessons he learned from being a founding member of The Christian Northwest Spiritual Work Mission. Because of the work of the Holy Spirit, he said, the northwest mission founded more than ten churches in Xinjiang with the congregation continuing to grow and flourish between 1948 and 1950. But the major co-workers were generally ignorant of what was happening in the broader

83   1 Corinthians 3:7.

country especially in terms of political transformation. The missionaries were thus not well-equipped spiritually and intellectually to meet the challenges such as the conflicts between atheism and Christianity. They thought that the coming of the People's Republic would be beneficial to the further spread of the gospel. In mid-September 1949, the Nationalist Party was quickly losing power in Xinjiang. The military ordered Li Daosheng and his co-workers in Shule to leave within a week or face detention. A few days later, Li Daosheng was told that the Nationalist Party military officers suspected they were Communist Party members in disguise sent from Shandong. But after late September when the rule of the Nationalists was replaced by the Communists in Xinjiang, the situations became even worse for the church's existence.

Of course, Pastor Li and his co-workers were not the only group of Christians in China who were not acutely aware of and fully prepared for the rule of the atheist Communism. In fact, in the mid-twentieth-century China, the nation-and-human-centered ideology, which was unprecedentedly reinforced by both the national independence after being in the shadow of the increasingly Western dominance for nearly a century and the rising demagogic Marxism in the West and the wider world, became not only the soul of the political elite but fashionable in the broader society. In contrast, the God-centered Christianity was still limited to small communities scattered all over China. Although overseas missionaries played an undeniably important role in helping introduce and build the infrastructure of civilized communities in China such as universities, schools, hospitals, orphanages and media, their Christian faith was basically overlooked or rejected. It would be considered a tool of Western imperialism or simply a foreign religion or a superstition that had already been out-of-fashion.

It was in just such a hostile climate that Li Daosheng and his fellow Christians learned to reflect on their faith and the social realities. In a sense, the fact that they could stay alive and construct a non-state-run church in a state-run factory and—at long last—win government approval is the fruit of their life-long learning experience. The growth like this one is indeed fairly slow and almost unbearably painful. But it is perhaps not untypical at all for any living being with a long life to take root. In contrast, the fast spread and acceptance among world communities of atheist Communism or anything like it did not bear wholesome fruits that lasted long. It was just the disasters it brought during that speedy process that have led to its internal, though not yet final, collapse, and made room for anything with a long life to grow.

Thirty years after the Qiquanhu Church was founded at Pastor Li's home, the congregants are mainly the elderly people, many of them retired workers. Hundreds of parishioners have moved to other places in Xinjiang. A co-worker in a Turpan church, which Pastor Li helped establish, said Qiquanhu Church was like a theological seminary helping nurture younger Christians who would serve in other churches. And the story of Qiquanhu Church itself has already made an impact in the wider Christian community in China. Two articles of Pastor Li's memoirs, *Walking on the Highway to Zion*, appeared in the two issues of Shouwang Church's *Almond Flowers* magazine, first in 2009 about the tradition of house churches in China and then in 2010 regarding church building. The memoirs was published in Taiwan in 2009.

Chapter 10
From Saving a Nation to Saving a Life

Supper should have been the liveliest time in this courtyard.

It looks like that light has already been on. It's time for supper.

But why have parents not come back from work? Why have children not come back from school? Why has the dried bib not been brought in? Why is it that there are no babies crying?

Whichever city you go to in China seems to have apartment buildings like this one. Six floors. Grey exterior. Dim stairways. Dujiangyan Hardware Corporation Apartment Compound is but a different name.

The smells of stir-fried dishes would drop by between the rooms. At least because of this, the dim stairways would not be desolate. A rich flavor of life.

But not this evening. Without the smells of stir-fried dishes, it wasn't desolate either. With the smell of the disinfectant lotion assailing your nostrils, it was harsh and raw, many many times more desolate than desolate. It was May, the cruelest month of the year.

Light was not from the apartment building inside. That's the bleak and barren moon reflecting the light from the fire engine outside.

Everywhere in the courtyard were bricks, concrete floor slabs and metal bars. Only figures flashing on them were the evidence that it was still a human's world.

Yet, where were the people inside the building? Was there anyone left?

Except Zhang Xiaoping and his girlfriend Luo Qingfeng, I didn't know where their neighbors had gone.

The part they were in was hit hardest by the earthquake. It has not collapsed completely yet. But the six floors have shortened to five. The stairways of the first floor were buried underground.

The couple was the reason why the rescue team came here. Chen Xingming, the cousin of Luo Qingfeng, found them still alive two days after the quake.

No one could move the concrete floor slab covering them even after the rescue team arrived, even 129 hours after they were buried, even after Zhang Xiaoping was pulled out of the ruin alive but with his lower legs amputated.

129 hours are the time Zhang Xiaoping was trapped in the wreckage. That's five days and nine hours since the massive earthquake struck at 14:28 on May 12th, 2008. That's a record of life preservation. For Zhang Xiaoping and Luo Qingfeng, that's the last 129 hours the couple stayed together, 129 hours without sunlight.

Now, the couple is no longer in this world. Luo Qingfeng passed away in the ruin three days after the quake. Zhang Xiaoping was rescued alive. I planned to see him at West China Hospital in Chengdu, the provincial capital of the southwest province of Sichuan. However on the morning of the seventh day after the quake, I heard the news of his death from the television screen on a taxi in Chengdu. His heart stopped beating barely two hours after he was pulled from the ruin in Dujiangyan, about sixty kilometers west of Chengdu. That's just after midnight on May 18th when two Chengdu journalists and I were on the way back from the pitch-dark Dujiangyan to Chengdu. Afterwards, we knew just at that moment another aftershock was jolting the Chengdu Plain.

It is said that Zhang Xiaoping almost ran out of the building immediately after the quake. But Luo Qingfeng did not. As her boyfriend ran back, the concrete floor collapsed, obstructing their way out.

Did they talk with each other? What did they talk about? Could they see each other's eyes? Were they hopeless when they thought of each other at their last moment?

Though I refer to them as a boyfriend and a girlfriend, it is not as romantic as it sounds. Both were middle-aged. Zhang Xiaoping was already forty-six years old. And he was a laid-off worker. The apartment on the first floor here was Luo Qingfeng's. Both had divorced their former spouses before they lived together less than two years ago. Only Luo Qingfeng had a child who was not with her.

Is it true that these two ordinary lives have thus ended outright? Is it sheer absurdity? What on earth were they here for? It is true that many people say they do not care about for ever and ever, so long as once had. Yet, what on earth did the couple once have? Even if there's something they once had, is the death like this what they deserved to have?

A Matter of Life and Death

Three months on since I left the Dujiangyan courtyard, sometime each day I would feel I was still standing among those heaps of rubble visualizing how they spent their last hours in the dark. It's hard to imagine that scores of people of my trade coming from across China were standing at the home gate of these two strangers witnessing a ten-hour rescue effort of other scores of people, mainly firefighters led by a major general of the People's Liberation Army.

Zhang Xiaoping and Luo Qingfeng had never received such a nationwide attention the whole of their lives. But what could be brought to them with such last attention?

For those who could not enter the ruin to the rescue, what could be done to help the victims?

Prayer appears to be one of the words passed on most frequently between people in China since the quake. But to whom we pray? Who will listen to our prayers? Is it because our prayers were heard that Zhang Xiaoping could be finally pulled out of the wreckage? Is it because our prayers were not heard that his heart eventually stopped beating less than two hours later?

Many people admit that they are powerless after the quake. What could be admitted other than admitting powerless? Who could prevent death from coming when it comes? When each and every life is born, death is coming. Day by day. Minute by minute. There may have been numerous uncertainties in life. The certainty of death, though, has been without exception. What is uncertain is sooner or later.

Death looks elusive when people are preoccupied with life of the present. Such might be the case for many people of the current generation in China before the temblor rocked much of East Asia at 14:28 on the 12th of May 2008.

It only takes a few seconds for death to preoccupy the life of anyone, whatever you do, whoever you are. All are equal before the death.

One of the most widespread impacts the Sichuan Earthquake has made on China may have been the plain fact that in a year that would mark the rise of modern China, with holding the Olympic Games on the top agenda after three decades of continued economic growth, so many living creatures stopped living abruptly in broad daylight across so large a land almost simultaneously, with numerous images beaming across the world by various media of, in particular, those artless school children and their teachers who perished in the collapsed school buildings, and other ordinary Chinese like Zhang Xiaoping and Luo Qingfeng locked up in their home-turned-into-hell.

Facing the abyss that never returns, who would be unmoved?

The government responded swiftly with uncharacteristic openness with its premier arriving in Sichuan from the country's capital of Beijing within several hours after the quake; hence the rescue and relief efforts that involve local, national and international organizations the world has witnessed since then.

It is in a stark contrast with not only China's neighboring Myanmar in the response to the cyclone disaster in early May, but also China itself in the past. In the summer of 1976 when an earthquake of similar magnitude hit the northern Chinese city of Tangshan, the same Communist government refused to accept international aid and wouldn't send its premier to the disaster zone that's less than 200 kilometers northeast of Beijing until six days after the quake.

Thirty years of the Reform and Opening-up policy which was adopted two years after the Tangshan Earthquake has been attributed to the big changes since then.

What kind of changes would happen after the Sichuan Earthquake? What kind of changes would take place in the next thirty years?

The clue to the answer may have something to do with the theme of both earthquakes. It is a matter of life and death.

While making the second visit to the Sichuan disaster zone in late May, Wen Jiabao, the Chinese premier, wrote down a phrase on a blackboard at a makeshift middle school. Literally, it reads, "Much distress regenerates a country."

So far, it has generated somewhat heated online debates about the meaning and even the relevance of the phrase.

For generations of Chinese elite in living memory, how to regenerate China against the backdrop of the rise of the West and its dominance of world affairs has been a recurrent theme. A current that moves below the surface is that of how to pursue life over death out of fear that China, long self-viewed as the middle of the land under heaven, might be eliminated through world competitions.

In the aftermath of the Sichuan Earthquake, both the current and the undercurrent have been evident.

Saving the life was atop the agenda throughout days and nights immediately after the quake. Numerous rescuers from home and abroad working around the clock to free people trapped in the wreckage such as the ones in the Dujiangyan courtyard may have been the most unforgettable images besides the victims themselves.

And the three days of national mourning for the tens of thousands of quake deaths, set up by the government when the Olympic torch relay was suspended along with other public amusement, is another sign showing the Chinese elite have probably begun thinking seriously about the role of saving the life in saving the country.

A Bruised Reed He Will Not Break

But how to save the life? Does it just mean stop someone from dying physically?

For those who live on after the Sichuan Earthquake, the question of life and death is a matter of pressing concern. Though it's not Auschwitz, the Sichuan Earthquake is tragic enough to press the survivors to address the Adorno-style question: Can one live after the Sichuan Earthquake?

For one thing, attention has been focused on the shoddiness of school and ordinary residential buildings. As some parents sobbed with the pictures of their children who had died in the collapsed schoolhouses, the cause of the deaths is more a man-made calamity than natural disaster. So, the premier demand upon all the construction industry and the relevant government departments is that these man-made calamities not happen again. In short, it is a matter of conscience.

For another, attention has also been drawn to the deeper meaning of life and death. In much of Chinese history, the question of death more or less remains a taboo. Confucius, arguably the most influential thinker in Chinese history, was quoted by his students in the Lunyu or Analects as saying, "While you do not know life, how can you know about death?" The view, fairly typical of Chinese elite of many generations, may sound reasonable in normal times. When it comes to catastrophe of various kinds, though, more convincingly relevant arguments are much-needed. In the aftermath of the Sichuan Earthquake, how to articulate the meaning of life and death seems to constitute a critical part of bringing real comfort to survivors.

Standing before the twisted buildings that trapped Zhang Xiaoping and Luo Qingfeng, I found two "I"s, or two Zhang Xiaopings, two Luo Qingfengs.

One is the mortal I. However I pray, I would receive no response awaiting the death that puts an end to me. What a grief. Despair.

I tried to imagine that I was trapped like Zhang Xiaoping in the building before my eyes with the loved one just at my side but unable to rescue her from the wreckage. In the end, though, I still couldn't imagine how dark would be the dark around him.

What I could imagine is that both the sun and the stars would be the same with their light going out of its way to the earth. By crawling along the surface of this Sichuan building regularly, it informs people outside the building when the night goes and when the day comes. I was once one of the people outside. Yet now, how many times brighter would be the night outside than the day here?

But faintly, I found it was not the whole of me. I might have underestimated my life.

When thinking of the loved one just at my side, when the endless night has become the daily life, when the metal bars and concrete floors have been part of the furniture, when the floor slabs over the legs have grown eternal, when the tears have dried up, when the dust has settled, my eyes may be the clear creeks. And my heart may be the quiet Don River.

I might have underestimated my life indeed. The 129 hours of life, a record Zhang Xiaoping had set, was broken a number of times in the days that followed by people who were freed from the wreckage. They later spoke about how they had cherished the hope that they would be freed and how they had quenched their thirst by drinking their own urine.

I still might have underestimated my life indeed. Are the lives of those who're not freed from the ruin definitely not saved?

What on earth happened at the last moment? Who knows except I who would go?

Man is not the creator of his own. Man doesn't know when he is to be born. How could he know when he is to go?

Perhaps it is not an end. Don't people refer to death as just leaving this world or simply passing away? If so, death is a new beginning. If it is a new beginning, it is not an end to everything. If it is not an end to everything, it is not an end at all.

Perhaps all this is but an imagination. But, is imagination itself not a miracle? Is there anyone who could say where imagination is in the world? Is it the invisible out of the visible body? Does the invisible not exist?

Imagination is by no means the only invisible that exists. In this huge disaster relief endeavor, love is probably the only really effective power that is believed could relieve quake victims.

We have witnessed numerous actions of love. And yet, can we tell the whereabouts of love?

Quite a number of survivors have expressed a kind of faith by saying, "I definitely believed I could be freed. I definitely believed I could be saved."

How could they say they "definitely believed" they would be saved before they were saved?

"Faith is being sure of what we hope for and certain of what we do not see."[84] Someone who lived more than one thousand years ago explained why one could have such definite faith. Is it still faith if one has already seen or been saved?

And didn't many people recently say that they believe their loved ones who had perished in the disaster were on the way to Heaven?

They haven't seen Heaven but believe in Heaven feeling that would be the best place for people to go.

84   Hebrews 11:1.

Why is it the case? What brought them to believe in Heaven despite the country they live in rarely attaches importance to the knowledge about Heaven?

What if Heaven has told them the truth?

I believe in Heaven, too, not because I just believe so but because I believe someone who's in charge of everything including Heaven of course has told us the truth by giving us his promise. It's just in that book explaining the meaning of faith that God the Creator who's also called Love has given us his promise.

> "A bruised reed he will not break,
> And a smoldering wick he will not snuff,
> till he leads justice to victory.
> In his name the nations will put their hope."[85]

As the amputated Zhang Xiaoping was carried through a narrow tunnel dug by the rescuers out of the ugliest building I've ever seen, a big round of applause was given to him and his rescuers. As I later heard the news of his death, my heart ached. Yet I still believe the promise God in Heaven has made to his children will not fail.

In ancient times, China was once called the Land of God, a name that has been long taken for granted. Will China truly become God's land?

It may be uncertain whether much distress can regenerate a country. But as the aftermath of the Sichuan Earthquake shows, saving the life will surely help save the country. By whom the life can be saved? The country that can host the Olympics? Or someone else? Someone above? Someone within? Until it hears the promise and depends on it, China still has a long way to go.

---

85   Matthew 12:20–21.

Chapter 11
Why There Is (Surprisingly) No War in China

It is in peace that people tend to take the peace for granted.[86] How to talk about war in a largely peaceful country? That does not mean that China has never been at war with itself or with others. Indeed, a largely peaceful China is a rarity.

Among the lists of wars and armed conflicts by death toll,[87] World War Two is usually ranked the first, which is immediately followed by the four other biggest wars in human history that all happened in what is today's China or its neighbors.

They are: the Anshi Rebellion in the Tang Dynasty in the mid-eighth century, the Mongol Conquests from the thirteenth to fifteenth centuries, the Manchu Conquest of the Ming Dynasty in the seventeenth century, and the Taiping Peaceful Heavenly Kingdom Rebellion in the Manchu Qing Dynasty in the mid-nineteenth century.

An estimated 100 million people died during those four periods of wars and armed conflicts. And if we add the number of the casualties in China from World War Two and World War One, China is a country that has been the most affected by human violence.

It is against this somber backdrop that we now see a surprisingly largely peaceful China over the past thirty years.

There are a number of factors that have led to the unusual realization of peace in China, of which two appear to have figured prominently. One is the global trend for peace and for economic development in recent

---

86 This chapter was originally a talk delivered at The Media Project's 2009 Jakarta workshop on August 17–21, 2009.

87 For an example, see http://en.wikipedia.org/wiki/List_of_wars_and_disasters_by_death_toll .

decades. The other is the fact that China has gradually and decisively changed the way it views itself and its place in the international society.

In the years after World War Two, and especially in the last thirty years, the world seems to have focused on spreading peace and development across much of the globe. This also is surprising when one considers that, after World War One, there was no peace at all like this. Rather, an even much crueler World War Two followed with a gap of only twenty years.

Live and Let Live

Behind this rough road from war to peace, there might lie a significant shift in the way of thinking and living in terms of gain and loss.

In a society where force and violence prevail, the dominant attitude is that if you want to win you must defeat any potential competitor or enemy, otherwise you will be defeated. In game theory, it is called zero-sum thinking.

But what on earth brought an end (though strictly speaking never once and for all) to the zero-sum mentality and gave rise to what is now widely known as win-win thinking?

If we look back on what has happened over the past hundreds of years globally, there has been a powerful undercurrent of cooperative interests among people in spite of wars and various forms of conflicts. This undercurrent first became something of a mainstream in Britain, other parts of Western Europe and much of North America where the rule of law and freedom of trade, speech and religion gradually took root from the seventeenth century and increasingly influenced the twentieth century.

The breakthroughs in science and technology in almost exactly the same period have made a huge difference to the way the world works.

It is probably these scientific and technological advances rather than anything else that first shocked, or to a considerable extent impressed, China and possibly many other countries.

China's attitudes towards science, technology and everything else coming from the West have been quite complicated. For centuries, China has called itself, and considered itself, the "Central Nation" or "Middle

Kingdom" under heaven. Out of the blue, that attitude started seeming out of line with reality.

Paradoxically, the West's military exports as well as invasions contributed to the continued bloodshed in China. And the massacres between the Western countries themselves like the two world wars serve as a reminder that peace is hard to make and maintain anywhere on the planet.

In the long run, though, the willingness to learn everything superior from the West and other parts of the world was gaining ground among the Chinese elites, despite numerous changes in who actually held power over the past century and a half.

From military muscle, technology, science, economy, and the arts to law, politics and even religion, China's learning road continues until today.

The road came to be nearly irreversible in the late 1970s when China—at long last—put an end to almost thirty years of a "closed-door" policy and totalitarian rule.

The Inside Story

Such a change of heart is seemingly strange. After the Second World War, China's own civil war did not end until the Western-supported Nationalist Party government troops were defeated by the then-Soviet-supported Communist Party guerrillas in 1949. For many people then, the time had finally arrived that China could build a new country on its own after countering foreign invasions and different projections of foreign interests that had humiliated China for as long as a century.

Yet that golden opportunity turned out to be a nearly unprecedented man-made disaster in Chinese history. Although there was no all-out war, tens of millions of lives are believed to have perished in various kinds of human catastrophe in the first thirty years of Communist rule in China.

It is perhaps beyond what everyone expected or could even imagine at the time that the bloody internal struggle without the presence of foreign interests helped the Chinese elite come to believe only an "Reform and Opening-up" policy could save the country from self-destruction.

What makes this different from the previous open-door policy before the 1949 revolution is that the decision to open up and learn from others was made out of China's own choice, not out of the presence of outsiders, their demands or their persuasion.

Of course, this does not mean that the pressure for change for the better from the outside is unimportant. If universal lessons could be learnt from the story of cultural change and openness in China, one of them would be that the pressure for change for the better from the inside is even more crucial than pressure for change from the outside.

In fact, the two world wars, and the years between and after them, were also a painfully crucial moment for the West in terms of soul-searching, and the prosperous reconstruction of Japan and Germany as well as the stunning collapse of central planning in the Soviet bloc helped the further expansion of win-win thinking.

Although history provides sad and hard lessons, peace remains hard to make and maintain—as can be seen currently in the Middle East, Sudan, Somalia and North Korea. If people themselves do not value peace from the bottom of their hearts, peace may come—but it will disappear sooner rather than later.

So, how long will the peace last in China? If history is any guide, caution must be constant. The Anshi Rebellion, which according to some statistics claimed perhaps the largest number of human lives only after the Second World War, erupted at the apex of the Tang Dynasty, which is often viewed as the most successful dynastic rule in Chinese history.

The eye-popping riots in China's western Xinjiang region in early July 2009, the seemingly ever more reports of local protests and conflicts, and the escalating clampdown on dissent ahead of the sixtieth anniversary of the People's Republic of China are just part of living proof of the need for constant caution.

Chapter 12
How Not to Defame Religions
and Their Defamers

Religion has basically not been a big concern in China.[88] One recent example is that since the United Nations began discussing the resolutions of what they called "combating defamation of religions" in 1999, no major Chinese media reports or articles have ever appeared about the topic. They include both state and private media.

However, it does not mean that religion would be worthy of no consideration either in China or when it comes to China. In fact, the Chinese government has consistently voted for the resolutions at both the UN Human Rights Council and the UN General Assembly.

It shows that the top decision-makers in China have had a consistent policy over religion and religion-related issues. Such a policy serves to illustrate the subtle place of religion in China's society.

If the policy is viewed in the context of the international community, the subtlety will become somewhat noticeable. The states which voted for the resolutions with their Chinese counterpart are generally the governments of the non-Western world. The March 2010 vote at the UN Human Rights Council is the latest one. All the twenty states that voted in favor of the resolution are of mainly Muslims or Africa or Asia or Latin America or (ex) Communists. The majority of the seventeen states voting against the resolution are of the West or Europe.

In 1999, the "combating defamation of religions" motion was first brought before the then UN Commission on Human Rights by Pakistan

---

88   This chapter was originally a talk given at The Media Project's 2010 Jakarta workshop on August 12, 2010.

on behalf of the Organisation of Islamic Conference(OIC), an international organization with fifty-seven member states. Originally, the draft resolution was introduced with the title "Defamation of Islam." It was later suggested to include all religions.

The move aimed at having the United Nations combat what the OIC said "Defamation of Islam." Both the first resolution and the ones that followed expressed "deep concern in this respect that Islam is frequently and wrongly associated with human rights violations and terrorism." Islam has been basically the only religion specifically mentioned in these resolutions.

The responses from the Western governments and non-governmental organizations have been generally that, in the words of Angela Wu at the Washington-based Becket Fund for Religious Liberty, "the concept of 'defamation of religions' undermines the foundations of human rights law by protecting ideas instead of people, and empowering states instead of their citizens."

Not only in this case but also in almost all issues concerning faith and speech and assembly, the difference between Western and non-Western countries has been evident. The Western governments would highlight the individual freedom, while the non-Western ones the state authority.

It is true that Islam is neither the state religion of China nor the country's religion of majority. And the reasons why the Chinese government has supported the resolutions sponsored by the Islamic group may be various. But one thing could be certain. The authority in China favors what the OIC does to try and keep an ideology from defamation by resorting to making laws. For now, the "combating defamation of religions" resolutions are non-binding and yet the sponsors clearly want them to become international law.

For anyone holding any belief, they would not be happy to hear or see their belief come under attack no matter if it is right or wrong. It is understandable that people would use some means to prevent such attacks or even punish those who launch an attack. An unavoidable question would be: how to keep justice for both sides?

In this regard, to strike the right balance between state authority and individual freedom may be crucial. For any society, it won't be easy.

There would be either the abuse of state power or that of personal liberty. Or there are both. They are perhaps just the two sides of a coin.

Separation of State and Religion

History has witnessed many efforts to achieve this goal. Among them, the First Amendment to the United States Constitution may have proved most beneficial to bringing somewhat widespread and lasting justice to both state authority and individual freedom.

It reads as follows, "Congress shall make no law respecting an establishment of religion, or prohibiting the free exercise thereof; or abridging the freedom of speech, or of the press; or the right of the people peaceably to assemble, and to petition the Government for a redress of grievances."

This amendment was put forward and adopted together with the rest of the Bill of Rights in late 1780s and early 1790s. For the sponsors, it provided adequate guarantees for civil liberties, which the Constitution lacked.

At that time, Christianity was apparently the dominant religion among the residents in North America. But it would not become the state religion. The First Amendment was helpful in preventing it from becoming so.

Yet, it was not just through a passing of a bill that what was later widely known as the "separation of state and religion (or church and state)" has been basically established. For any law to be effective, there has to be general consensus between members of the society. For example, if the Christian churches were in fact funded by the state, then it would not be right to say the separation of church and state took effect.

For any religion or any belief system that is dominant in society, it would be almost impossible for it not to get involved with state power. Instead, it would be very easy for such a belief system to gain favoritism from the state and even to use state power to silence criticism of any kind.

History shows that the separation of church and state has helped Christianity have a relatively dynamic growth in America or at least more dynamic over recent centuries than in many European countries where Christianity was or has been the state religion for quite a while.

Of course, this does not mean that the separation of church and state has been the only reason for the more robust growth of a religion. This only means that the separation of state and religion could help keep any religion or belief system from being gravely corrupted by the abuse of power and liberty.

No religion or belief system could be free from criticism or even defamation. The point is how to deal with any opinion about the religion in a fair way. And especially when the defamation is indeed defamation, what should the followers of the religion do?

For the real truth, no defamation could reduce it to untruth. So defamation may have harmed one religion or another but it cannot change the fact that the truth is the truth. In this sense, it would be unnecessary for the members of a religion to use anything including state power to defend itself against defamation.

Yet of course, anyone who does defamation should be responsible for what one says. To what extent he or she could be treated fairly depends considerably upon the extent the separation of state and religion is carried out. Imagine how different it would be between what an alleged defamer could face under the rule with the separation of state and religion and under the rule without the separation.

Separation of State and Party

In China, on the surface there is no religion that is dominant in both social and personal life. So the question of the separation of state and religion appears irrelevant. But a closer look may reflect a very different reality.

For example, Communism, which covers almost all aspects of individual and social life with atheism and party/state ownership as the well-known characteristics, is the belief system of the Communist Party of China that has been the only ruling party in the country since it took power in 1949. This only ruling party has used state power (both hard and soft power) it monopolizes to keep their belief system dominant. In much of the past sixty years, anyone who challenges or criticizes the ruling system may risk losing freedom or even life because of charges of, say, defamation.

It seems improbable for any other group with a different belief system to grow and spread in such an iron grip of a strong ruling political party with a strong belief system. For many years, it was indeed unlikely. In China, the question of the separation of state and religion may have been if it is possible to separate state and party, and how.

Over the recent years, many changes have taken place. They came perhaps very unexpectedly after the ruling party initiated what is called "Reform and Opening-up" policy in late 1970s when the ten-year Cultural Revolution and the previous highly centralized planned economy were put to an end in catastrophe. Private business and private ownership have gradually been allowed and even some private-run media have appeared and gained in popularity.

Yet even more surprisingly, the market of belief systems has also begun prospering. The religions and philosophies that once were popular and even dominant in Chinese society have had a revival to some degree. They include Buddhism, Confucianism and Taoism. And various schools of thoughts from abroad have also been introduced to China after a thirty-year hiatus.

All these, though, came still less surprisingly than the rise of a seemingly foreign religion and its followers. It is the Christian house church. Many house churches started from a small Bible study group in a family, instead of being planted by foreign missionaries who played an important role in introducing Christianity to China and were expelled after 1949. Many early house church planters were baptized at the state-sanctioned Three-Self churches and then left to establish independent churches. Many house churches have rented office buildings and even started purchasing a space for worship. A probably unprecedented number of people in China from all walks of life with many of them young people have converted to Christianity.

An interesting point is that these house churches have grown and spread despite the fact that the government almost consistently refuses to recognize their legality and tries to prevent them from mere existence or further growth. Some house churches have applied to register with the government as an independent church, but the government asked them to first join the official Three-Self church, which has been funded by the state and whose leaders are also members of the government-controlled legislative or political consultative bodies. These house churches have appealed to the government to revamp its religion policy by asking for the realization of the separation of church and state.

In a symbolic article published in a house church's magazine in 2008, the author who is also the founding pastor of the church elaborated the church's stance on registration. In his words, "the realization of the principle of the separation of church and state is the key to solving the house church issue."

According to the article, the house church believes that the government "has gone beyond its limits of power meddling with the internal affairs and belief of the church" when it demanded the non-Three-Self churches join the Three-Self ones. The house church also holds that if the Three-Self also makes the same demand then it clearly shows the Three-Self is but an extension of the government.

Although many are home-grown, these house churches have resorted to the seemingly alien principle of the separation of state and religion to help solve the issue of their legality. As shown above, this principle could be traced back to the founding era of the United States. It is quite possible that this principle along with other ideas regarding the relationship between state and religion has been introduced or re-introduced to China since the policy of "Reform and Opening-up" was started up in late 1970s.

The Word Became Flesh

But in fact, the principle of the separation of state and religion was not invented by the American founders despite their crucial contribution to helping put it into practice through amending the constitution of a big new country. The Bible, which the followers of Jesus Christ (Christians) believe is God-breathed, tells its own story of the principle.

One of the most famous teachings is "Give to Caesar what is Caesar's, and to God what is God's."[89] That is when Jesus was asked by the Pharisees if it was right to pay taxes to Caesar (the title of many Roman emperors). Another instance is that Jesus withdrew to a mountain by

89   Matthew 22:21.

himself when he knew the people who saw the miraculous sign that he had done intended to make him king by force. And Jesus also made it clear to Pontius Pilate (then the Roman governor in Judaea province) that his kingdom was not of this world.

It would take many years or decades or even centuries before a principle like the separation of state and religion was made known to and started putting into practice in the world. The separation has generally brought benefit to both the state authority and the individual freedom of faith, expression and assembly.

The principle will perhaps take root in a changing China with the potential further growth of the independent Christian church. And in the longer term, China may come up with some constructive ideas like the separation of state and religion when it comes to international resolutions regarding religion and defamation. At that time, the role of religion may become more noticeably important in the shape of the Chinese society and the broader world.

Chapter 13
How Far Still Are the Chinese
from Being Creative?

If you go shopping around the world, you would find one thing in common: a wide range of goods from clothing to electronics that carry a mark of "Made in China." In contrast, it would not be very easy to get a local product. However, it might be somewhat equally difficult to buy any modern product that is "Created in China." And the situation of the kind looks likely to last for a while at least.

In spite of a number of vicissitudes, the Chinese over the recent one hundred years have basically been on the road of learning from what they call the developed societies. Imitation seems inevitable in this learning process, which itself is hard to come by. Yet, imitation is not creation. The learning process will not definitely result in creating something.

The gap between imitation and creation might be like the one between a book and its translation. A book about technology that was translated into Chinese in 2010 is such a case. The gap might not only be related to the time difference but also to the ideas about creation.

Out of Control

Kevin Kelly is the founding Executive Editor of *Wired*, an American magazine devoted to reporting on the trends in technology and how they affect the broader society. When his new book *What Technology Wants* was published in October 2010, one of Kelly's old works just came out in Chinese.

It is *Out of Control: The New Biology of Machines, Social Systems, and the Economic World*, published in America as early as 1994. In the eyes of Chris Anderson, the incumbent Editor of *Wired*, *Out of Control* is perhaps the most important book of the 1990s. Some significant worldwide phenomena such as the rise of the Internet and the diffusion of democracy and decentralization since the mid-1990s were both anticipated and illuminated in this book.

In late 2010, Kelly visited China promoting the Chinese edition of *Out of Control*. The Chinese audiences began to know about Kelly's ideas. In addition to *Out of Control*, some of the interviews and articles about him in English were translated into Chinese.

So far, the media reports in the Chinese-speaking world about Kelly and his ideas are largely a basic introduction. It is not uncommon for the people who're interested in the current trends in technology to start speaking about this "éminence grise of Silicon Valley." But as for what on earth Kelly's ideas are about, what background they are situated in and what they would mean to one's own life, it appears not very clear.

For those who have heard of Kevin Kelly may have known about his somewhat legendary experience. In 1952, Kelly was born in the northeastern US state of Pennsylvania. He dropped out of University of Rhode Island at the age of 19. For the following nearly eight years, Kelly was an independent photographer. He travelled in more than ten Asian countries. In 1979, he visited Jerusalem. He became a Christian after a conversion experience there. Then, he rode a bicycle across the continental U.S.

In 1992, Kelly helped found *Wired* magazine. Before that, he had various jobs like launching *Walking Journal*, the first American magazine dedicated to recreational walking, and editing *Whole Earth Review*, a magazine about technological innovation. From 1990 to 1994, he researched and wrote *Out of Control*, initially subtitled *The Rise of Neo-Biological Civilization*.

For most of his contemporaries in China, Kelly's life experience would sound very different. Even for the younger generation, perhaps still not many people would lead a life like Kelly's. His dropping out of college would remind people of two better-known dropouts in his generation: Bill Gates and Steve Jobs, who founded Microsoft and Apple respectively.

Throughout his journey across many countries after leaving

school, Kelly wanted to explore some fundamental questions of life. Some major questions: Is God real? If he is real, then how could people ignore him?

After his years-long Asia tour, Kelly was in Jerusalem on Easter in 1979. Like in many other places, he planned to photograph yet another religious ceremony. Well beyond his expectation, the Jerusalem visit would change Kelly's life forever.

Nearly twenty years later, in 1997, Kelly told America's *National Public Radio* (*NPR*) about his experience in Jerusalem. "And then for various reasons I got locked out of my hostel room. They had a curfew and I didn't make it back in time." Kelly recalled, "I was in quite a fix because I was a stranger in this very strange town. I didn't have enough money to stay elsewhere, nor did I even have knowledge of where to go, so I wandered the old town of Jerusalem."

Kelly wandered around for a number of hours. He felt it was getting colder. Finally, he found himself at a place that was still open. That was a church. He entered the building. He was very tired and slept on a slab. That slab is believed to be a spot where Jesus was crucified.

Early next morning, Kelly woke when people started coming in. He said, "I went out and followed the crowd where it was going. They were going out to the tombs area, in Jerusalem. And I went out, and there were some chairs set up, folding chairs set up in front of this tomb area. And as the sun was coming up on that Easter morning, I was staring at empty tombs."

Kelly sat on a chair contemplating a view of the early morning sun coming into the empty tombs. For a reason even he himself does not understand, Kelly realized that all the major questions he had been wrestling with for many years were resolved. Not only is it that God is real, but also he believed that Jesus had indeed risen from those tombs.

All this would sound a very personal experience. Kelly himself acknowledged it was hard to figure out how the change happened. Despite this, the change did have an evident and far-reaching impact on Kelly. He felt that he was going to die in six months. He wanted to go home and be with his parents. This came as a big surprise. He thought that, given six months to live, he would climb Mount Everest or he would go scuba diving into the depths of the ocean.

So, Kelly went back home. He stayed with his parents in New Jersey for three months. He helped them do household chores. "And yet I found myself relishing the ordinariness, and finding it in some ways as exotic as anything I had traveled to see," said Kelly.

In the next three months, Kelly visited his four brothers and sisters on a bicycle. They were scattered all across America. Kelly's trip covered some eight thousand kilometers. By the end of the three months, he returned to his parents. He anonymously gave the money left to those who were in need. He was ready to die. And yet, he remains alive.

Nowadays, Kelly's interview with *NPR* about this experience can still be heard on the Internet. When he said that he opened his eyes in the morning he thought he would have died, his voice choked with emotion. He had to pause for several times. If you listen with earphones, you would perhaps be surprised why it was so difficult for him to continue. Though each pause is no longer than ten seconds, each one sounds a very long time.

In fact, Kelly himself did not expect the fact that he could wake in an ordinary morning turned out to be a moving miracle for him. In his words, "There was nothing special about the day. It was another ordinary day. I was reborn into ordinariness. But, what more could one ask for?"

Finding a miracle in ordinariness may have been the experience of many people who grew from ignorance to maturity. A young man or woman would eventually realize that novelty was relative. While young, he or she might want to be different. When it is time to get married, a more or less stable family life seems inevitably desirable for many people. In this sense, Kelly's change might be one of the numerous stories of the kind in human history.

It is true that after spending most of his twenties on the road, Kelly gradually settled down. At age thirty-five, he married Gia-Miin Fuh, a biochemist from Taiwan. They have two daughters and a son. In the meantime, he helped launch *Wired* magazine at the age of forty and was its first Executive Editor for almost seven years.

Creation's Deeper Meaning

And yet, there is more about Kelly's change. To find a miracle in ordinariness is not having to do as others do. Kelly kept on his exploration.

He once told *Christianity Today* magazine that he "was science nerd in high school." The change he experienced in and after Jerusalem has apparently helped shape his thinking about science and technology. He studied only one year at University of Rhode Island. He has no college or university degrees. But much of his life after Jerusalem has had something to do with expounding his ideas about science and technology.

If it is fair to say that dropouts like Jobs and Gates unconventionally helped grow the computer and Internet technology in their business, it might be equally fair to say that Kelly unconventionally helped develop a deeper understanding of the Internet and the wider technology. The *Wired* magazine he co-founded has become a window into how technology is changing the world. If you read his articles in *Wired* and the books he wrote, you would find his views about technology are quite different from conventional wisdom you have heard.

Perhaps the most unique view is that for Kelly, technology is "a living, evolving organism." His two best-known books come straight to the point right from their covers: *What Technology Wants; Out of Control: The New Biology of Machines, Social Systems, and the Economic World* or *The Rise of Neo-Biological Civilization*. Technology is more than just things people invent but "anything that springs from the human mind." That Kelly is interested in what technology wants shows that he cares about how the human mind can be creative.

From this perspective, technology is an extension of a creative living being. It can be seen from history that the growth of technology to a considerable extent depends on the social and individual circumstances. What Kelly means by "Out of Control" is not that humanity will collapse into chaos because of the flourishing technology. Rather, it means the free growth of technology is the reflection of the free growth of a creative living being. [A more exact Chinese translation of *Out of Control* than 失控 (Shikong) might be: 走出控制 (Zouchu Kongzhi), *The Emergence from Control, or Walking Out of Control*]

To Kelly, the creative living beings don't live in a top-down system with a center of control, but in a bottom-up, diverse, distributed and complicated world with numerous self-governing members who are highly connected. The creative nature of human beings is not a result of human decisions. Both why humans can be creative and how they create are beyond their own control.

If going further simply by this way of thinking, the picture of creation might still be of chaos. What Kelly has seen is more than just a world of humanity and nature. Yes, humans can be creative. Yet, humans themselves are also a kind of creation. The creativity of humanity comes from that of the one who created humanity. This idea is what the Bible shows. It says God created humans in his own image. Though the world of creative humans is beyond their control, it is under the rule of their creator.

In this sense, technology is more than just an extension of human beings, but that of a living being who created humans. For Kelly, the reason why he is so fascinated with technology "is that every individual human has a certain God-given set of talents that require things like technology in order to be expressed." He says, "technology is actually a divine phenomenon that is a reflection of God."

In addition, one could make sense of some deeper meaning of creativity from God's creation of humans. When humans were created, he or she was endowed with a character that is closely linked with creativity: freedom. Without freedom, it would be impossible for humans to be creative. But to endow humans with freedom means their creator needs to take a huge risk.

With freedom, humans as a creation would be different from other creations. He or she would be free to think and do. Of course, it does not say that other creations do not have any freedom at all. Some creations do have some freedom. For example, some creatures can choose when to hop and when to fly. But humans apparently have much more freedom.

The question is, different thinkings and doings would entail different outcome. Humans and the world they inhabit would be faced with a variety of possibilities. Some think it would be good for them. Others would think otherwise. Humans even have the freedom to doubt whether they were created or to deny they were creations. Despite all this, the creator still endowed humans with freedom. In Kelly's eyes, humans should follow their creator's example by doing creation.

For those who are not familiar with Kelly's ideas, the thoughts above would sound strange or even incredible. But any response would be understandable. All sorts of ideas just show the freedom of human beings. On the other hand, Kelly's ideas may be unique and yet they are not alone. They appear to have benefited from a long tradition of creativity.

Accumulating a Tradition of Creativity

The idea that humans model on their creator in creating things could be found long ago in Europe where a series of science and technological revolutions took place over recent centuries. One notable instance is Charles Babbage (1791-1871), considered a "father of the computer."

In an article entitled "God Is the Machine" for the December 2002 issue of *Wired*, Kelly mentioned Babbage. He wrote, the English inventor "saw the world as one gigantic instantiation of a calculating machine, hammered out of brass by God. He argued that in this heavenly computer universe, miracles were accomplished by divinely altering the rules of computation. Even miracles were logical bits, manipulated by God."

Throughout the revolutions to which Babbage contributed, to endow the creations with more freedom is a common goal. The more automatic the creation is, the more creative the creation could become. To a considerable extent, the ever continued emergence of new tools since the industrial revolution is a result of the progress of automation. An ever growing network of automation is connecting up numerous aspects of global life.

A seemingly unnecessary concern is, will the growing automatic creations come to rebel against their creator? For technology thinkers like Kelly, it would be possible. It is perhaps an inevitable price a creative being would have to pay. From the Bible, Kelly sees a creator who inevitably has embraced the uncertainty creativity brought.

In the Bible, the creator of human beings resolved the problem of hostility by resorting to a way well beyond the imagination of humanity. The creator humbled himself "being made in human likeness," was crucified by the humans he created, rose from the dead. Then he appeared to humans showing he was their creator and redeemer and anyone who believed in him would be reborn in him and stay with him forever.

The war between humans and their creations is a theme in a 1999-2003 film trilogy, *The Matrix*. It is partly under the influence of the biblical views. Interestingly, the directors of the film asked Keanu Reeves and other actors to read Kelly's *Out of Control* and two other books about creation and psychology before opening the original script.

Prior to the making of *Minority Report* in 1999, film director Steven Speilberg invited Kelly and some other futurists to contribute ideas about what the year 2054 would be like. This film, which was released in 2002, had a theme of free will and determinism.

All this seems too far from what is happening in daily life. In much of the world, people from all walks of life appear to be preoccupied with things of the present. It is indeed a part of the story. And yet, what is called daily life has already also involved those things that are seemingly far away. What is far from some people is perhaps very near to others. What is far from some people right now may be very near to them at other moments.

Kelly's ideas were accumulated in his daily life. They may have had an impact on the daily life of a couple of film directors. Their films, in turn, may have played a role in the daily life of millions of souls. Even without these films, the *Wired* magazine Kelly co-founded, his books and his website (www.kk.org) have in fact been connected with the daily life of many people. The Internet, magazines and films are also things created and promoted quietly in daily life.

Of course, both what Kelly has seen and where he lives may still look far from China. In some sense, it is also true. But his experience and his ideas have begun to be heard in China. When he visited China in December 2010, some people went to his talk and asked him questions. Some have kept in touch with him. And the Chinese translation of *Out of Control* was done by a group of Chinese who volunteered to collaborate with one another via the Internet.

And yet, all this might still count for nothing. Out of control, is not done overnight. Kelly has had a long walk. It is after spending huge amounts of time on the road alone that beyond his expectation Kelly eventually experienced what he called being "reborn into ordinariness." Now, another thirty years have passed.

Anyway, Kelly has spent those numerous ordinary days sharing the miracles he saw with his fellow inhabitants of the world. In China, there are people who might be inspired by his story or even would also experience an unexpected rebirth.

In 2007, Kelly sent a Christmas card to family and friends expressing his gratitude to the living being who created humans and the wider universe. It was entitled "The Universe Is Conspiring to Help Us." This discovery might not be good luck only Kelly has met. What do you think?

Chapter 14
The Unfashionable Peter Drucker

In a 1989 interview with American magazine *Christianity Today*, the first question for Peter Drucker was: "After a lifetime of studying management, why are you now turning your attention to the church?" Drucker answered by saying he "became interested in management because of my interest in religion and institutions."[90]

For those who have heard of Peter Drucker, this brief round of question and answer might sound odd. For years, Drucker has been known as the father of modern management. Even after his death on November 11, 2005, Drucker seems to continue to be one of the most popular management consultants. His books in different languages remain on the list of management bestsellers and can still be seen in airport bookstores worldwide. Yet, very few people may have known how Drucker's interest in religion and institutions exerted an influence on his contributions to management.

On November 19, 1909, Drucker was born in Vienna, the capital of Austria. His father, Adolph Drucker, was a senior civil servant at the Austrian ministry of finance and would later teach international economics and European literature at universities in America. His mother, Caroline Bond, was one of the first women in Austria to study medicine. They held weekly gatherings joined by politicians, academics and artists. Among them were economists like Ludwig von Mises, Joseph Schumpeter and Friedrich von Hayek. At the age of eight, Drucker was led to see a friend of his parents, Sigmund Freud, the founder of psychoanalysis. And Drucker's paternal grandmother was a pianist who once worked with such musicians as Johannes Brahms and Gustav Mahler.

---

90   A Chinese version of this chapter was published in the April 5, 2009 issue of *Global Entrepreneur* magazine.

It seems that in a family like this one would need nothing else. However, there was Lutheran Protestantism in Drucker's childhood. But, in the eyes of Drucker, the Christian faith of his household "consisted of little more than a tree at Christmas and Bach cantatas at Easter." The class of religion, which was two hours a week, was still mandatory when Drucker attended school. Yet, the pastor who taught the class "hardly aimed much higher."

At barely 18 when finishing high school, Drucker did not go to university. He moved to Hamburg, a northern German city, as a trainee at a cotton-export company. It was just what he wanted to do from as early as about 14: getting out of school, getting out of Vienna and Austria. "By that time I had become weary of being bored by bored teachers," recalled Drucker in *Adventures of a Bystander*, his autobiography first published in 1979, "indeed the one point of agreement between my faculty and myself was that I had sat long enough. I would be an adult among adults—I have never liked being young, and detested the company of delayed adolescents as I thought most college students to be. I would earn a living and be financially independent."

Getting out of school and one's home country would not necessarily mean getting out of boredom. Still, the life as a firm trainee in Hamburg "was terribly boring." Copying invoices was his main responsibility. But he did not have to be busy. He read a lot, mainly European literature and history. And a city library was very close to his office. He also had time to go to the opera. The one that impressed him the most was Falstaff by the Italian composer, Giuseppe Verdi. It was based on Shakespeare's *The Merry Wives of Windsor* and was Verdi's last opera. Drucker was astonished to learn that the masterpiece with "incredible vitality" was composed when Verdi was in his ninth decade.

The opera and literature combined, though, were still unable to fill the vacuum in Drucker. He came across a small book called *Fear and Trembling*. It was based on a chapter of Genesis, the first book of the Bible, and discussed how Abraham, by faith, stood the test of God by being willing to sacrifice his son Isaac as a burnt offering. The influential work was first published in 1843 and the author was Søren Kierkegaard, a Danish theologian who died on November 11, 1855. The title came from a verse in a letter from the apostle Paul to his Christian friends in

Philippi, Greece: "continue to work out your salvation with fear and trembling." For Drucker, the appearance of Kierkegaard was more than an accident, but a providence. It would be many years later when Drucker could make sense of what had happened. "But I knew immediately that something had happened. I knew immediately that I had found a new, a crucial, an existential dimension," Drucker wrote at age eighty-three.

That dimension, Drucker explained, was one that "transcends society." Back in 1928 when he read *Fear and Trembling*, Drucker realized that his life would have to have that dimension even though his work would be in society. He clarified the dimension in "The Unfashionable Kierkegaard," an article first published in an autumn 1949 issue of *The Sewanee Review*, which was founded in 1892 and is America's oldest continuously published literary quarterly. That was when Drucker was forty and just four years after the end of World War II. He said the article was written "out of despair" and "to affirm hope."

For Drucker, Kierkegaard helped him to see a broader picture of human existence. Besides the existence in time or in society, a human being also exists in eternity or in spirit. It is not enough for a human being to live and die in society. The basis of the meaning and ethics in time or society lies in eternity or spirit. What Drucker called "a new, a crucial, an existential dimension" is an existence where society is not a totally human-made environment but also in spirit.

It follows that the dimension Drucker saw through Kierkegaard has gone beyond what he had seen in Vienna. In the words of Kierkegaard, it might be called "a leap to faith," or "a leap of faith," a term attributed to the Danish writer. From this leap, it is not just that both boredom and despair could be overcome and the source of vitality was known, but the place of a human being in the universe was clear: "The opposite of Sin (to use the traditional term for existence purely in society) is not Virtue; it is Faith. Faith is the belief that in God the impossible is possible, that in Him time and eternity are one, that both life and death are meaningful. Faith is the knowledge that man is creature not autonomous, not the master, not the end, not the center—and yet responsible and free. It is the acceptance of man's essential loneliness, to be overcome by the certainty that God is always with man, even 'unto the hour of our death.'"

In "The American Genius Is Political," a piece published in 1953, Drucker went on to highlight the dimension as part of the Judaeo-Christian tradition. He said "it is in the Old Testament that the Lord looked upon his material creation and saw that 'it was very good.' Yet the creation is nothing without the Spirit that created it. And it is man's specific task, his own mission and purpose, to make manifest the creator in and through the creation— to make matter express spirit."

The two articles would be part of *The Ecological Vision: Reflections on the American Condition*, a book published in 1992 when Drucker was 82. This collection of essays may have been one of the least popular books Drucker ever penned. But it is a book that could perhaps best display Drucker's vision as a social ecologist, a term he used to describe his profession which is "concerned with man's man-made environment the way the natural ecologist studies the biological environment."

In the discipline of social ecology, Drucker commented, the greatest document was French thinker Alexis de Tocqueville's *Democracy in America*. And the man whom Drucker viewed was closest to him "in temperament, concepts, and approach" was Walter Bagehot, an English journalist and chief editor of *The Economist* in the 1860s-70s. Like Bagehot, who first saw civil service and cabinet government as cores of a functioning democracy and banking as the center of a functioning economy, Drucker considered himself the first to identify management as the new social institution of the emerging society of organizations, knowledge as the new central resource, and knowledge workers as the new ruling class of a society.

Behind those social phenomena, Drucker was concerned about the health of human existence. He said the tension between the need for continuity and the need for innovation was central to civilization. It is a tension reminiscent of the one Drucker learned from Kierkegaard: "human existence is possible only in tension—in tension between man's simultaneous life as an individual in the spirit and a citizen in society ... the tension as the consequence of man's simultaneous existence in eternity and in time." As a social ecologist, Drucker was not confined to the human-made society. And it is what the title of the last part, which contains "The Unfashionable Kierkegaard," of *The Ecological Vision: Reflections on the American Condition*, refers to: Why Society Is Not Enough.

After encountering the dimension that transcends society, Drucker started a long journey that would take him to different societies and various social sectors. While still in Hamburg, he began studying law at Hamburg University. After staying in Hamburg for fifteen months, he moved to Frankfurt, a city in southwest Germany. He first worked as a trainee at a brokerage company. It went bankrupt during the Wall Street Crash in October 1929, one of the biggest financial crises in human history. On his twentieth birthday, Drucker became a journalist at a Frankfurt daily newspaper responsible for writing financial and foreign affairs stories. He transferred his study from Hamburg University to the University of Frankfurt where he earned a doctorate in 1931. He did not have to attend a class. It was enough to take an examination at a year's end. He studied international law and international relations, social and legal history, and finance. And at the University of Frankfurt, he met Doris Schmitz, a nineteen-year-old student from a nearby city of Mainz, whom he would marry in 1937 and stayed together until 2005 when Drucker died.

In 1933, Drucker went to Britain where he worked at an insurance company and then a small merchant bank. That came after Adolf Hitler was appointed as Chancellor of Germany on January 30, 1933. Hitler's Nazi or National Socialist German Workers' Party became the largest party in the German parliament in July 1932 when an election was held. In spring that year, Drucker had told a close friend that he would leave Germany if the Nazis came to power. Meanwhile, he was beginning to write *Friedrich Julius Stahl: Conservative Theory of the State and Historical Development*. It was a short monograph about Friedrich Julius Stahl, a nineteenth-century German political thinker. Drucker called Stahl "Germany's only Conservative political philosopher."

Like eighteen-year-old Drucker, Stahl had what Drucker called a "religious experience " and converted to Protestantism from Judaism in 1819 when he was seventeen. For Drucker, Stahl's "whole life and his whole doctrine are founded on this step and the obligation it imposed." In terms of politics, Stahl's theory holds that the state must be prevented "from becoming the only obligation, from becoming the 'total state'; for the state is an order of this world, an institution arisen out of the dissolution of a supreme, timeless order, a kingdom with a human goal and meaning. And this meaning and goal, that is to say, power, is evil and demoralizing, destructive, if it is not bound to a divine, immutable order, if it is not bound to God's plan for the world." Because of such a Christian worldview and the fact that Stahl was a Jew, the essay that came out in April 1933 was banned and burned by the Nazis.

While being forced to leave Germany due to the rise of the Nazis, Drucker would gain a lot from his four-year stay in Britain. Through the director of the bank where he worked as an economist, Drucker was able to attend British economist John Maynard Keynes's seminar at Cambridge University in 1934. Recalling the seminar in the early 1990s, Drucker wrote in *The Ecological Vision* that sitting in Keynes's lecture helped him realize that he was not an economist: "all the brilliant economics students in the room were interested in the behavior of commodities while I was interested in the behavior of people." But this does not mean Drucker would no longer have interest in economics. Instead, it shows that Drucker saw the world in a way that was different from Keynes and similar economists. Drucker said that he was "deeply interested in economics as a social dimension ... as the symbol around which social and political issues can be organized ...as an expression of social and political views and values."

Compared to Keynes, Joseph Schumpeter and the like were the economists whom Drucker held in much higher regard. Both Schumpeter and Keynes were born in 1883. In an article marking their centenary, Drucker described them as the greatest economists in the twentieth century. But, "Keynes and Schumpeter replayed the best-known confrontation of philosophers in the Western tradition—the Platonic dialogue between Parmenides, the brilliant, clever, irresistible sophist, and the slow-moving and ugly, but wise Socrates. No one in the interwar years was more brilliant, more clever than Keynes. Schumpeter, by contrast, appeared pedestrian—but he had wisdom. Cleverness carries the day. But wisdom endured."

Nevertheless, Schumpeter himself was not the same type of person throughout his sixty-six years. He came to know Drucker's father, Adolph, at age nineteen when studying at the University of Vienna. Seven years Schumpeter's senior, Adolph Drucker taught economics part-time at the university. On January 3, 1950, Adolph and his son went to see Schumpeter who was a professor at Harvard University. Drucker's father asked his friend if he still talked about what he wanted to be remembered for. "You know, Adolph, I have now reached the age where I know that being remembered for books and theories is not enough. One does not make a difference unless it is a difference in the lives of people," replied Schumpeter, who was then very ill. Before that, the Austrian economist had been known for wanting to be remembered as "Europe's greatest lover of beautiful women and Europe's greatest horseman—and perhaps also the world's greatest economist." Five days later, Schumpeter died.

In April 1937, Drucker and his bride Doris Schmitz emigrated to America. Apart from remaining as an economist for the bank in London, he wrote for a group of British and American newspapers and magazines. In the spring of 1939, Drucker's first book, *The End of Economic Man: The Origins of Totalitarianism*, was published. It was finished by the end of 1937. But Drucker started it as early as 1933 shortly after Hitler became the German chancellor. Reminiscing about the origin of the book in October 1994 before it was reissued, Drucker wrote: "An early excerpt—the discussion of the role of anti-Semitism in the Nazi demonology and the reasons for its appeal—was published as a pamphlet by an Austrian Catholic and anti-Nazi publisher in 1935 or 1936." The excerpt was *The Jewish Question in Germany*, published in 1936 by Gsur u. Co. in Vienna. A Nazi stamp can be seen on a surviving copy of the article kept in The Drucker Institute, a think-tank based at Claremont Graduate University, America's oldest all-graduate institution. It is where Drucker taught management from 1971 until his death in 2005.

In *The End of Economic Man*, Drucker treated society as "ecology"—"the environment of that very peculiar critter, the human being," and "Nazism—and totalitarianism altogether" as a disease across Europe. Totalitarianism denies all the traditional ideas in West and offers no positive ideology. In particular, Drucker considered that the failure of Marxism—a social movement as a new savior of humankind popular in the decades before World War I in Europe—was a major reason that made the masses "easy prey to totalitarian demagoguery and demonology." Three years later, Drucker published an essay "The Freedom of Industrial Man" in the Autumn 1942 issue of *The Virginia Quarterly*

Review, an American literary magazine founded in 1925. Much of the article would become a part of Drucker's second book, *The Future of Industrial Man: A Conservative Approach*, which came out in the same year. For Drucker, it was his most ambitious work and the only one that mapped out his social theories. For many of his friends and critics, it was Drucker's best book. Drucker used both the article and the book to warn his readers not to fight totalitarianism by resorting to any "equally absolutist, equally despotic revolutionary creed of our own," for that "could only lead to the substitution of one totalitarian despotism by another." Here, the dimension Drucker saw at the age of eighteen played a critical role in shaping his social theories: "The only basis of freedom is the Christian concept of man's nature: imperfect, weak, a sinner, and dust destined unto dust; yet made in God's image and responsible for his actions."

Drucker went on to suggest the vital significance of the Bible in the history of freedom and an early fruit it bore: "The roots of freedom are in the Sermon on the Mount and in the Epistles of St. Paul; the first flower of the tree of liberty was St. Augustine." The Sermon on the Mount is the longest piece of teaching from Jesus who told his disciples on a mountainside in Galilee of northern Israel about being a person God created in his own image. Paul is one of the most influential theologians and missionaries in the history of Christianity. He has been widely believed to have authored thirteen letters recorded in the New Testament dealing with various aspects of being a follower of Jesus. Augustine of Hippo in north Africa, a theologian in the late fourth century and early fifth century, is best known for his *City of God* and *Confessions*. For Drucker, it was Augustine and the Western tradition his thoughts helped shape that moulded Kierkegaard when it came to human being's simultaneous existence in eternity and in time. In "The Unfashionable Kierkegaard" that appeared in 1949, Drucker said "Kierkegaard stands squarely ... in the tradition of St. Augustine" and "concerns himself with the specific disease of the modern West: the falling apart of human existence, the denial of the simultaneity of life in the spirit and life in the flesh, the denial of the meaningfulness of each for the other."

When his first two books were published in the late 1930s and early 1940s, Drucker's life as the father of modern management had barely begun. But the dimension he learned from Kierkegaard, Augustine, Paul, and Jesus and the tradition they passed down from generation to generation served to equip Drucker to open up a new discipline in social studies. In 1943, Donaldson Brown, a vice chairman of General Motors—the world's largest manufacturing company then—invited Drucker to study its managerial policies as a social scientist. This came after Brown read Drucker's *The Future of Industrial Man*. After staying in the company for eighteen months, Drucker wrote *Concept of the Corporation*, which was published in 1946. It proved to be a seminal work in modern management. It is not particularly about GM or even business but about what Drucker called "organization," especially concerning how an organization really works.

For Drucker, what matters is management, because "Management is the organ of institutions, the organ that converts a mob into an organization, and human efforts into performance." Again, Drucker likened human institutions to a living body. Interestingly, the word "organization" derives from "organ." To grow healthily, a living body needs to have living organs that themselves grow healthily and interact with one another healthily. So it is no surprise at all that Drucker held that management was "at bottom a clinical discipline."

Again, the dimension Drucker saw at eighteen is evident in his ideas about management. In his eyes, a person working in an organization is not just an executive or a worker but a human being created by God and yet fallen. In 1954, Drucker's *The Practice of Management* came out. It is deemed to be the first book to look at management as a whole. The author explored the origin of work by quoting Genesis, the first book of the Bible, and claiming work was "both the Lord's punishment for Adam's fall and His gift and blessing to make bearable and meaningful man's life in his fallen state." So, "Only the relationship to his Creator and that to his family antedate man's relationship to his work; only they are more fundamental. And together with them the relationship to his work underlies all of man's life and achievements, his civil society, his arts, his history."

Over the later decades, Drucker would define management as "a liberal art." In a traditional sense, "liberal arts" refer to the education worthy of a free person. In *The New Realities: In Government and Politics/In*

Economics and Business/In Society and World View, a book published in 1989, Drucker elaborated on the definition of management as a liberal art: "'liberal' because it deals with the fundamentals of knowledge, self-knowledge, wisdom, and leadership; 'art' because it is practice and application." An educated free person needs to draw on all the knowledge and insights he or she learns to deliver effective and responsible results on a specific practice. Drucker said that his decades-long experience of working with managers of various kinds of organizations indicated that "management is deeply involved in spiritual concerns—the nature of man, good and evil."

The various kinds of organizations Drucker consulted with range from such leading businesses as General Electronic and IBM to the government of the United States, youth organizations like Girl Scouts of the USA, universities and churches. But writing and teaching accounted for much of his career. He authored about forty books and many other articles. Before lecturing at Claremont Graduate University in California from the age of sixty-one on, Drucker spent nearly thirty years teaching, first at Bennington College in the northeastern state of Vermont and then at New York University. At age ninety-one he taught his last class at Claremont, where his courses were the most popular.

In the same year, one of his last articles appeared in the February 2002 issue of *Harvard Business Review*. Entitled "They're Not Employees, They're People," the essay reminded the business world of the everlasting importance of treating employees as whole-person people. For Drucker, this was not just a traditionally moral issue but that of productivity any organization would face: "since it is impossible, according to the laws of statistics, for an organization to hire more than a handful of 'better people,' the only way that it can excel in a knowledge-based economy and society is by getting more out of the same kind of people— that is, by managing its knowledge workers for greater productivity. The challenge, to repeat an old saying, is 'to make ordinary people do extraordinary things.'"

In fact, even what is called "better people" share the same nature of their ordinary counterparts. In Drucker's own words, the nature of human beings is certain: "imperfect, weak, a sinner, and dust destined unto dust; yet made in God's image and responsible for his actions."

What could make people with this nature extraordinary is, "the Spirit that created" creations. Ordinary people could do extraordinary things, as long as he or she comes to realize that the mission and purpose of one's existence is "to make manifest the creator in and through the creation." In this regard, Drucker's own experience is a perfect example. A dimension that transcends society not only helped raise a eighteen-year-old trainee from boredom but served to get more out of the man and manage him for lifelong productivity. Despite this, Drucker acknowledged that he would be a hopelessly poor manager and a company job would bore him to death. He described himself as "a loner" who worked best outside.

On November 11, 2005, Drucker died in his sleep at his home in Claremont, only eight days shy of his ninety-sixth birthday. Exactly on this day 150 years before, Kierkegaard died—but at only age forty-two. On an afternoon three days later, a private memorial service was held at the local St. John's Episcopal Church. According to Frances Hesselbein, who attended the funeral and once was the CEO of Girl Scouts of the USA, just twenty-five people were present. They included Drucker's wife, Doris, their four children and six grandchildren and some close friends. "Amazing Grace," arguably the best-known hymn in the English-speaking world, was sung at the end of the liturgy. Years before his death, Drucker told Rick Warren, the founding pastor of Saddleback Church in California who was visiting his home, about how he came to accept Jesus Christ as his savior: "The day that I finally understood grace, I realized I was never going to get a better deal than that."

Chapter 15
How the Big Corporations Lost Their Way

"It is critically important for China to distinguish good capitalism from bad," the eighty-year-old William Hopper tells me.[91] With his brother Kenneth, eighty-three, William has been creating a buzz in business and management circles, thanks to their 2007 book, *The Puritan Gift: Triumph, Collapse and Revival of an American Dream*, named by the *Financial Times* one of that year's Top Ten Business Books.

For its 2009 reissue in paperback, the book was re-titled *The Puritan Gift: Reclaiming the American Dream Amidst Global Financial Chaos*. Not surprisingly, the financial crash has boosted interest in this book. In an article for the magazine *strategy+business*, British management thinker Charles Handy hailed the new version of *The Puritan Gift* as one of the top leadership books of 2009. According to Handy, leadership was in short supply in the year-long aftermath of the crisis on Wall Street and the Hoppers' book served as an ideal reminder of where the business world truly stood.

In the January 2010 *Harvard Business Review*, executive editor Sarah Cliffe described it as "this astonishing book about American managerial culture." She added, "I've never read a business book that packed so much information, history, and insight into one compact volume."

Older brother Kenneth, once a department head at Procter & Gamble, has decades of industrial and management consulting experience under his belt. Younger brother William, an investment banker, has served in the European Parliament. The insights their book has to offer,

---

91   This chapter first appeared in the March 8–17, 2010 issue of *Vista*, a leading Chinese-language news and general-interest magazine in China. It was translated into English by Stephanie Schubmehl.

though, are not simply a product of their professional lives. More importantly, the brothers are seeking an ultimate solution to the chaos that has engulfed the corporate and business sectors.

Today the Hoppers are busier than ever, constantly updating their blog, fielding lecture and interview requests, and corresponding with readers. Between February and March 2010, William was blogging almost daily. One item that caught his attention was Toyota CEO Akio Toyoda's acknowledgment before a U.S. Congressional hearing that the company had "lost its way during a period of rapid growth." The apology came as no surprise to William. He says Japan's corporate sector began to lose its way years ago, when it retreated from the corporate system and workplace values imported during the U.S. occupation (1945–1952). "That," William says, "was good capitalism." As for the bad kind, the brothers blame post-war American business schools, particularly after the 1970s. As curricula became dominated by "financial engineering," profit and performance were prioritized before all else.

A Foreseeable Crisis

When the book's first edition came out three years ago, William and Kenneth made a point of raising concerns about Toyota. They believed the automaker—like Sony, Hitachi, Mitsubishi, Panasonic and other Japanese brands once synonymous with quality—was losing its focus. As William points out, the evidence was emerging long before the brothers completed their book in 2006.

According to James P. Womack, who made a name for himself studying Toyota's "lean production" practices, the carmaker's troubles began in 2002. That was the year Toyota rolled out plans to expand its share of the global market from 11 percent to 15 percent. Womack derided the scheme as "just driven by ego," calling the fifteen percent goal "totally irrelevant to any customer."

William Hopper's analysis goes a step further. Back in 1993, he says, U.S. auto analyst Maryann Keller was already admonishing Toyota to take a long, hard look in the mirror. Keller's book criticized Toyota for trimming vital "middle management" positions even as headquarters tightened its control company-wide. A top-down, hierarchical approach replaced what had been a bottom-up, participatory managerial culture; attention to detail and quality suffered as the company's expansion picked up speed.

Many management experts would stop there, but, for the Hoppers, Toyota is only an example. They have a much broader vision. The Toyota scandal, the achievement and shattering of the American Dream, good and bad managerial cultures, the global financial crisis—at first glance, it is difficult to see what any of these has to do with a book titled *The Puritan Gift*. Take a moment to think about what the title is saying, however, or engage more closely with the authors, and the connections become clear. What's more, this book touches on many aspects of the globalized world we live in—and more importantly, on our own individual lives.

In a sea of information, history, and concepts, the Hoppers seek the answer to a single question: what factors create a work environment that promotes well-being? In other words, why and how do people work? This is a fundamental question, because without such an environment, no company can experience sound growth. Some, like Toyota, may enjoy a moment of glory, but it will not last.

And so the Hoppers take their readers on a journey across centuries of history. One important conclusion they reach is this: the factors most conducive to the sound, sustained development of a work environment originate with a singular worldview—one handed down from a group of migrants who left Europe for North America more than four hundred years ago.

They were known as Puritans: a people who believed in stripping away man-made conceits and giving oneself over to the will of God. This God was supremely powerful, and as the word of God revealed to mankind, the Bible was the final arbiter in all matters. Puritans crossed the Atlantic in droves during the early seventeenth century, spurred on by their opposition to the way religion was practiced in England and throughout Europe. In North America, they intended to create a new homeland, one that would allow them to do God's work.

As the Hoppers see it, this endeavor essentially laid the foundation for the modern free-market society. The values inherited from the Puritans are sharply distinct from those of other peoples and places. Despite their relatively small numbers, the influence of the Puritans is felt everywhere from education (they founded the Ivy League schools of Harvard, Yale and Princeton) to organizational management (the Presbyterian Church, republican government, the parliament, the board of directors). Here the authors would seem to be crossing into historical or even theological territory, which may come as a surprise for those accustomed to more traditional business fare. But the Hoppers have much more to show their readers.

Why Do People Work?

Both in their eighties, the brothers believe that the sustained, healthy development of a work environment is a product of spiritual and historical traditions. They learned this first-hand, which may be why the autobiographical portions of their book are so engaging. Kenneth and William are the sons of a chemist. Trained as an engineer, the youthful Kenneth went to work for a branch of Procter & Gamble after a colleague of their father's touted it as the best-run industrial firm in the U.K. Kenneth found himself fascinated by P&G's workplace culture, which contrasted sharply with his experiences in two British firms. Despite the company's complex structure, decisions on points of detail were handled with great efficiency.

That experience planted the seeds for the book Kenneth would complete at the age of 80. He wanted to find out what was going on in the world. Later, Kenneth's professional life became what amounted to an extended global tour of workplace cultures. Working in Ireland, he witnessed the rebirth of the Irish economy. He also watched continental Europe rebuild itself after World War II. In the United States, he had the chance to observe the Golden Age of the American corporation. And he was in Japan as that nation was shaping itself into the world's second-largest economy.

Throughout his long working life, Kenneth occasionally took time to write about his experiences, whether for newspapers or academic journals. Later, he planned to integrate these pieces into a single work, but health problems prevented him from completing the project. Fortunately, his brother William helped put the book back on the agenda. William's experience as an investment banker on both sides of the Atlantic, and as a member of the European Parliament, served to broaden Kenneth's outlook.

He also introduced Kenneth to a friend who would prove critically important to the brothers' work: Peter F. Drucker, a pioneer in modern management theory. In a letter dated October 3, 1983, Drucker expressed his eagerness to read Kenneth's forthcoming book, which he intended to order from the publisher as soon as it came out. Kenneth still has the letter. As it turned out, the book would not be completed until after Drucker's death in 2005. Kenneth still regrets that his friend, who dedicated his life to bettering society, never saw the book in its final version.

Aside from his friendship with the brothers, Drucker contributed indirectly to *The Puritan Gift* by making a pivotal introduction. It was through Drucker that the Hoppers met three American engineers who had played a central role in Japan's postwar reconstruction. This gave them the opportunity to examine Japan's transformation and offered a new perspective on the United States.

Another friend whose help shaped *The Puritan Gift* was American management guru W. Edwards Deming. Deming, too, had helped rebuild Japan after the war, and he is still remembered in the Japanese business world for his role in convincing manufacturers to prioritize the pursuit of quality management.

In the course of discussions with these eyewitnesses and their own work in Japan, the brothers formed a conclusion: it was thanks to the influence of Puritan values that Japan had been able to develop its impressive postwar line-up of quality brands. Furthermore, the social changes that later swept the so-called Asian Tigers and the Chinese mainland signified the spread of these values.

William's recent blog commentary on the Toyota scandal revisits territory covered in the new edition of the book. The current scandal, he says, is actually a reflection of a much larger crisis, one aspect of which is the decline in "middle management" mentioned earlier. As the Hoppers see it, Japan began to turn away from Puritan values in the 1990s, when many young Japanese were setting their sights on an American MBA degree—one of them being Akio Toyoda, the face of

Toyota's younger generation, who was twenty-six when he graduated from a Massachusetts business school in 1982. In contrast to older generations, they had little first-hand knowledge of the industries they were working in.

Part of the blame for Japan's corporate crises, the Hoppers argue, lies with the curriculum that has dominated American business schools since the 1970s. To an even greater degree, this helped bring about the sub-prime mortgage crisis in the U.S. and Europe. These failures, they go on to explain, began when business education departed from its original Puritan ethos. To a typical Puritan, work was not simply a way to earn a living, to amass wealth, or to display one's talents; rather, it was a "vocation" or "calling."

Central to the concept of "vocation" is the idea that people do not work for themselves, or because they have no choice but to work. They do so in order to fulfill a God-given mission, for the good of themselves and of others. As for human needs, the Creator has promised to provide for all those who do His work.[92] Just as the historical influence of the Puritans has spread into every industry, the blessings of this all-powerful Creator extend far beyond what any individual can conceive. Toyota was fixated on becoming the world's biggest automaker; Wall Street was busy amassing paper wealth through complex feats of "financial engineering." Viewed in this light, they have been straying farther and farther from their roots.

---

92 Matthew 6:24–33 "No one can serve two masters. Either he will hate the one and love the other. or he will be devoted the one and despise the other. You cannot serve both God and Money. Therefore I tell you, do not worry about your life. what you will eat or drink; or about your body, what you will wear. Is not life more important than food, and the body more important than clothes? Look at the birds of the air; they do not sow or reap or store away in barns, and yet your heavenly Father feeds them. Are you not much more valuable than they? Who of you by worrying can add a single hour to his life? ... So do not worry, saying, 'What shall we drink?' or 'What shall we wear?' For the pagans run after all these things, and your heavenly Father knows that you need them. But seek first his kingdom and his righteousness, and all these things will be given to you as well."

The Cult of the Business School

Over recent decades, the authors write, business education has lost sight of its own values; as education became increasingly focused on landing a decent job, the big questions were shunted aside. Aware only that the subject was gaining in popularity, students and their instructors had no intrinsic motivation which would tell them why they ought to work, giving rise to professional managers whose only goal was making money.

The Hoppers have dubbed this phenomenon "the Cult of the (so-called) Expert." Cults, in one form or another, have wrought havoc throughout history. In the political sphere, they have been known to threaten popular wisdom, and the same holds true for economics. Of course, as the Hoppers acknowledge, the business school did not create this cult in and of itself. But as educational institutions, business schools—along with the entire university system—are responsible for molding new generations of professionals.

The problem is with the notion that a prestigious business degree is an instant ticket to the top—when in fact, any job at all presents an opportunity to develop expertise. The dot-com bubble, the Enron scandal and now an epic financial crisis have given the business world a wake-up call. Goldman Sachs, for instance, reduced the proportion of MBA graduates among its new hires in 2000, from seventy-five percent to twenty-five percent. The consulting firm McKinsey is also recruiting fewer MBAs.

But it isn't just the corporate world that's in trouble, according to Kenneth and William. Corporations are only one facet of society. The Toyota scandal and the Credit Crisis, for example, have something in common. As companies began sacrificing quality in favor of performance and rapid growth, there were insiders who recognized that something was gravely wrong. Yet they failed to bring their concerns to management's attention, or failed to make management take them seriously. For a worker to deliver bad news directly to a superior requires uncommon courage; character of this sort is rooted in an individual's fundamental attitude toward work, which in turn is rooted in prevailing social mores.

The Hoppers support a view that Peter F. Drucker came to hold in his later years: fixing the corporate sector will require a society-wide revival of spiritual values. Just as it took nearly two centuries to establish the United States, such a revival will not happen overnight. It took the Hoppers a lifetime simply to write their book. But perhaps their story is cause for optimism: late in their lives, they have given us an extraordinary gift. The Hopper brothers have never forgotten that a society, once it has managed to achieve prosperity, must decide where to turn next.

Chapter 16
How to Grow up before Growing Old

To write about the state of a country in terms of any aspect in a couple of pages would be no more than catching a fleeting glimpse of a cosmic world.[93] But if such a glimpse is based upon more than ten years of observation on both the inside and outside, it might be a sample worthy of attention.

Like almost any other modern profession, journalism was not born in China. It was introduced by Christian missionaries coming from Europe and North America in the nineteenth century. Before that, China did not have media or journalists as they are today. A similar form of journalism is that from perhaps as early as in the second century B.C. on, China's central government in different dynasties or political systems has sent reports to the local governments about its new decisions and everything officials might be required to know. With the arrival of Christian missionaries like Robert Morrison from Britain in the early nineteenth century, newspapers and magazines in their modern forms began to be produced and circulating among the people who were not necessarily government officials. More than two centuries later, the state-run media remain powerful. Non-government-sponsored media companies were not allowed to grow until the late 1990s when part of the market started opening to the private investment. That came after decades of the state monopoly in almost all social fields beginning in 1949 when the Communists came to power and a relatively free flow of information over the previous decades was put to an end. They initiated what they call "reform and opening-up policy" in the late 1970s. The policy was

---

93 This chapter was originally written for The Media Project's 2012 Coaching and Leadership Fellowship.

at first focused on economy and confined to some designated sectors and regions. It later spread to other fields like culture but is still largely off-limits to politics.

In this sense, journalism in China is a profession that is under heavy influence of the state-dominated ideology combined with profit-oriented privatization. For journalists living in such an environment, they seem to be more like those who work at government agencies or commercial organizations. Power, money and fame seem the ruling factors few journalists could entirely ignore. One would survive or even thrive if he or she could meet the challenges rightly. Of course, they would have different opinions as to what constitutes a right way. Some would think it inevitable to seek power and money and fame. Some would consider seeking these things to be the undoubted enemy of independent journalism.

Yet, behind these noticeable phenomena, one slice of life may have been either unseen or underestimated. It may have gone deeper and beyond the perspectives of politics, economy, or independent journalism. It concerns the growth of a journalist or any other professional as a person: Among the people I have met throughout the past twelve years as a journalist at a state-run television station or writing for different privately-owned magazines or doing independent research and writing, too many people seem to have grown old before (or instead of) growing up. In China, a thirty-year-old journalist would be viewed by oneself and/or one's colleagues as an old journalist. He or she at around the age of thirty would be a leader of a team with different sizes in a media organization whether it be government-owned or privately-held. Or one would become a celebrity. For the rest, one would be a mere journalist. Being a mere journalist could mean one would not have much power, money, fame. Of course, a mere journalist still would have a chance of getting richer by, say, accepting what is called "red envelopes" or bribes. But whoever they are and whatever they do, one who remains in the media industry at thirty would be considered to be "old" in the eyes of anyone who practices or is familiar with the journalistic profession in China.

What has made such a situation is partly that the loosening up of China's media sector has a short history of just more than ten years. Those who have worked for more than ten years or a little less in the media are the first generation of journalists who have witnessed the historic change. It would be natural for them to become the backbone of the industry's new growth. Those who have more than fifteen or twenty years of media experience may have remained in the sector but would perhaps be not at the forefront of the new part. Some of them would be officials at the government-run media organizations. Some others would be semi-retired or already retired. A few of them, who were not content with the old media system, would try and establish privately-held media companies. Compared to the ever growing number of younger media professionals, they are increasingly becoming a minority. Yet, the ever more younger journalists would find it difficult to grow up in an environment where, to a considerable extent, the tradition of arbitrary and authoritarian rule remains. In order to survive, they would have to, the sooner the better, grow "old" enough to fit in with the circumstances. That comes despite a sense of frustration prevalent among them.

But against this backdrop, is it possible to grow up rather than simply grow old? In fact, I felt sort of semi-retired at the age of twenty-nine when I was to make a final decision to quit my job at the state-run broadcaster where I had worked for less than six years. Six years after leaving there, I now find myself much "younger" but at the same time more mature. There may have been a variety of elements that have worked. A major one might be that the Christian faith, a faith in a transcendent or transcendental dimension I came to see at around 30, has helped me to become increasingly less influenced by the prevailing mindset of the media sector where I work. This faith has led me to see a broader picture of being a journalist as a person. It includes not only what I have learned and continue to learn from the discipline and practice of journalism but also some perennial issues that a journalist as a person needs to know such as truth, freedom, hope and love. In terms of growing up instead of growing old, this faith has been guiding me to learn to be patient and to know how to grow step by step. This kind of quality might be critical given that younger journalists are under pressure to seek becoming famous as young as possible. One would think either too highly or too lowly of oneself if he or she does not know clearly and firmly about his or her due place in the world.

And this process of learning to grow up would not just concern oneself. In the first couple of years since leaving the state-run broadcaster, I found myself alone on the journalistic journey without finding anyone with similar faith among the Chinese colleagues I had known. But a few years later, in a non-government-run church I started attending in 2006, more than ten are journalists working at different media organizations, most of whom are in their twenties or thirties. Some of them are in the English Bible study group I have helped facilitate since 2010. I have also come to know some journalists who attend other non-government-run churches. In May 2010 in Beijing, we had the first ever Chinese Christian journalists meeting sponsored by The Media Project, a non-profit educational and research organization for journalists worldwide. And in April 2011, the second meeting was held in America, co-sponsored by The Media Project and Purdue University. Such domestic and international connections have paved the way for my colleagues and I to learn to connect up and help one another. This new community is still very small. But in a country where people seem prone to seek making it big and strong as quickly as possible, starting small and growing patiently is what could make a real difference.

Chapter 17
How "Serve the People" Would Not Be a Cliché

An effective way to get familiarized with an unfamiliar world might be through one you are familiar with who has already known about the world.[94] Before receiving a copy of Max De Pree's *Leadership Jazz: The Essential Elements of a Great Leader* from Caroline Comport of The Media Project in November 2011, I had never got a chance of reading the book. It came as a joy to see the name of Peter Drucker on the cover of *Leadership Jazz* and his acclaim for it, "Read this slowly. This book is wisdom in action." Drucker was an Austrian American who died in late 2005 and has been known as "the father of modern management." I wrote an article about Drucker's spiritual journey and how it shaped his management thinking in a column at *Global Entrepreneur*, a leading Chinese business magazine, in 2009, which marked his centenary.

It turned out that I had no other choice but to read De Pree's book slowly even though there was no ample time left before the mid-December deadline for finishing a piece about it. This appears a small book with less than 200 pages. Its language is casual and easygoing. And yet it addresses a big and difficult subject: the essential elements of a great leader. I once tried and read it fast, only to find that it was like drinking concentrated fruit juice. A single drop may require a period of time to savor with not just your tongue but brain and heart. A Washington Post review of De Pree's previous bestseller *Leadership Is an Art* seems right for this book as well, "Small and soulful enough to be carried around like a prayer book—and, in some respects, it is."

---

94 This chapter was originally written for The Media Project's 2012 Coaching and Leadership Fellowship.

There are numerous drops in *Leadership Jazz*. The title of the book is perhaps the first or even the foremost one. In the introduction to the 2008 edition, De Pree explained its origin by saying it was his friend and mentor, Peter Drucker who inspired the notion. In the eyes of Drucker, leading an organization is like directing a symphony orchestra. De Pree suggested a similar comparison. It was a jazz band, "because performers in organizations are often called on to make their own variations on a tune, to improvise as part of a team, to innovate in concert with others." Both similes are intended to bring the substance of being a real leader to the world's attention. In them, leadership is not a superior position but a job serving others. In De Pree's own words, "A jazz band is an expression of servant leadership. The leader of a jazz band has the opportunity to draw the best out of the other musicians."

But an obvious question is how. Too many leaders in world history have claimed their mission was to serve others. For example, one of the best-known slogans of the ruling Communist Party in China, the globe's most populous country, is "Serve the People." Yet it may have long become more than a bit of a cliché. As one who lives in such an environment, I would have to be wary of simply talking about servant leadership. It was a relief to see the author of *Leadership Jazz* acknowledging this: "Groups around the world value real leaders, and it seems to many people that real leaders are now scarcer than ever." However, it was a bigger gain to read De Pree's detailed answer to the question of how.

Unlike Drucker, De Pree is not a writer by profession. He is chairman emeritus of Herman Miller, a top American manufacturer of furniture perhaps most notable for introducing such modern furniture products as the office cubicle and the Aeron chair. Born in 1924, De Pree is a son of D. J. De Pree, the founder of Herman Miller. He and his older brother Hugh began managing the company in the early 1960s. In the Harvard Business School database of American business leaders, De Pree is described as one who "grew the small family-owned business into the second largest furniture maker in the world. Under De Pree's leadership, Herman Miller had the unique distinction of being named to three *Fortune* Top 10 lists—most admired companies, most innovative companies, and best managed."

For De Pree, at the heart of becoming a real leader is "the need always to connect one's voice and one's touch." The voice manifests one's beliefs. The touch is about action. How to connect them? De Pree found the connection not directly in his company but at a hospital. His granddaughter, Zoe, was born prematurely. A neonatologist said she only had at most ten percent chance of living three days. A nurse, Ruth, asked De Pree to caress Zoe as the surrogate father. Zoe's biological father had jumped ship the month before she was born. More than this, De Pree was asked to tell Zoe over and over how much he loved her while caressing. By doing this, Zoe would be able to connect the voice and the touch. Four years later when *Leadership Jazz* appeared, Zoe was flourishing. "These days, her voice and touch are as important to me as my voice and touch were to her four years ago. This interdependent relationship, it seems to me, is one of the results of trying to be a good leader, of composing voice and touch," concluded Zoe's grandfather.

Beyond my expectation, De Pree's story about connecting voice and touch helps me further recover due respect for leadership and makes me want to learn more about being a real leader. De Pree said in his book that the best description of servant leadership was found in the Gospel according to Luke: "The greatest among you should be like the least, and the one who rules, like the one who serves."[95] The story of De Pree and his little granddaughter Zoe is one of the best descriptions I have ever heard of such a real leadership in daily life. The ultimate example here is not any person but the one who created humans and other beings. In the same response to a dispute among his disciples as to which was considered to be greatest in Luke, Jesus said he was among them as one who served. For De Pree, not only Zoe but his colleagues and friends are part of the same family where God is the Father. "We are dealing with God's mix, people made in God's image, a compelling mystery," he highlighted.

In this sense, it is understandable that the author valued "vulnerability" as an essential quality of leadership. This is a sharp contrast to the conventional wisdom about leadership. Instead of almost unavoidably encouraging self-expression, vulnerability allows others to realize their

95 Luke 22:26.

potential. A leader is required to understand weakness, strength, cares, yearnings and struggles of the human spirit. De Pree went further to point out a paradox in the human nature: "Leaders are fragile precisely at the point of their strengths, liable to fail at the height of their success." So, leadership is not just a job, but a delicate one—"as delicate as Mozart's melodies." It "exists and it doesn't." It "means nothing until performed and heard."

That is why De Pree offered more than just principles. He had more questions than answers. How often do I say "I don't know"? Who matters? What matters? Do I realize that special insight often comes out of silence? Have I learned to stop? Do I stop to talk or listen, or simply out of curiosity? Do I have a nose for stale air? Have things become mechanical? When did I last spend three full hours with someone from research and development? Has anyone in this place confided in me lately? Do faculty want me to share in their departmental celebrations? Do people here avoid risk like the plague and isolate themselves? Have we stopped hiring people better than we are? Followers sometimes treat leaders like an emperor. Do I have my clothes on? Do people tell me when I'm naked? Have I made it possible for the institution to succeed after I leave? These are just part of questions De Pree posed that have impressed me the most. And asking questions itself and facing up to hard facts may reflect yet another leadership element De Pree stressed: courage.

De Pree is a man of questions. He is also a man of many lists, as some of his friends call him. His list of real leadership traits would go on without an end. He said a list might help one "coalesce" one's thinking about leadership. On the one hand, this is a holistic approach to a complex concern. "One quality of leadership always implies another," said De Pree towards the end of *Leadership Jazz*. On the other, this demands a habit of "live and learn." De Pree admitted that leadership was something one could never totally understand. In Epilogue, one would see a very short story about oak trees that lived in southern England for a century prior to being used to help restore a roof that had been built at Oxford nearly five centuries before. For De Pree, that is about how the voice and touch of architect Sir Gilbert Scott, what the author called "a distant leader," had been joined. (It might be better if the author elaborated on this distant leader and the story itself.) To me, the century-long growth of a tree symbolizes one's lifelong learning not necessarily as a leader but a living being.

A weak point of De Pree's book might be that there are too many lists or points to illustrate a focus to the full. The stories or examples the author used seem thin and need further details. It might be an example of the paradox De Pree pointed out about strength and weakness. For a reader who does not have a career of managing a leading company or any other kind of organization, he or she might find it difficult to digest so many thoughts in a single small book coming from decades of practice and reflection. But in another light, these lists and points could serve as a constant reminder on one's long road of learning real leadership. One might add his or her own stories and observations from ever growing practice and reflection. This would imply an insight in the book that could help encourage a beginner like me: learning leadership from trying to be a good follower. It is partly from a requirement that a real leader should know the perspective of followers. It is also from the reality that since leadership is but a job serving others, any leader could also be served by others or any leader could have one's leaders. In my life so far, I have had lots of leaders serving me. Now, I am called to learn to serve others by following the good examples of the leaders I have met.

To be frank, I never had thought as seriously as now of learning leadership before despite having written a piece about how to help create and select a real leader in my *Global Entrepreneur* column in late 2008, just after the US presidential elections. This was considerably due to the environment of "Serve the People" I mentioned earlier. Another element was that I considered myself unfit for leadership. That started to change after I came to further understand the unique idea of leadership in the Bible. For example, learning to lead a Bible study group was and remains an important part of the change. Another was a small group doing a research and writing project that tentatively began life in the spring of 2011. The 2012 Media Project Coaching and Leadership Fellowship and De Pree's book bring further opportunity and impetus to taking a long hard look at this challenging subject. It is beginning to become a necessary discipline and practice (these two words are borrowed from the two books I recently got benefits from besides De Pree's, Richard Foster's

Celebration of Discipline: The Path to Spiritual Growth and Brother Lawrence's *The Practice of the Presence of God*) for me after I spent some not-so-easy time preparing this writing. I look forward to identifying two younger colleagues and learning to help and serve them with sharing the gains I have received from all who have helped and served me including those from De Pree and his *Leadership Jazz*.

Chapter 18
Why the Medium Is the Message

Creations, seem always prone to become better-known than their creator. For example, while numerous people may have heard or spoken of "the global village," few would have known who coined the catchphrase. It might make no difference if one knows or not. But to take a closer look at the creator could help one better understand his creations.

Marshall McLuhan is commonly credited with both coining and popularizing "the global village" and anticipating the era of the Internet. In the 1960s, American journalist Tom Wolfe regarded McLuhan as a thinker on a par with Newton, Darwin, Freud, Einstein, and Pavlov. He was adopted by *Wired* magazine as its patron saint in its debut 1993 issue. That was thirteen years after the Canadian media thinker died of a stroke on the last day of 1980.

As early as in a 1959 letter to a magazine editor, McLuhan used the term "the global village" to describe a pattern of the world that "is caused by the instantaneous movement of information from every quarter to every point at the same time." In the same letter, McLuhan also wrote, "The globe becomes a very small village-like affair, under electronic conditions, in which whatever happens to anybody, happens to everybody." In 1962, he elaborated on the global phenomenon in *The Gutenberg Galaxy: The Making of Typographic Man*, a book that immediately won Canada's highest literary award, the Governor General's Award for English-language non-fiction.

According to Marshall McLuhan's son, Eric McLuhan, James Joyce's *Finnegan's Wake* and P. Wyndham Lewis' *America and Cosmic Man* may have played a role in inspiring his father about conceptualizing "the global village." In the former work that was published in 1939, the Irish novelist used two phrases allusive of the Pope's annual Easter and

Christmas messages, Urbi et Orbi, which means "to the City of Rome and to the World." In the latter book published in 1948, the English artist claimed "the earth has become one big village, with telephones laid on from one end to the other, and air transport, both speedy and safe."

Another well-known aphorism attributed to McLuhan is "The medium is the message." It was first introduced in his most popular book, *Understanding Media: The Extensions of Man*, which came out in 1964. What makes the idea different from the conventional wisdom is that for McLuhan, "it is the medium as an environment of services that produces the effects. The 'message' is the total happening, as it were, and not a special bit of data or a special point of view." And the medium McLuhan refers to is not only that of communication but also any technological extension of the human body, which includes language, number, clothing, housing, money, means of transportation, weapons and automation.

What might have made an impact on McLuhan's understanding of medium and message? Two quotations that have not received widespread attention could provide a surprising clue to the mind of McLuhan. One is, "In Christ, Medium becomes message. Christ came to demonstrate God's love for man and to call all men to Him through himself as Mediator, as Medium. And in so doing he became the proclamation of his Church, the message of God to man. God's medium became God's message." The other, "In Jesus Christ, there is no distance or separation between the medium and the message: it is the one case where we can say that the medium and the message are fully one and the same … In fact, it is only at the level of a lived Christianity that the medium really is the message."

The former was recorded in a footnote of W. Terrence Gordon's *Marshall McLuhan: Escape into Understanding*. It comes from Raymer B. Matson's "The Christian and McLuhan," an article published in a 1968 issue of *Dialog: A Journal of Theology*. The latter was what McLuhan told Pierre Babin, a French Catholic media analyst in 1977, which was included in *The Medium and the Light: Reflections on Religion* published in 1999.

For the readers of McLuhan's major works like *The Gutenberg Galaxy* and *Understanding Media*, his comments on medium and message from the viewpoint of Christianity may be alien. McLuhan consciously avoided expressing his Christian faith in his public and academic statements. In a letter to American anthropologist Edward T. Hall, McLuhan once wrote that "I deliberately keep Christianity out of all these discussions lest perception be diverted from structural processes by doctrinal sectarian passions. My own attitude to Christianity is, itself, awareness of process."

But as his writing to Hall and his discussion with Babin indicate, the relationship between faith and media studies is evident in McLuhan's private correspondence and conversations. In the eyes of biographer Philip Marchand, "His faith ... provided the foundations for his work." McLuhan's son, Eric, once told me that he had frequently heard his father express those sentiments of the two quotations. Yet, even McLuhan himself did not expect his faith would play a foundational role in his thinking career. In fact, for Eric, "Perhaps the person most surprised by Marshall McLuhan's conversion to Catholicism was Marshall himself."

In his 1970 account, McLuhan said he did not have any religious belief when he began to be interested in Catholicism. That was despite being brought up in a community of Protestantism such as the Baptist, Methodist and Anglican churches. McLuhan was born on July 21, 1911, in Edmonton, the capital of Canada's western province of Alberta. His father sold insurance after his real estate business collapsed with the outbreak of the First World War. His mother was a school teacher who later became an actress. According to W. Terrence Gordon's *Marshall McLuhan: Escape into Understanding*, McLuhan's parents and their original families were both Baptists with practicing "a religion of faith, hope, and charity" varying "little from one generation to the next."

McLuhan went to church and attended Bible class almost every Sunday, even while he was at university. But his diaries at that time show Bible classes often disappointed him and sermons exasperated him. On January 11, 1931, McLuhan wrote, "I was disgusted by a sermon that could have been preached to a 14th century audience without causing offence to their narrowed orthodox minds. It was nothing less than a rant upon the futile and childish subject of Foreknowledge, Predestination, Election, Justification and Glorification." And on July 5, 1931, "[The preacher] delivered himself of a quantity of balderdash and rigmarole that was nothing short of shameful."

However, McLuhan did not give up Christianity, although he did give up the Baptist church. On February 14, 1931, he wrote, "As long as the example of Jesus Christ stands before us, let everyone be ashamed of even a moment of self-complacency." And he even came to a conclusion that the uniqueness and dynamism of Christianity sprang from Pentecost—the day when the Holy Spirit began to come on the followers of Jesus Christ after he was resurrected and taken up into heaven—and that the materialism of Western culture was the cause of a general neglect of Pentecost. In the words of McLuhan's son Eric, it was "the Church and its claims" that "repeatedly intruded on his attention while he was trying to focus on other, scholarly, matters—so often and so powerfully that he eventually felt forced to 'deal' with them."

In 1928, McLuhan enrolled as an engineering major at the University of Manitoba in the southern Canadian city of Winnipeg. Yet, he found his true calling was not in engineering despite the fact that he liked boatbuilding and sailing. A year later, he moved to a program of English literature, history, and philosophy. Thomas Carlyle, Thomas Macaulay, Samuel Johnson, James Boswell, George Macaulay Trevelyan, William Thackeray, William Shakespeare, Charles Lamb, Matthew Arnold became his early favorites. Later favorites would include Thomas Aquinas, a thirteenth-century Italian theologian. The Bible was also what he read often. He began to see the hundreds of years of English literature in relation to Christianity.

The writer who would exert the greatest influence on the whole life of McLuhan is G. K. Chesterton, an Anglican-turned-Catholic. Initially, McLuhan did not have any high regard for the English author. In the diary of June 17, 1930, he "found him somewhat tautological in his analogies" after reading Chesterton's preface to Charles Dickens' Great Expectations. Just one year later, McLuhan's fellow Manitoba student, William Thomas Easterbrook, gave him Chesterton's *What's Wrong with the World?*. On July 31, 1931, he was excited to declare, "No matter what, G. K. had [something] to say on any subject however irrelevant in such a manner as to make the connection at once obvious and important. Few writers, yes I can say, no other writer, has ever before been able to arouse my enthusiasm for ideas as has G. K."

Even before getting to know Chesterton, England had fascinated

McLuhan with its rich spiritual and intellectual resources. It was evident in his diary of February 10, 1931: "How I long to get across to that wee island, to talk with the living, to visit, read, absorb, and revere the past, places, the books, the spirit of the great past, and the aspirations for the future." His dream came true in the summer of 1932 when he and his friend Easterbrook made a visit to England. With a pair of purchased old bicycles, they toured the country for three months. In October 1934, McLuhan began to pursue study at Cambridge University. In an evening next June, he saw Chesterton in London when the 61-year-old Englishman spoke to the Distributist League, a group Chesterton helped establish to promote a third-way economic philosophy that was different to both capitalism and socialism. That was a year before Chesterton died.

In a letter to his mother written on September 5, 1931, McLuhan explained why he was converted to Catholicism and why Chesterton was a decisive factor: "The Catholic religion is the only religion—all sects are derivative. Buddhism and similar oriental philosophies and mythologies are not religions in any sense. They have no covenants and no sacraments and no theology ... The Catholic Church does not despise or wantonly mortify those members and faculties which Christ deigned to assume. They are henceforth holy and blessed. Catholic culture produced Chaucer and his merry story-telling pilgrims. Licentious enthusiasm produced the lonely despair of Christian in *Pilgrim's Progress*—what a different sort of pilgrim! Catholic culture produced Don Quixote and St. Francis and Rabelais. What I wish to emphasize about them is their various and rich-hearted humanity. I need scarcely indicate that everything that is especially hateful and devilish and inhuman about the conditions and strains of modern industrial society is not only Protestant in origin, but it is their boast(!) to have originated it. You may know a thing by its fruits if you are silly enough or ignorant enough to wait that long. I find the fruits and the theory of our sects very bitter. Had I not encountered Chesterton I would have remained agnostic for many years at least. Chesterton did not convince me of religious faith, but he prevented my despair from becoming a habit or hardening into misanthropy. He opened my eyes to European culture and encouraged me to know it more closely. He taught me the reasons for all that in me was simply blind anger and misery."

McLuhan's criticism of Protestantism and endorsement of Catholicism sounds too extreme. But it might be understandable if one takes into account McLuhan's personal experience, especially the long tradition of Protestantism where he grew up. In the same letter, he said his "religion-hunting" began with "culture-hunting": "I simply couldn't believe that men had to live in the mean mechanical rootless joyless fashion that I saw in Winnipeg. And when I began to read English literature I knew that it was quite unnecessary for them so to live. You will remember my deep personal enjoyment of Tom Brown's Schooldays in grade 8. It brought me in contact with things for which I was starved—things which have since disappeared from England. All my Anglo-mania was really a recognition of things missing from our lives which I felt to be indispensable. It was a long time before I finally perceived that the character of every society, its food, clothing, arts, and amusements, are ultimately determined by its religion. It was longer still before I could believe that religion was as great and joyful as these things which it creates—or destroys."

In this sense, the religion of McLuhan determined the character of his thinking about media. He found that people would be prone to focus on the things the media carry but ignore the media themselves. He suggested the world be seen in a holistic way. He was led to see not only the richness in English literature but also what had produced such richness. In a 1937 letter to Maurice, his younger brother, McLuhan wrote, "To explain reality is to unfold ... 'the ground of everything which is real' which is God. So to explain is to reveal or expose God." In 1974, he told *The Globe and Mail*, a Canadian newspaper, that "belief in God alters existence ... making it mystical and converting a leaden uninspired human into something lyrically superhuman." By mystical, McLuhan meant "the daily miracles of sense and consciousness" revealed by one like Chesterton who believed in God. About what faith means to him, McLuhan once told Derrick de Kerckhove, his colleague at the University of Toronto in the 1970s, that "faith is paying attention, not to the clichés of religion only, but to the ground of the total man, which is the archetype. You come to the faith by prayer and by paying attention." In a 1977 interview with Babin, McLuhan said "prayer and liturgy (which are inseparable) are the only means of tuning in to the right wavelength, listening to Christ, and of involving the whole person."

For McLuhan, Christ is not only God's message (Word) to human beings but the medium (Mediator) between God and his creations. He believed what the Bible says about how God created and saved the world: through Christ all things were made and whoever believes in him shall not perish but have eternal life. For McLuhan, it is not enough for human beings to simply listen to the message from God. They should hear the message, which would pass into their daily life. "Only then do you get the message, that is, the effect [that is, conversion]. Only in that moment do medium and message unite," said McLuhan to Babin in a 1977 interview.

In order to hear the message, one needs to acknowledge one is a dependent creature, owing one's entire being to God and relying on Christ, the medium, to get united with God. But even for McLuhan himself, it would not be easy to make such an acknowledgment. On September 5, 1935, he wrote to his mother Elsie from Cambridge, "I need scarcely point out that religious enthusiasm (in which I am lamentably weak) has rarely directed the erratic and leaping feet of the inebriated one along the slow and arduous path that leads from a meeting-house to the Church—I mean the Catholic and universal Church, the visible body of Christ. Now religion-hunting even in its worst phases is yet a testimony to the greatest fact about man, namely that he is a creature and an image, and not sufficient unto himself ... The great difficulty about Truth is that it is not simple except to those who can attain to see it whole."

Before he was baptized in 1937, McLuhan wrote to his younger brother Maurice, "My malady is of the marrow. It is a hunger in the bone for something which cannot be satisfied by flesh and blood." That was almost six years after he read Chesterton's *What's Wrong with the World?* and a year after *G. K. Chesterton: A Practical Mystic*, his first academic article, was published. Less than two years later, McLuhan told his fiancée Corinne Lewis in a letter about being a Catholic, "You see, to hear Mass and/or to receive communion are spiritual acts ... The merit of these acts does not, and this is crucial, proceed from the person performing the act. Since human merits, all of them in their entirety from the beginning of history, are not sufficient to compensate for the tiniest sin. For even the tiniest sin constitutes an act of spiritual rebellion against God ... Thus the merit, to return to the first point, of spiritual acts is derivative. It is derived from Christ. The infinite merit of His Incarnation, His infinitely humbling Himself, was alone sufficient to 'liquidate' all human sins for all time. But the subsequent acts of His life have a mysterious value (a mystery is, strictly, not something queer or hidden, but something unfathomably and inexhaustibly rich in meanings) which naturally (in their very nature) dwarf every historical event and every philosophical or scientific truth."

And four decades later, McLuhan said in a 1977 interview with Edward Wakin, a Fordham University communications professor, "I never came into the Church as a person who was being taught. I came in on my knees. That is the only way in. When people start praying, they need truths; that's all. You don't come into the Church by ideas and concepts, and you cannot leave by mere disagreement. It has to be a loss of faith, a loss of participation. You can tell when people leave the Church: they have quit praying." Given that he has been known for his ideas and concepts like "the global village" and "The medium is the message," what McLuhan shared about his spiritual journey makes himself an apparent paradox. Yet, this paradox is not paradoxical at all. The man who was the greatest influence on McLuhan, Chesterton, had already been famous for using paradox. And this impressed McLuhan the most. In *G. K. Chesterton: A Practical Mystic*, he commented, "All profound truth, philosophical and spiritual, makes game with appearances, yet without really contradicting common sense." In McLuhan, ideas and concepts are but the appearances of his creativity. What matters more is what lies beneath. For McLuhan, Chesterton, or anyone like him, "is original in the only possible sense, because he considers everything in relation to its origins."

Chapter 19
But What on Earth God Looks Like

"Man approaches God most nearly when he is in one sense least like God." Clive Staples Lewis made this discovery in *The Four Loves*, a book published in 1958 when the Irish-born British writer was fifty-nine years old. Five years before his death, this paradox staggeringly wrecked Lewis' previous efforts to write about love. Lewis, better known as C. S. Lewis and for his earlier works such as *The Chronicles of Narnia, The Screwtape Letters* and *Mere Christianity*, had thought he would easily distinguish between these two types of love: God's love as gift and Man's love as need; and the former is obviously far better than the latter. But he later found love as need was not necessarily "mere selfishness."

When I first came across Lewis' find, I was standing in a subway train on a late Monday afternoon in February 2011. A copy of *The Four Loves* in my hands would be given as a birthday gift to a member of my English Bible study group a couple of hours later. A year or so before, a friend in Boston brought it to me from America. For the most of the following 12 months, it would lie on my bookshelf. I read part of the book. And yet, Lewis' insight did not come to my notice until I was to give it over to another person. Before that, my impression about the two loves had been almost the same as Lewis' erstwhile one. But out of the blue, the paradox that changed Lewis caught my eye that dusk. I continued to read the book during supper at a small restaurant before I joined the friend's birthday party. I told the partygoers about this fresh unexpected experience. I don't remember how they responded. Nodding and smiling, perhaps. What I do remember is that I was still digesting what I had just learned as I was sharing. And I knew that I would keep on ruminating over this manna from heaven for at least a while.

It was more than eight months later that I was able to start writing about the event. To me, this was a period of time when I began consciously reflecting on not just the two loves Lewis referred to, but how a human being could follow his or her God. The surprise conclusion Lewis came to in his later years helped me take note of a difference there might be between following God and following anyone who is not God. Compared with following God's example, following the example of anyone who is not God is a far more familiar sight within my memory. It would be desirable for the one who wants to follow one's example to be like the example. And it seems so when it comes to following an example who is God. But what does Lewis mean by saying "Man approaches God most nearly when he is in one sense least like God"?

Lewis's find lays bare a dimension that would be overlooked in the relationship between an example and its follower. For the follower, it is no doubt important that one needs to know how to be more like one's example. And it is perhaps no less important to know how unlike one might be in comparison to one's example. In the relationship between one and one's example, the most difficult imitation for a human being might be the imitation of one's creator. In *The Four Loves*, Lewis sighed, "For what can be more unalike than fullness and need, sovereignty and humility, righteousness and penitence, limitless power and a cry for help?" In this sense, it is simply in vain for any limited being to be like an limitless one. That's despite numerous limited beings in human history who have been worshipped as limitless ones. However, it does not necessarily mean it would be hopeless and meaningless for a human being to follow God. For Lewis, the God he believes in is the one who himself calls human beings to follow him and be with him. But to follow God and be with him does not mean that he or she would be the same as God, but that first of all, one would acknowledge he or she needs God as one's God. This acknowledgement involves accepting a situation where one is unable to follow God and be with him unless God wills. In this acknowledgement, one not only comes to know the distance between the limitless and the limited but also begins to respond to God's call by asking for his help. By such acknowledgement, one might turn out to be surprisingly closer to God than one thinks he or she could be through mere imitation.

In this light, Lewis no longer sees need as just selfishness but a necessary bridge connecting one and one's God. It is as a baby needing its mother. It is also as a mother needing her baby. In Lewis's own words, "There is the paradox. It is a Need-love but what it needs is to give. It is a Gift-love but it needs to be needed." For me, the discovery of the significance of need in following God and becoming his imitator seems but a return to common sense; and yet this common sense gives me both comfort and confidence that being unlike God is what I look like, but it unexpectedly awakens my need to long for God's help.

Despite this, might it be contradictory when one takes into account what the Bible says about the origin of human beings, "God created man in his own image, in the image of God he created him; male and female he created them"?[96] If one is made in God's likeness, why is it difficult to be like him? A proposed answer might be that a creation, though created in the image of the creator, still cannot be the same as the creator himself. Yes, like father, like son. But however alike they are, father and son are different persons. Another point might be about the issue of freedom. Compared with other creations, human beings enjoy much more freedom. They might even include the freedom to be like the creator or not. But there might still be another aspect of the possible answer. That human beings are made in God's image does not mean the creations know what the creator's image really looks like.

The Bible throughout its sixty-six books indicates the creator keeps revealing his image to the creations he made in his image, with a climax that he himself became a human being. Yet, the human beings he created in his likeness sentenced him to death, accusing him of passing himself off as God. Only after he resurrected, showed himself to his followers and his spirit descended upon them, were they truly able to come to believe in him and do what he told them to do. Only because of this did they see what on earth God's image looked like: "(Jesus Christ) Who, being in very nature God, did not consider equality with God something to be grasped, but made himself nothing, taking the very nature of a servant, being made in human likeness. And being found in appearance as a man, he humbled himself and became obedient to death—even death

96   Genesis 1:27.

on a cross! Therefore God exalted him to the highest place and gave him the name that is above every name, that at the name of Jesus every knee should bow, in heaven and on earth and under the earth, and every tongue confess that Jesus Christ is Lord, to the glory of God the Father."[97]

Other than this description from one of the apostle Paul's letters in his later years, John, another apostle, wrote towards the end of his life: "No one has ever seen God, but God the One and Only, who is at the Father's side, has made him known."[98] According to what these followers of Jesus saw, the image of God appears a paradox. The heart of God's image turns out to lie in that God makes his God's image nothing, he takes the form of a servant, he is found in the likeness of a human being, and he volunteers to be crucified by human beings who are made in God's image but are blind to the image.

From this and the rest of the Bible, one could further see God's image in terms of not only God's relationship with human beings but also his inner workings. It is the Father who sends the Son, Jesus Christ, who shows God's image and promises the Spirit, who, the Father sends in the name of the Son, teaches God's followers all things and reminds them of everything the Son says to human beings. And it is intriguing to read what God said when he created human beings, "Let us make man in our image, in our likeness."[99] This is different from what God said when he made previous things, such as, "Let there be light"[100] or "Let the land produce living creatures according to their kinds."[101] Bible commentaries from theologians like John Calvin and Matthew Henry consider the difference to be that between consultation and commanding. God's image, in greater detail, is the image of the Father, the Son, and the Spirit. In God, there are three members but they are one.

For the creations even made in their creator's likeness, the image of a triune God might look elusive. How to make sense of a God with three members in one? From human beings, it seems impossible to see or

97   Philippians 2:6–11.
98   John 1:18.
99   Genesis 1:26.
100   Genesis 1:3.
101   Genesis 1:24.

imagine any image like this one. It only becomes possible if God shows human beings the image in a way they could understand. This accessible way is the Son, one member of the triune God. He is the Word of God, the radiance of God's glory, the exact representation of God's being, the firstborn over all creations, and the image of the invisible God. It is he who tells his creations that God is spirit. But he has a body so that his creations made in his image could see the image. And yet, his appearance has no beauty or majesty to attract his creations to him. However, the Father makes it clear he is his Son whom he loves and with him he is well pleased. The reason is that the Son completely does the will of the Father. This is the example the human beings, sons and daughters of the Father, are called to follow.

One would find it still difficult to be like God even if he or she believes Jesus in the Bible is the image of the invisible God, and the Spirit he promised would be the ever-present help. But the account of Jesus shows that even the Son himself was overwhelmed with sorrow to the point of death in the lead-up to his crucifixion, and he said to the Father that if possible the hour might pass from him. And the Son, as the creator, knows the most about the difficulties facing human beings. Among the parables he told his disciples, one is about how a father warmly welcomed back his younger son who asked his father to give him his share of property but squandered his wealth in a distant country. The younger son thought he was no longer worthy to be his father's son because he sinned against heaven and his father. But his father saw him and then ran out from home to him while the son was still a long way off. He embraced him and kissed him. He asked his servant to bring the best robe, a ring and sandals for his younger son. A fattened calf was killed for a feast in celebration of the younger son's return. Yet, the older son got angry at how his father treated his younger brother. He complained to his father by saying that he never disobeyed his orders, but not even a young goat was given to him. His father went out pleading with the older son who refused to go in, "My son, you are always with me, and everything I have is yours. But we had to celebrate and be glad, because this brother of yours was dead and is alive again; he was lost and is found."[102]

102 Luke 15:31–32.

In this story, the father accepted both his sons who could accept neither himself nor his brother and both became his heirs. It shows an image of the Father who longs for his children to be with him however far they wander from him.

The image the Son reveals is not just how he follows the Father but how the Father is with the Son and embraces his children. When the Son said to the Father about his weakness before he was to be betrayed by one of his followers, an angel was sent from heaven to strengthen him. According to the apostle Paul, the Spirit will be sent to help humans in their weakness even though they do not know what they ought to ask the Father: "the Spirit himself intercedes for us with groans that words cannot express."[103] Paradoxically, this is just how one could start bearing God's image. If one gives up relying on oneself and believes in the work in him or her of the Spirit promised by the Son and sent by the Father, one's new life comes into being. In this sense, it is no wonder why Paul said he delighted in weakness. Three times he pleaded with his God to take away a thorn in his flesh. But his God responded, "My grace is sufficient for you, for my power is made perfect in weakness."[104] For Paul, it was just in weakness that the Son was crucified and yet the Son lives by the power of the Father. In other words, weakness or frailty would not constitute an insurmountable obstacle in one's path to following God. On the contrary, it would be taken advantage of for manifesting a new life out of the Spirit. In this light, the profound significance of the opening remarks of Jesus's Sermon on the Mount may become noticeable— "Blessed are the poor in spirit, for theirs is the kingdom of heaven. Blessed are those who mourn, for they will be comforted. Blessed are the meek, for they will inherit the earth. Blessed are those who hunger and thirst for righteousness, for they will be filled."[105]

In the eyes of humans, the weakness the Son was in might appear extremely perplexing or shocking. It would be incredible to believe what Isaiah, an ancient Hebrew prophet, penned was an image of one member of the triune God: "He grew up before him like a tender shoot, and like

---

103 Romans 8:26.
104 2 Corinthians 12:9.
105 Matthew 5:3–6.

a root out of dry ground. He had no beauty or majesty to attract us to him, nothing in his appearance that we should desire him ... He was despised and rejected by men, a man of sorrows, and familiar with suffering ... yet he did not open his mouth; he was led like a lamb to the slaughter, and as a sheep before her shearers is silent, so he did not open his mouth. By oppression and judgment he was taken away. And who can speak of his descendants? For he was cut off from the land of the living; for the transgression of my people he was stricken ... Yet it was the LORD's will to crush him and cause him to suffer, and though the LORD makes his life a guilt offering, he will see his offspring and prolong his days, and the will of the LORD will prosper in his hand ... he poured out his life unto death, and was numbered with the transgressors. For he bore the sin of many, and made intercession for the transgressors."[106] Here, the LORD is a translation of God's name in such popular English versions of the Bible as King James Version, New International Version, and English Standard Version. In Exodus, Moses once asked the one who claimed he was the God of the Israelites about his name. "I AM WHO I AM" was the response.[107] The Hebrew for LORD sounds like and may derive from the Hebrew for I AM. The LORD's will is the will of the triune God, not only the Father, but the Son and the Spirit.

No one but God himself could really understand why God's will was like this one. But his purpose is clear. It is to bear the sin of humans, die with them and give them a new life with his own life. It is God's salvation of humans. Or in a sense, it may still be a part of God's creation of humans according to his image. In Genesis, "the LORD God formed the man from the dust of the ground and breathed into his nostrils the breath of life, and the man became a living being ... the LORD God made a woman from the rib he had taken out of the man."[108] Yet, the creation seems not to stop here. It continues until the life of the Son himself, the image of God, is formed in dust/rib-made creatures. This stage of creation requires a response from human beings. With the work of the Spirit, he or she would confess with one's mouth that Jesus is Lord and believe

106 Isaiah 53:2–12.
107 Exodus 3:14.
108 Genesis 2:7, 22.

in one's heart that Jesus was raised from the dead. The outcome of this response, according to the apostle Paul, is that one's old self was crucified with Jesus and the new self was born with the resurrection of Jesus. It is this new self, not the old one, that bears the genuine image of God. But interestingly, this does not mean the old self is meaningless. Yes, it is perishable and it does not acknowledge its creator. Yet, it could be raised imperishable and be united with its creator. As Paul's first epistle to the Christians in Corinth shows, the transformation from the old self to the new one is a course of history a human being who is saved by one's creator would face: "'The first man Adam became a living being'; the last Adam, a life-giving spirit. The spiritual did not come first, but the natural, and after that the spiritual. The first man was of the dust of the earth, the second man from heaven ... And just as we have borne the likeness of the earthly man, so shall we bear the likeness of the man from heaven."[109] It is also in this course of events that a paradox similar to the one C. S. Lewis found is revealed. The apostle of Jesus wrote in the same letter: "The body that is sown is perishable, it is raised imperishable; it is sown in dishonor, it is raised in glory; it is sown in weakness, it is raised in power; it is sown a natural body, it is raised a spiritual body."[110]

109 1 Corinthians 15:45–49.
110 1 Corinthians 15:42–44.

Chapter 20
How to Live in the Two Worlds at Once

"In fact, both this shore and the other shore are in the same world. What differentiates the two is that one is visible and the other invisible. Even living in the visible part of the world, one would be under the influence of the invisible one." This is part of an essay I received in an afternoon of January 2012. The author is Sun Yi, an elder of the church which I am in and the chief editor of the church magazine, *Xing Hua* or *Almond Flowers*. He shared with his editorial colleagues of the journal some of his thoughts during the traditional Chinese new year holidays or Spring Festival. Sun Yi, also a professor at Renming or People's University in Beijing, has been under house arrest since April 2011 when the church was forced to leave its rented indoor space and hold outdoor worships.

For nearly a year before seeing Professor Sun's article, my attention had been drawn at times to the idea of living in the two worlds simultaneously. One day in early 2011, I visited the home of a member of our church who has been a business consultant. With several other church friends, we watched a few clips of films. One was the start of The Seventh Seal, a 1957 Swedish movie written and directed by Ernst Ingmar Bergman, a world-renowned film director. The scene of a medieval knight playing a chess game on a desolate beach with Death, personified as a black-cowled figure with a pale face, unexpectedly made me think of an opening scene of Job, a book in the Old Testament of the Bible. That is about a dialogue between God and Satan. God allowed Satan to test Job's faith in God by afflicting him. What Job endured in the visible part of the world was under the influence of what happened in the invisible one. From then on, the relationship between the two worlds or the two parts of the world seemed to come to form a conscious part of my mind.

In early November in the same year, I made another visit to the home of this business consultant. But his home was not the same one. He and his wife were forced to move out of their rented place because of taking part in the church's outdoor worship. With another member of the church, we watched the start of another film, *The Tree of Life*, written and directed by American film director Terrence Frederick Malick. The movie won the Palme d'Or at the Cannes International Film Festival in 2011. We were not able to see the whole film due to lack of time that day. But like it was with *The Seventh Seal*, the opening scene of *The Tree of Life* enabled me to think of the two worlds again. The movie began with a shot of light and then a quotation from what God answered Job in the Bible: "Where were you when I laid the earth's foundation ... while the morning stars sang together and all the sons of God shouted for joy?"[111] A son of a mother died at the age of nineteen. The mother prayed and asked God, "Why?" It was followed by an approximately twenty-minute visual history of the formation of the universe, reminiscent of God's long and seemingly irrelevant response to Job from chapter 38 through chapter 41 in the Book of Job, including about how the universe was formed and how nature worked. In a sense, it was through a visible way that a voice from the invisible world was shown.

Experiences like these woke me up to facing both the visible and invisible parts of the world. One surprise benefit I got is that, a little more than five years after being baptized, I found faith a more necessary part of my daily life. It seems more and more that faith, as "being sure of what we hope for and certain of what we do not see,"[112] is what one must learn to consciously live in the two worlds at once. With faith, one

---

111 Job 38:4,7.

112 Hebrew 11:1. Some theologians also gave their definition of faith, *e.g.*, for John Calvin, faith is "a firm and certain knowledge of God's benevolence toward us, founded upon the truth of the freely given promise in Christ, both revealed to our minds and sealed upon our hearts through the Holy Spirit." John Calvin, *Institutes of Christian Religion* (Westminster John Knox Press, 2006), 551; in a note of *The ESV (English Standard Version) Study Bible*, faith is "the known and received body of truth about Jesus and salvation through him," *The ESV Study Bible* (Crossway, 2008), 2449.

would be certain of what one does not see. With faith, one's eyes would be opened to the invisible part of the world. But here of course, one needs to know how he or she could be certain that with faith one would be certain of what one does not see. For me, it is about one's basic attitude towards not just the verse about faith in a letter in the Bible but the Bible itself. As a Christian, I accept that the Bible is "God-breathed"[113] and God's word recorded in the words of human beings "carried along by the Holy Spirit"[114] who "searches all things, even the deep things of God."[115] It is through the Holy Spirit of God that one can see "the deep things of God" or "the thoughts of God,"[116] which are invisible. And faith is what God gives his people[117] through his Spirit to see what is unseen. In other words, because of the Holy Spirit working in his or her life,[118] one would gain faith that is certain of what is invisible.

However, faith itself is not always certain in my life even more than five years into baptism. For example, it is not that whenever I read the Bible I would consciously believe that I am reading the word coming from God. At times, I would still find it difficult to relate the Bible to the complicated reality of the world. This situation has begun changing to a significant extent since late 2010 and early 2011 when I studied the apostle Paul's letter to the Colossians along with my English Bible study group. One verse caught my eye and it has kept coming back to me from time to time since then. The verse is "the reality, however, is found in Christ."[119] In other widely-circulated English Bible translations such as the King James Version or English Standard Version, this verse is rendered as "the body is of Christ" or "the substance belongs to Christ." What the body or substance contrasts with is the shadow or the form. But the reality appears more than just the body or the substance. The New International Version of this verse, "the reality, however, is found in Christ," helps me seem to see both the visible and invisible parts of

113 2 Timothy 3:16.
114 2 Peter 1:21.
115 1 Corinthians 2:10.
116 1 Corinthians 2:11.
117 1 Corinthians 2:12; 2 Peter 1:1; Jude 1:3.
118 Ephesians 3:7.
119 Colossians 2:17

the world together.[120] To put it in another way, a specific help I have got is that the visible and invisible parts are not worlds apart, for both are the reality which is found in Christ. Here, a crucial point concerns the relationship between the reality and Christ. How could the reality be found in Christ? Elsewhere in the Bible, Christ is described as "the image of the invisible God"[121] and "by him all things were created ... visible and invisible ... and in him all things hold together."[122] Given this, it would be understandable to acknowledge that the reality is found in Christ or God. But the question remains: how and so what. One could still be puzzled as to how to find out the reality in the world he created. Even if one knows, then so what?

In this regard, help came in late 2011 when I read a *Christianity Today* interview with Mark Noll, an American historian of Christianity, about his new book, *Jesus Christ and the Life of the Mind*. I found this whole paragraph illuminating: "The whole point of the book is that believers in Christ should take seriously who Christ is and what Christ has done. As a historian, I've been drawn to the great Christian creeds as the most succinct and powerful statements of who Christ is and what Christ has done. The great relevance of the Nicene Creed and the Chalcedonian definition is to affirm that Jesus Christ was fully human and fully divine in one integrated person. But we know from moral and ethical reasoning that God and humans are different. God is the Creator, and humans are the creatures. There's a huge gap between humanity and divinity. Yet Christianity says that in Christ, that gap doesn't exist. The lengthy debate leading up to Nicaea and Chalcedon was over how to state that what can't be together really was together."[123] What Noll wrote about Christ

---

120 The original Greek version of this verse is "ἅ ἐστιν σκιὰ τῶν μελλόντων, τὸ δὲ σῶμα τοῦ Χριστοῦ." "σῶμα" has a number of meanings. These two are the major ones: 1, body (both that of people and animals); 2, an entire thing. For more details, see http://en.wiktionary.org/wiki/σῶμα . Also see http://scripturetext.com/colossians/2-17.htm in which the meaning of the body as a sound whole is highlighted.

121 Colossians 1:15.

122 Colossians 1:16–17.

123 For more details, see http://www.christianitytoday.com/ct/2011/august/nollfoundationmind.html.

is not new. And yet, the simultaneously fully divine and fully human natures of Christ the Notre Dame University professor highlighted with his new book helps me see a clearer picture of the reality and its relationship with God. Christ himself has set the example for anyone who wants to learn how to live in the two worlds or the two parts of the world simultaneously. He said his kingdom was not of this world.[124] But he also made it clear that his coming to this world was of supreme significance. He said he came to the world to bear witness to the truth.[125] And his witness is nothing but enabling those who were made in God's image to see "the image of the invisible God," i.e., the truth incarnate. In him, what one would see is not only the reality to the full but also the truth to the point. For him and in him, both visible and invisible are important. He is the mediator between the two parts of the world, through whom the otherwise impossible togetherness of simultaneously full divinity and full humanity in a person proves not only possible but real. It is in the visible human form that the invisible God manifests himself fully.[126]

But, Christians are not Christs. What a Christian can do is no more than become a faithful follower of Christ, "God the One and Only."[127] The question of living in the visible and invisible worlds at once turns out to be that of living in Christ. And the former question is just a part of the latter one. Yet, the emergence of this specific question in my awareness seems to enable me to see one more side of the manifold life in Christ. And to what extent this side of the life in Christ is grown would affect the growth of Christ's body that includes the body's different members across the visible world. The way of being in this world but

---

124 John 18:36.

125 John 18:37.

126 Colossians 1:25–27. See also the notes about Philippians 2:10–11 in *The ESV Study Bible*: "While Christ now bears the divine name Yahweh ('Lord'), he is still worshiped with his human name, Jesus, since it was in the flesh that he most clearly displayed his divine glory to the world. This astounding union of Jesus' divine and human natures is reinforced by the allusion to Isaiah 45:23 in the words every knee should bow … and every tongue confess, which in Isaiah refer exclusively to Yahweh." *The ESV Study Bible* (Crossway, 2008), 2283.

127 John 1:18

not of this world comes from the way of Jesus Christ himself and what he prayed to the Father for his followers: "My prayer is not that you take them out of the world but that you protect them from the evil one. They are not of the world, even as I am not of it. Sanctify them by the truth; your word is truth. As you sent me into the world, I have sent them into the world. For them I sanctify myself, that they too may be truly sanctified."[128] To be sanctified by God's word is key to this way of life. In its original Greek or Hebrew,[129] to be sanctified means to be separated or set apart. How to be in the world but not of the world? It is to be sent into the world by God as the Son by the Father and at the same time, to be set apart from the world by the Son who is the word of the Father.

---

128 John 17:15–19.

129 The Greek word for "sanctify" is ἁγιάζω or in transliteration, hagiazó. The Hebrew is שָׁדַק ׳ or in transliteration, qadash. See https://biblehub. com/greek/37.htm, https://biblehub.com/hebrew/6942.htm.

Epilogue
The Reality of Politics

A Preliminary Reading of Eric Voegelin and Ellis Sandoz

It was a day in early September 2012. I went to see a friend at All Sages Bookstore, perhaps the most popular bookshop among intellectuals in Beijing. A few small black noticeboards were placed at the door. On them were the new titles and authors the bookstore recommended to the readers. On the middle one were written in Chinese: Ellis Sandoz, *The Voegelinian Revolution: A Biographical Introduction (Second Edition)*.

Before that, I had seen the Chinese version of this book. It was the translator, Mr. Xu Zhiyue or Daniel Hsu, who sent it to me by express. Other than All Sages Bookstore, the website of China's official news agency, *Xinhua* or *New China,* and *Southern Weekend*, a leading Chinese newspaper in China, made their respective recommendations in August and October. In an interview concerning the role of reason in Chinese history, a professor at Central Party School of China's ruling Communist Party had a passing reference to Voegelin's comments on China. This interview was published in the website of China's state newspaper, *People's Daily.* [130]

Why *The Voegelinian Revolution* caught my eye is that it was its author, Professor Ellis Sandoz, who mailed me by air an autographed copy of the original English version along with many other books in 2006. From this book and others I began hearing about the name of Eric Voegelin and his place in the world of political thought in America and Europe.

---

130 http://news.xinhuanet.com/book/2012-08/02/c_123514825.htm ; http://www.infzm.com/content/82349 ;http://theory.people.com.cn/n/2012/1022/c49157-19340054.html .

Erich Hermann Wilhelm Voegelin was born in the western German city of Cologne on January 3, 1901. His father was a civil engineer, his mother a Viennese. In 1910, he moved with his family to the Austrian capital of Vienna. Voegelin studied in the law faculty of the University of Vienna from 1919 and obtained Dr. rer. pol. only three years later. He then became an assistant to Professor Hans Kelsen (1881-1973), who helped draft the Austrian constitution of 1920 and was one of the most influential legal scholars in Europe and America of the twentieth century.

Facing Nazi persecution, Voegelin and his wife Lissy Onken (1906-1996) emigrated to the United States in 1938. Voegelin mainly worked at Louisiana State University, University of Munich, University of Notre Dame and the Hoover Institution, Stanford. Notably, Voegelin accepted an invitation in 1958 to establish an institute of political science and fill the chair left vacant since the death of the German sociologist Max Weber (1864-1920).

From 2007 on, the Chinese editions of Voegelin's works have begun to appear in China's mainland. They include the first two volumes of the five-volume *Order and History, Israel and Revelation, The World of the Polis*; six volumes of the eight-volume *History of Political Ideas, Hellenism, Rome and Early Christianity, The Middle Ages to Aquinas, The Later Middle Ages, Religion and the Rise of Modernity, Revolution and the New Science, Crisis and the Apocalypse of Man*; and *Modernity without Restraint.*

These are part of the thirty-four-volume *The Collected Works of Eric Voegelin.* Its general editor is Ellis Sandoz who has worked with many of his American and international colleagues since Voegelin died in his Stanford home on January 19, 1985. Sandoz set up the Eric Voegelin Institute at Louisiana State University in March 1987. He studied political science under Voegelin at Louisiana and Munich during undergraduate and doctorate years. Sandoz is Hermann Moyse Jr. Distinguished Professor of Political Science and director of the Eric Voegelin Institute at Louisiana. Before the publication of the Chinese translation of *The Voegelinian Revolution* in 2012, Voegelin's *Autobiographical Reflections* based on the interviews Sandoz conducted in 1973 was also translated by Daniel Hsu who published it in 2009. Autobiographical

Reflections is a major part of the thirty-fourth and final volume of *The Collected Works of Eric Voegelin*, which came out in 2006.

With all these thirty-four volumes, one might be all at sea even if he or she is interested in politics. For Chinese readers, *Faith and Political Philosophy: The Correspondence Between Leo Strauss and Eric Voegelin, 1934-1964,* which appeared in Chinese in 2007, might be of help in comparing the two political philosophers. The works of Leo Strauss (1899-1973) entered China much earlier than those of Voegelin. The earliest one seems to be the Chinese edition of *History of Political Philosophy* in 1993, sixty years after it first appeared in English. It was co-edited by Strauss and his then Chicago University colleague, Joseph Cropsey (1919-2012). From their correspondence, one could see how the two German-American political thinkers thought differently about the issues of mutual concern.

In comparison, *Autobiographical Reflections* and *The Voegelinian Revolution* provide a general introduction to Voegelin's life and thought through the philosopher himself and his student who was also his life-long friend. And in the thirty-fourth volume of *The Collected Works of Eric Voegelin*, "Glossary of Terms Used in Eric Voegelin's Writings" in thirty-seven pages explains what Voegelin could mean by the words he would use, especially the Greek ones.[131] Without this help, readers in not just the Chinese mainland but also America and Europe, might find Voegelin's books not an easy read.[132] There is a world of difference between Voegelin and many other popular political scientists in writing and thinking.

Nevertheless, even without the glossary, Voegelin's life itself could still

---

131 Eric Voegelin, *The Collected Works of Eric Voegelin: Volume 34, Autobiographical Reflections: Revised Edition, with a Voegelin Glossary and Cumulative Index* (Columbia, Missouri: University of Missouri Press, 2006), 149–86. This glossary is based on Professor Eugene Webb's compilation in his book *Eric Voegelin: Philosopher of History* (Seattle: University of Washington Press, 1981), 277–89; Webb's book was translated into Chinese by Cheng Qing and was published in 2011.

132 Barry Cooper and Jodi Bruhn, eds., *Voegelin Recollected: Conversation on a Life* (Columbia, Missouri: University of Missouri Press, 2008), 49–52.

touch a chord with Chinese mainland readers. It might be just this aspect that first holds the Chinese attention. In his preface to the Chinese edition of *The Voegelinian Revolution,* Professor Sandoz points out the background Voegelin was in: "Voegelin himself, of course, wrote in the shadow of the great totalitarian tyrannies of the 20th century, Bolshevism and National Socialism, and was personally victimized by the latter."[133] On March 11, 1938, Nazi[134] Germany occupied Austria. Voegelin's 1936 book, *The Authoritarian State: An Essay on the Problem of the Austrian State,* was banned. On April 23, 1938, the commissary dean of the faculty of law and political science at Vienna University wrote to Voegelin notifying him that the Austrian education ministry had revoked his right to teach.

In the twenty-ninth volume of *The Collected Works of Eric Voegelin,* one could see the photocopy of this letter of dismissal where "Heil Hitler!" is striking.[135] On July 14 in the same year, Voegelin fled to Zurich, Switzerland. A week later, his wife, Lissy, joined him in Zurich. On September 8, the Voegelins left Paris for America. Voegelin told Sandoz what it was like on his last day in Austria, "The emigration plan almost miscarried. Though I was politically an entirely unimportant figure, and the important ones had to be caught first, my turn came at last. Just when we had nearly finished our preparations and my passport was with the police in order to get the exit visa, the Gestapo[136] appeared at my apartment to confiscate the passport. Fortunately, I was not at home, and my life [Lissy Onken Voegelin] was delighted to tell them that the passport was with the police for the purpose of getting the exit visa, which satisfied the Gestapo. We were able, through friends, to get the passport, including the exit visa, from the police before the Gestapo got it—that all in one day. On the same day, in the evening, with two bags, I caught a train to Zurich, trembling

133 Ellis Sandoz, Xu Zhiyue trans., *The Voegelinian Revolution: A Biographical Introduction* (Second Edition) (Shanghai: Shanghai Joint Publishing Company, 2012), 7. There is some change to the Chinese translation in the Chinese version of this writing.

134 Nazi is short for Nationalsozialist, National Socialist.

135 Eric Voegelin, *The Collected Works of Eric Voegelin: Volume 29, Selected Correspondence, 1924–1949* (Columbia, Missouri: University of Missouri Press, 2009), Letter of dismissal.

136 Gestapo is short for Geheime Staatspolizei, Secret State Police.

on the way that the Gestapo after all would find out about me and arrest me at the border. But apparently even the Gestapo was not as efficient as my wife and I in these matters, and I got through unarrested."[137]

It was in such personal experience that Voegelin devoted himself to exposing "the shadow." Even before fleeing from Austria, Voegelin had already started trying to do that. For him, "ideology" makes up part and parcel of "the shadow." *The Authoritarian State* was Voegelin's "first major attempt to penetrate the role of ideologies, left and right, in the contemporary situation."[138] Voegelin used this book to show the difference between authoritarian state and total state. While an example of the former is the 1934 Austrian constitution and its government after the civil war, an instance of the latter is such radicals as National Socialists who were ready to seize power then. Voegelin considered an authoritarian state "would keep radical ideologists in check" and "was the best possible defense of democracy."[139] For Voegelin, such totalitarianism as National Socialism is "the totality of ideology" where one would accept the supremacy of Volk as both people and nation not passively from the outside but voluntarily, "intellectually and spiritually from the inside." Political rule like this is not confined to keeping social order but already a spiritual force, a religion.[140] Voegelin went on to elaborate on this point in *The Political Religions*, which was confiscated by the Gestapo immediately upon publication in April 1938. He wrote in its epilogue: "The inner-worldly religiosity experienced by the collective body—be it humanity, the people, the class, the race, or the state—as the *realissimum*[141] is abandonment of God."[142]

---

137 Eric Voegelin, Ellis Sandoz ed., Xu Zhiyue trans., *Autobiographical Reflections* (Beijing: Huaxia Press, 2009), 43. There is some change to the Chinese translation in the Chinese version of this writing; Eric Voegelin, *The Collected Works of Eric Voegelin: Volume 34, Autobiographical Reflections: Revised Edition, with a Voegelin Glossary and Cumulative Index* (Columbia, Missouri: University of Missouri Press, 2006), 71.

138 *Ibid.*, 69.

139 *Ibid.*, 69.

140 Eric Voegelin, *The Collected Works of Eric Voegelin, Volume 4, The Authoritarian State: An Essay on the Problem of the Austrian State* (Columbia, Missouri: University of Missouri Press, 1999), 73.

141 Literally, realissimum means the most real.

142 Eric Voegelin, *The Collected Works of Eric Voegelin, Volume 5, Modernity*

However, Voegelin later would not use "religions" to make sense of various ideologies. He thought the term "too vague and already deforms the real problem of experiences by mixing them with the further problem of dogma or doctrine."[143] Despite this, Sandoz viewed *The Political Religions* as "a new turn in the development of Voegelin's thought." It is not just because the 1939 new edition of *The Political Religions* was the first work published after Voegelin arrived in America, but that the "central ground of all his later work is clearly at the root of his argument" in this small book of less than sixty pages. In the eyes of Sandoz, "Voegelin in this brilliant essay sketches the problem of the ideologies in terms of the disease of the spirit whose cure lies in rediscovery of the order of the soul as a major task of his new science of politics."[144]

In Autobiographical Reflections, Voegelin described ideology as "the deformation of existence, which leads to the construction of ideological systems."[145] He made this statement about the nature of ideology when speaking of philosophy of history. For Voegelin, "Philosophy of history as a topic does not go further back than the eighteenth century. From its beginning in the eighteenth century, it became associated with the constructions of

    without Restraint: The Political Religions; The New Science of Politics; and Science, Politics, and Gnosticism (Columbia, Missouri: University of Missouri Press, 2000), 71.

143 Eric Voegelin, Ellis Sandoz ed., Xu Zhiyue trans., *Autobiographical Reflections* (Beijing: Huaxia Press, 2009), 51; Eric Voegelin, *The Collected Works of Eric Voegelin: Volume 34, Autobiographical Reflections: Revised Edition, with a Voegelin Glossary and Cumulative Index* (Columbia, Missouri: University of Missouri Press, 2006), 78.

144 Ellis Sandoz, Xu Zhiyue trans., *The Voegelinian Revolution: A Biographical Introduction (Second Edition)* (Shanghai: Shanghai Joint Publishing Company, 2012), 81–82. There is some change to the Chinese translation in the Chinese version of this writing; Ellis Sandoz, *The Voegelinian Revolution: A Biographical Introduction* (New Brunswick, New Jersey: Transaction Publishers, 2000), 65.

145 Eric Voegelin, Ellis Sandoz ed., Xu Zhiyue trans., *Autobiographical Reflections* (Beijing: Huaxia Press, 2009), 103. There is some change to the Chinese translation in the Chinese version of this writing; Eric Voegelin, *The Collected Works of Eric Voegelin: Volume 34, Autobiographical Reflections: Revised Edition, with a Voegelin Glossary and Cumulative Index* (Columbia, Missouri: University of Missouri Press, 2006), 127.

an imaginary history made for the purpose of interpreting the constructor and his personal state of alienation as the climax of all preceding history. Until quite recently, philosophy of history has been definitely associated with the misconstruction of history from a position of alienation, whether it be in the case of Condorcet, Comte, Hegel, or Marx. This rigid construction of history as a huge falsification of reality from the position of an alienated existence is dissolving in the twentieth century."[146]

"Ideology" derives from a French word, "idéologie," which is the combination of two Greek words, ἰδέα (idea) and λόγος (logos). It means science of ideas. The French philosopher Destutt de Tracy (1754-1836) is widely believed to have first coined the word "ideology" in 1796. De Tracy's goal was to free human beings from what he saw as the slavery of theology through his "ideology," and to place the science of ideas as "the greatest of the arts [...] that of regulating society [...]." For de Tracy, ideas come from a sense that is a function of human faculties, and thus to study ideas is to study human faculties.[147] In a wider sense, de Tracy proposed that "ideology is a part of zoology."[148] Briefly, the French philosopher held that social scientists should follow the natural scientists' example to be neutral and objective, rather than like theologians and metaphysicians who are opinionated and subjective. Among the thinkers who had made a serious impact on de Tracy are the British philosophers Francis Bacon (1561-1626) and John Locke (1632-1704), and the French philosophers René Descartes (1596-1650) and Étienne Bonnot de Condillac (1715-1780).[149] Thomas Jefferson (1743-1826) is perhaps the first

---

146 *Ibid.*, 103. There is some change to the Chinese translation in the Chinese version of this writing.
147 Emmet Kennedy, The secularism of Destutt de Tracy's "IDEOLOGY" http://www.geisteswissenschaften.fu-berlin.de/v/grammaire_generale/Actes_du_colloque/Textes/Kennedy/Emmet_Kennedy.pdf .
148 Robert J. Richards, "Ideology and the History of Science," in *Biology and Philosophy*, 8 (1993), 103–108 http://philosophy.uchicago.edu/faculty/files/richards/Ideology%20and%20the%20History%20of%20Scie nce.pdf .
149 B. W. Head, *Ideology and Social Science: Destutt de Tracy and French Liberalism* (Dordrecht, The Netherlands: Martinus Nijhoff Publishers, 1985), 25–34.

person who introduced "ideology" into the English-speaking world. The author of the Declaration of Independence, who served the U.S. as minister to France between 1785-1789, published in 1817 his translation of the fourth volume of de Tracy's Eléments D'idéologie or Elements of Ideology.[150]

It appears that Voegelin never talked about de Tracy. But the French philosopher, Nicolas de Condorcet (1743-1794), Voegelin often mentioned is contemporary with de Tracy. Both experienced the French Revolution (1789-1799). Condorcet's best-known work might be his *Esquisse d'un tableau historique des progrès de l'esprit humain* or *Sketch for a Historical Picture of the Progress of the Human Mind.* Along with the French philosopher Auguste Comte (1798-1857), and German philosophers Georg Wilhelm Friedrich Hegel (1770-1831) and Karl Marx (1818-1883), de Tracy and Condorcet are thinkers whose thoughts are typical of the Enlightenment.

In *The World of the Polis* published in 1957, Voegelin pointed to the similarity between the Sophists in the fifth century B.C. and the Enlightenment in the eighteenth century. That is, "insensitiveness toward experiences of transcendence." To Voegelin, this insensitiveness "has the same result of destroying philosophy—for philosophy by definition has its center in the experiences of transcendence."[151] In *Israel and Revelation* which came out a year earlier, Voegelin explained what he meant by "transcendence" when defining ideology and philosophy: "Ideology is existence in rebellion against God and man. It is the violation of the First and Tenth Commandments, if we want to use the language of Israel order; it is the nosos, the disease of the spirit, if we want to use the language of Aeschylus and Plato. Philosophy is the love of being through love of divine Being as the source of its order. The Logos of being is the

---

150 The Count Destutt Tracy, Thomas Jefferson trans. and ed., *A Treatise on Political Economy, To which is prefixed a supplement to a preceding work on the understanding or, Elements of Ideology* (Georgetown, D. C.: Published by Joseph Mulligan, Printed by W. A. Rind & Co., 1817) http://mises.org/books/tracy.pdf .

151 Eric Voegelin, *The Collected Works of Eric Voegelin: Volume 15, Order and History: Volume 2, The World of the Polis* (Columbia, Missouri: University of Missouri Press, 2000), 349.

object proper of philosophical inquiry; and the search for truth concerning the order of being cannot be conducted without diagnosing the modes of existence in untruth. The truth of order has to be gained and regained in the perpetual struggle against the fall from it; and the movement toward truth starts from a man's awareness of his existence in untruth."[152]

From this, one could see that "the shadow" Voegelin tried to expose is not confined to the recent centuries of European history. The disease of the spirit he tried to diagnose is not just the modern European problem. Apart from the Sophists' "insensitiveness toward experiences of transcendence" in ancient Greece, the shadow of ideology could also be found in ancient West Asian political order. Voegelin told Sandoz: "By transcendental representation I mean the symbolization of the governmental function as representative of divine order in the cosmos. That is the fundamental symbolism, back to the ancient Near Eastern empires where the king is the representative of the people before the god and of the god before the people. Nothing has changed in this fundamental structure of governmental order, not even in the modern ideological empires. The only difference is that the god whom the government represents has been replaced by an ideology of history which now the government represents in its revolutionary capacity."[153]

In particular, Voegelin pinpointed Gnosticism as a serious form of the disease of the spirit. This is most evident in his *The New Science of Politics* in 1952 and *Science, Politics, and Gnosticism* in 1959. Gnosticism originates from the Greek, γνωστικός (gnostikos) meaning learned, intellectual. By Gnosticism, Voegelin refers to "a type of thinking that claims absolute cognitive mastery of reality" and "considers its

---

152 Eric Voegelin, *Order and History: Volume One, Israel and Revelation* (Baton Rouge: Louisiana State University Press, 1994), xiv.

153 Ellis Sandoz, Xu Zhiyue trans., *The Voegelinian Revolution: A Biographical Introduction (Second Edition)* (Shanghai: Shanghai Joint Publishing Company, 2012), 94. There is some change to the Chinese translation in the Chinese version of this writing; Ellis Sandoz, *The Voegelinian Revolution: A Biographical Introduction* (New Brunswick, New Jersey: Transaction Publishers, 2000), 78.

knowledge not subject to criticism."[154] Voegelin listed six features of gnostic movements, "that, taken together, reveal the nature of the gnostic attitude." 1, he or she is not satisfied with one's situation; 2, the bad situation is attributed to the intrinsic problem of the world; 3, "salvation from the evil of the world is possible"; 4, "From this follows the belief that the order of being will have to be changed in a historical process"; 5, "With this fifth point we come to the gnostic trait in the narrower sense—the belief that a change in the order of being lies in the realm of human action, that this salvational act is possible through man's own effort"; 6, gnostics proclaim the knowledge of this change.[155] In exploring history, Voegelin found different branches of Gnosticism in Jewish, Christian, Islamic and other cultures.[156]

Voegelin later made further remarks about Gnosticism and the disease of the spirit. In 1973, he explained to Sandoz: "The application of the category of Gnosticism to modern ideologies, of course, stands. In a more complete analysis, however, there are other factors to be considered in addition. One of these factors is the metastatic apocalypse deriving directly from the Israelite prophets, via Paul, and forming a permanent strand in Christian sectarian movements right up to the Renaissance."[157] Metastasis literally means the spread of cancer to other parts of the body. To Voegelin, the metastatic apocalypse means "all unrealistically expected transformations of human beings, society, or the

---

154 Eric Voegelin, *The Collected Works of Eric Voegelin: Volume 34, Autobiographical Reflections: Revised Edition, with a Voegelin Glossary and Cumulative Index* (Columbia, Missouri: University of Missouri Press, 2006), 160–61.

155 Eric Voegelin, *The Collected Works of Eric Voegelin, Volume 5, Modernity without Restraint: The Political Religions; The New Science of Politics; and Science, Politics, and Gnosticism* (Columbia, Missouri: University of Missouri Press, 2000), 297–98.

156 *Ibid.*, 191, 296–97.

157 Eric Voegelin, Ellis Sandoz ed., Xu Zhiyue trans., *Autobiographical Reflections* (Beijing: Huaxia Press, 2009), 67. There is some change to the Chinese translation in the Chinese version of this writing; Eric Voegelin, *The Collected Works of Eric Voegelin: Volume 34, Autobiographical Reflections: Revised Edition, with a Voegelin Glossary and Cumulative Index* (Columbia, Missouri: University of Missouri Press, 2006), 93.

structure of existence."[158] Another factor Voegelin took note of is Neo-Platonism that was revived in Florence of the late fifteenth century. He said "the attempt to regain an understanding of cosmic order through a revival of Neo-Platonism miscarried; a revival of the divine order in the cosmos in the ancient sense would have required a revival of the pagan gods, and that did not work."[159]

In *Crisis and the Apocalypse of Man* that was finished in the 1950s, Voegelin used Comte's thought as an example to show all similar phenomena were "apocalypse of man" or "intramundane eschatology."[160] Voegelin developed a new concept, "egophanic revolt," in contrast to "theophany" when he wrote *The Ecumenic Age*[161] that was published in

158　Eric Voegelin, T*he Collected Works of Eric Voegelin: Volume 34, Auto-biographical Reflections: Revised Edition, with a Voegelin Glossary and Cumulative Index* (Columbia, Missouri: University of Missouri Press, 2006), 167–68; Eric Voegelin, *The Collected Works of Eric Voegelin: Volume 33, The Drama of Humanity and Other Miscellaneous Papers: 1939–1985* (Columbia, Missouri: University of Missouri Press, 2004), 90.

159　Eric Voegelin, Ellis Sandoz ed., Xu Zhiyue trans., *Autobiographical Reflections* (Beijing: Huaxia Press, 2009), 68. There is some change to the Chinese translation in the Chinese version of this writing; Eric Voegelin, *The Collected Works of Eric Voegelin: Volume 34, Autobiographical Reflections: Revised Edition*, with a Voegelin Glossary and Cumulative Index (Columbia, Missouri: University of Missouri Press, 2006), 93.

160　Other than Comte, Voegelin also referred to Marx, Lenin, Hitler. Eric Voegelin, *The Collected Works of Eric Voegelin, Volume 26, History of Political Ideas: Volume VIII, Crisis and the Apocalypse of Man* (Columbia, Missouri: University of Missouri Press, 1999), 5, 7, 9, 185, 193. *Crisis and the Apocalypse of Man* was published as *From Enlightenment to Revolution* in 1975. It was the only book published among the eight-volume *History of Political Ideas* before Voegelin died. Eric Voegelin, *From Enlightenment to Revolution* (Durham, North Carolina: Duke University Press, 1975).

161　"Ecumenic" derives from οἰκουμένη (oikoumene) in Greek meaning "(the) inhabited (world). In *The Ecumenic Age*, Voegelin examined its multiple layers of meaning: "The term *ecumene*, which originally means no more than the inhabited world in the sense of cultural geography, has received through Polybius the technical meaning of the peoples who are drawn into the process of imperial expansion. On this Polybian stratum of meaning could later be superimposed the meaning of the mankind under Roman

1974. Again Voegelin mentioned Condorcet, Comte, Hegel, Marx as well as three other German philosophers, Johann Gottlieb Fichte (1762–1814), Ludwig Andreas Feuerbach (1804–1872), and Friedrich Wilhelm Nietzsche (1844–1900).[162] Voegelin described "egophanic revolt" as "the best I can do terminologically at present."[163]

Where Voegelin introduced "egophanic revolt" or "egophany" as "the rejections of the theophany" is in Chapter 5 of *The Ecumenic Age, The Pauline Vision of the Resurrected.* He wrote: "when the varieties of

jurisdiction (Luke 2:1; Acts 17:6; 24:5), and ultimately of the messianic world to come (Heb. 2:5). " Polybius (c. 200 B.C.– 118 B.C.), a historian during the Hellenistic Period, wrote multi-volume Histories. For more details, see Eric Voegelin, *The Collected Works of Eric Voegelin, Volume 17, Order and History: Volume IV, The Ecumenic Age* (Columbia, Missouri: University of Missouri Press, 2000), 178–79. Regarding "Ecumenic Age," Voegelin referred to "the period in which a manifold of concrete societies, which formerly existed in autonomously ordered form, were drawn into one political power field through pragmatic expansions from the various centers. This process has a recognizable beginning with the Iranian expansion; and it has its recognizable end with the decline of Roman power, when the ecumene begins to dissociate centrifugally into the Byzantine, Islamic, and Western civilizations." *Ibid.*, 188. As for "the Iranian expansion," Voegelin referred to "the rise of the Persian Empire" in the book's second chapter. *Ibid.*, 167. In a chapter concerning China, Voegelin used "ecumene" to translate "t'ien-hsia" (all-under-heaven, below heaven, all below heaven, world). For Voegelin, in the cultural sense, "t'ien-hsia," "as the carrier of human society," is the exact equivalent of "oikoumene." *Ibid.*, 340–41, 352. Voegelin further pointed out that with the rise of Ch'in, the idea of "kuo" replaced "t'ien-hsia" and "the principle of force swallowed up the ecumene and its order." In the Han Dynasty that followed Ch'in, various movements and schools struggled to provide the spiritual substance of the power but the order of "t'ien-hsia" was never restored. *Ibid.*, 370.

162 Eric Voegelin, *The Collected Works of Eric Voegelin, Volume 17, Order and History: Volume IV, The Ecumenic Age* (Columbia, Missouri: University of Missouri Press, 2000), 326–27.

163 Eric Voegelin, *The Collected Works of Eric Voegelin: Volume 34, Autobiographical Reflections: Revised Edition, with a Voegelin Glossary and Cumulative Index* (Columbia, Missouri: University of Missouri Press, 2006), 94, 157.

egophanic history have come to dominate the climate of opinion, as they do in our time, not surprisingly the 'historicity' of Christ has become a problem for thinkers, including a good number of theologians, who have succumbed to the climate."[164] What Voegelin referred to is part of the apostle Paul's letters in the Bible concerning the resurrection of Jesus and his second coming, especially Chapter 15 of 1 Corinthians. What Voegelin focused on is the different responses to the resurrection of Jesus and his second coming.

In Voegelin's eyes, "the main Church had accepted Augustine's symbolization of the present, post-Christ period as the *saeculum senescens*,[165] as the time of waiting for the Parousia[166] and the eschatological events, while the more fervent expectations were pushed to the sectarian fringe of apocalyptic and Gnostic movements." One of "the more fervent expectations" Voegelin elaborated on is "a new pattern of expectations: The age of perfection, the *teleion*, would be an age of the Spirit beyond the age of Christ." A representative is the thought of Joachim of Fiore or Joachim of Flora (c. 1135/1145–1202), a monk born in southern Italy whose theology was influential in the twelfth-century Europe. For Joachim, "the flowering of the monastic life as the event that indicated a meaningful advance in the process of transfiguration" is "the approach of a Third Age of the Spirit, following the ages of the Father and the Son." In other words, the Age of the Spirit would be the age of perfection. Joachim and his followers even calculated the year 1260 or so as the start of the Age of the Spirit.[167]

Voegelin talked about Joachim in more than one of his works with

---

164 Eric Voegelin, *The Collected Works of Eric Voegelin, Volume 17, Order and History: Volume IV, The Ecumenic Age* (Columbia, Missouri: University of Missouri Press, 2000), 327–28.

165 Literally, *saeculum senescens* means age growing old.

166 Parousia, literally meaning presence, arrival, official visit, here refers to the second coming of Christ.

167 Eric Voegelin, *The Collected Works of Eric Voegelin, Volume 17, Order and History: Volume IV, The Ecumenic Age* (Columbia, Missouri: University of Missouri Press, 2000), 335. George H. Tavard, *The Contemplative Church: Joachim And His Adversaries* (Milwaukee, Wisconsin: Marquette University Press, 2005), 7–21.

the earliest being *The Political Religions.*[168] In *The New Science of Politics*, Voegelin spoke of a theologian who was earlier than Joachim. He is Johannes Scotus Eriugena (c. 810/815–877), "John, the Irish-born Gael."[169] Sandoz traced the movement of the Age of the Spirit back to an even earlier time when Montanus and his adherents were popular in the second century.[170] Montanus was said to be self-identified as "the Mouthpiece of the Holy Spirit." Montanism, known for advocating the new prophecy after the Bible, is widely considered to be a major heresy in early church and thereafter.[171]

Besides Joachim, Voegelin also mentioned Otto of Freising (c. 1114–1158), a German bishop, and Petrarca (c. 1304–1374), an Italian poet and scholar.[172] Some historians call Petrarca the "father" of modern humanism. Petrarca is believed to have first developed the idea of Dark Ages. He thought the ages from the collapse of the Roman Empire through his time were in the darkness. He hoped the "radiance" of the old Rome would reappear.[173]

168 Eric Voegelin, *The Collected Works of Eric Voegelin, Volume 5, Modernity without Restraint: The Political Religions; The New Science of Politics; and Science, Politics, and Gnosticism* (Columbia, Missouri: University of Missouri Press, 2000), 50–52.

169 *Ibid.*, 178–80, 184–85, 191; Johannes Scotus Eriugena, Christopher Bamford trans. and ed., *The Voice of the Eagle: The Heart of Celtic Christianity* (Great Barrington, Massachusetts: Lindisfarne Books, 2000), 53.

170 Ellis Sandoz, *Political Apocalypse: A Study of Dostoevsky's Grand Inquisitor* (Wilmington, Delaware: ISI Books, 2000), 135–36, 138–39; Ellis Sandoz, Xu Zhiyue trans., *The Voegelinian Revolution: A Biographical Introduction (Second Edition),* (Shanghai: Shanghai Joint Publishing Company, 2012), 123; Ellis Sandoz, *The Voegelinian Revolution: A Biographical Introduction* (New Brunswick, New Jersey: Transaction Publishers, 2000), 108.

171 Roger E. Olson, Wu Ruicheng and Xu Chengde trans., *The Story of Christian Theology* (Beijing: Peking University Press, 2003), 20–22; Roger E. Olson, *The Story of Christian Theology: Twenty Centuries of Tradition & Reform* (InterVarsity Press, 1999), 31–33.

172 Eric Voegelin, *The Collected Works of Eric Voegelin, Volume 17, Order and History: Volume IV, The Ecumenic Age* (Columbia, Missouri: University of Missouri Press, 2000), 335.

173 Carol E. Quillen, *Rereading the Renaissance: Petrarch, Augustine, and*

People like Joachim, Otto, Petrarca, in Voegelin's eyes, are forerunners of modern humanist intellectuals with Hegel coming at the climax. Voegelin wrote, "Hegel, finally, brought the potential to fruition by identifying revelation with a dialectical process of consciousness in history, a process that reached its *teleion* in his own 'system of science.' The Logos of Christ had achieved its full incarnation in the Logos of Hegel's 'absolute knowledge.' The transfiguration that had begun with the theophany in Paul's vision of the Resurrected was now completed in the egophany of the speculative thinker. The Parousia, at last, had occurred."[174]

One would feel unable to face such complex ideas and acts in history. A criterion might be of help in judging what is right or wrong. But people would not even agree on if such a criterion exists at all. Even if people agree on its existence, a criterion for one would not necessarily be for the other. All this would reinforce the impression about the complexity of the world. For Voegelin, what makes a big difference is whether the human being is the measure of all things, or God who created humans and everything else is the measure of all things. For those who live in today's world, "Man is the measure of all things" appears much better known than "God is the measure of all things." The former comes from Protagoras (c. 490–420 B.C.), an ancient Greek philosopher, and the latter, Plato (c. 428/427–348 B.C.). Voegelin more than once displayed the contrast between the two measures in his works including *Hellenism, Rome and Early Christianity, The New Science of Politics, The World of the Polis, Plato and Aristotle, The Ecumenic Age.*[175]

the Language of Humanism (University of Michigan Press, 1998), 8, 12; Theodore E. Mommsen, "Petrarch's Conception of the 'Dark Ages'" in *Speculum* Vol. 17, No. 2 (Apr., 1942), 226–42.

174 Eric Voegelin, *The Collected Works of Eric Voegelin, Volume 17, Order and History: Volume IV, The Ecumenic Age* (Columbia, Missouri: University of Missouri Press, 2000), 335–36.

175 Eric Voegelin, *The Collected Works of Eric Voegelin, Volume 19, History of Political Ideas: Volume I, Hellenism, Rome, and Early Christianity* (Columbia, Missouri: University of Missouri Press, 1997), 77; Eric Voegelin, *The Collected Works of Eric Voegelin, Volume 5, Modernity without Re-*

In his letter to Hannah Arendt (1906–1975) on March 16, 1951, Voegelin did this as well. He wrote, "whoever denies the Platonic 'God is the measure of all things' will find man as the measure."[176] Arendt was a Jew born in Germany. She escaped from the Nazi persecution and first arrived in France and then America. As a political theorist, Arendt published in 1951 *The Origins of Totalitarianism*, one of her most important works. She praised Voegelin's *Race and State* which appeared in 1933 as the "best historical account of race-thinking in the pattern of a 'history of ideas.'"[177]

Arendt sent a copy of *The Origins of Totalitarianism* via its publisher to Voegelin who was teaching at Louisiana State University. Voegelin's response to the book was a letter. Voegelin said Arendt had done a "penetrating (and incredibly detached, objective) treatment of the Jewish problem." Meanwhile, he suggested that Arendt go back to an earlier time saying "where modern anti-Semitism occurs it is a symptom of the decay of Christianity in the sociological sense, as a force that determines the character of civilization. The totalitarian movements would, in my opinion, have to be placed in the context of the decay of a Christian civilization; and the continuum of these destructive forces goes back to the medieval sectarian movement, at least as far back as the 12th century."

straint: *The Political Religions; The New Science of Politics; and Science, Politics, and Gnosticism* (Columbia, Missouri: University of Missouri Press, 2000), 142–43; Eric Voegelin, *Order and History: Volume Two, The World of the Polis* (Baton Rouge: Louisiana State University Press, 1957), 20, 109, 255, 273, 291, 295; Eric Voegelin, *The Collected Works of Eric Voegelin, Volume 16, Order and History: Volume III, Plato and Aristotle* (Columbia, Missouri: University of Missouri Press, 2000), 307–08; Eric Voegelin, *The Collected Works of Eric Voegelin, Volume 17, Order and History: Volume IV, The Ecumenic Age* (Columbia, Missouri: University of Missouri Press, 2000), 290–91.

176 Eric Voegelin, *The Collected Works of Eric Voegelin: Volume 30, Selected Correspondence, 1950–1984* (Columbia, Missouri: University of Missouri Press, 2007), 70.

177 Hannah Arendt, *The Origins of Totalitarianism* (Harvest Book, 1951), 158. Ellis Sandoz, Xu Zhiyue trans., *The Voegelinian Revolution: A Biographical Introduction (Second Edition)*, (Shanghai: Shanghai Joint Publishing Company, 2012), 303.

The "decay" Voegelin mentioned lies in the fact that "God is the measure of all things" was replaced by "Man is the measure of all things." For Voegelin, the relevant ideologies "were not harmless (and they still are not), but are symptoms of the kind of destruction of the person that is being carried out in the concentration camps."[178]

Such contrast is also presented in *Political Apocalypse: A Study of Dostoevsky's Grand Inquisitor*, a book Sandoz first published in 1971 based on his 1965 dissertation for the Dr. oec. publ. at the University of Munich. In the view of Sandoz, the nihilism, atheistic humanism, and socialism that Russian writer Fyodor Dostoevsky (1821–1881) faced in the 19th century is "in much the same way as" the Sophists Plato faced in the 4th century B.C. Confronting Protagoras' "Man is the measure of all things," Plato's "God is the measure of all things" echoed "like a thunderclap across more than twenty centuries of history, found consummate expression in the last great work of each writer, the *Laws* and *The Brothers Karamazov*."[179]

But despite of "God is the measure of all things," "Man is the measure of all things" seems to have been the mainstream of the world history. Even though the "apocalypse of man" has led to the "destruction of the person" on numerous occasions, "egophany" appears inevitable all the time. Even if Jesus Christ declared some two thousand years ago that "My kingdom is not of the world,"[180] there have always been people who, either voluntarily or involuntarily, have taken pains to build the kingdom of God in this world. What on earth could one do otherwise in this world?

In a 1965–1966 term lecture at the University of Munich, Voegelin spoke of Lamentations by quoting *Doctor Faustus* by German writer Thomas Mann (1875–1955). Voegelin pointed out that Mann's *Doctor Faustus* published in 1947 was "the great lamentation of a German over Germany." Yet, the lamentation "is not to be understood in any

---

178 Eric Voegelin, *The Collected Works of Eric Voegelin: Volume 30, Selected Correspondence, 1950–1984* (Columbia, Missouri: University of Missouri Press, 2007), 70.

179 Ellis Sandoz, *Political Apocalypse: A Study of Dostoevsky's Grand Inquisitor* (Wilmington, Delaware: ISI Books, 2000), xvii.

conventional sense" but "in the sense of the Biblical Lamentations of Jeremiah." It concerns not only "the atrocities of lesser evils of a period, but lamentations about man and his falling away from God." Voegelin went on to mention a few verses quoted from Lamentations in *Doctor Faustus*, "Why should a living man complain letter ... about the punishment of his sins? Let us test and examine our ways, and return to the Lord. We have transgressed and rebelled, and thou hast not forgiven. Thou hast wrapped thyself with anger and pursued us, slaying without pity. Thou hast made us filth and refuse among the nations."[181] For Voegelin, "Lament is not the return itself, but the insight into the defection and thus the beginning of the return ... lament is the language of suffering from estrangement—the Ecce-Homo stance."[182]

Ecce Homo, coming from John 19:5, is translated as "Behold the man" in the Bible of King James Version. It is what Pontius Pilate, the Roman governor of Judea, told the crowd who asked Jesus to be crucified. Before that, Pilate said: "Look, I am bringing him out to you to let you know that I find no basis for a charge against him." Then, "Jesus came out wearing the crown of thorns and the purple robe." That is when Pilate said this, "Behold the man!" The crowd's response, "As soon as the chief priests and their officials saw him, they shouted, 'Crucify! Crucify!'"[183] For Mann, lamentations are "a constant, inexhaustibly accentuated lament of the most painful Ecce-Homo variety." Voegelin's explanation is, "This suffering, however, belongs to the essence of man, for though it is man's destiny to be *imago Dei*, the possibility is also present not to live up to it—to fall away from it and to close oneself off. The dignity of the *imago Dei* encompasses the suffering of the Ecce-Homo."[184]

Here, Voegelin highlighted the serious corruption of language. Contrary to a corrupted language, in lament, "language restores itself through

---

180 John 18: 36.
181 Lamentations 3:39–45. Eric Voegelin, *The Collected Works of Eric Voegelin: Volume 12, Published Essays, 1966–1985* (Baton Rouge: Louisiana State University Press, 1990), 17.
182 *Ibid.*, 17.
183 John 19:4–6.
184 *Ibid.*

insight into its own character as expression of reality."[185] Voegelin said he lived "in an age of linguistic corruption."[186] Linguistic corruption lies in the fact that language and the thought it carries fail to reflect reality. It is a symptom of the spiritual disorder. The language of German philosopher Martin Heidegger (1889-1976) is an example Voegelin gave in his lecture about the German spiritual problem and the rise of National Socialism in Germany. Voegelin did not mention the name of Heidegger, but only said he was a famous philosopher and the author of Being and Time. And Voegelin deliberately did not choose "one of his pronouncements from the National Socialist period" but a part of *Being and Time* first published in 1927 that concerns "the nature of a sign." Voegelin pointed out that the philosophical language of Heidegger "transposes factual relationships of our everyday world into a linguistic medium that begins to take on an alliterative life of its own, and thus loses contact with the thing itself. Language and fact have somehow separated from one another, and thought has correspondingly become estranged from reality."[187]

Linguistic corruption is not alone. Voegelin also brought to mind religious corruption among the Christian church in Germany. An example in this regard is Martin Niemöller (1892–1984), a Lutheran pastor who had voted for Hitler but later was arrested because of his opposition to Hitler's control of the church. Niemöller is believed to be the original author of the famous statement "First they came ..." that repented of the inactivity of German intellectuals during and after the Nazi rise to power.[188] A source Voegelin used is an observer's report of the Niemöller trial in 1938. The report called Niemöller "a National Socialist." According to

185 *Ibid.*
186 *Ibid.*, 10.
187 *Ibid.*, 8–10.
188 Leo Stein, *Hitler came for Niemoeller: the Nazi War against religion* (New York: Fleming H. Revell Company, 1942; Gretna, Louisiana: Pelican Publishing Company, 2003); Milton Mayer, *They Thought They Were Free: The Germans, 1933–45* (Chicago: The University of Chicago Press, 1955, 1966), 168–69; Professor Harold Marcuse at University of California explored the origin of "First they came ...": http://www.history.ucsb.edu/faculty/marcuse/niem.htm.

this report, Niemöller "described how since 1924 he had always voted for the Nazi party" and he "read aloud two pages from *Mein Kampf*, then a chapter from the New Testament, and finally a sermon from the year 1932 on the leader question (*Führerfrage*)." Regarding the Jews, Niemöller "finds [them] foreign and distasteful." In his eyes, God's revelation "in the Jew Jesus of Nazareth" is "very painful and vexing state of affairs" but "must be accepted for the sake of the gospel." For Voegelin, Niemöller's problem is due to his juxtaposition of the word of the leader (*Führer*, referring to Hitler herein) and that of God and his interpretation of the Incarnation as God's revelation in a Jew instead of a human being. This distortion of the spirit no longer reflects a proper God-human relationship and thus this Christian faith is no longer the reality of faith.[189]

Throughout his life, "reality" was a word Voegelin used constantly. From his first book, *On the Form of the American Mind*, published in 1928, to his last article, "Quod Deus Dicitur," which he revised even in the afternoon before his death in the morning of January 19, 1985, Voegelin seemed to have always talked about the question of reality.[190] On November 22, 1978, Voegelin gave a talk at York University in Toronto, Canada. He explained that the word "reality" he used had a Greek root, ἀλήθεια (aletheia), literally meaning "unhidden" or "uncovered."[191]

189 Eric Voegelin, *The Collected Works of Eric Voegelin: Volume 12, Published Essays, 1966–1985* (Baton Rouge: Louisiana State University Press, 1990), 10–12; Eric Voegelin, *The Collected Works of Eric Voegelin: Volume 31, Hitler and the Germans* (Columbia, Missouri: University of Missouri Press, 1999).

190 Eric Voegelin, *The Collected Works of Eric Voegelin: Volume 34, Autobiographical Reflections: Revised Edition, with a Voegelin Glossary and Cumulative Index* (Columbia, Missouri: University of Missouri Press, 2006), 456–57; Eric Voegelin, *The Collected Works of Eric Voegelin: Volume 1, On the Form of the American Mind* (Baton Rouge: Louisiana State University Press, 1995), 12–271; Eric Voegelin, *The Collected Works of Eric Voegelin: Volume 12, Published Essays, 1966–1985* (Baton Rouge: Louisiana State University Press, 1990), 376–94.

191 Eric Voegelin, *The Collected Works of Eric Voegelin: Volume 34, Autobiographical Reflections: Revised Edition*, with a Voegelin Glossary and Cumulative Index (Columbia, Missouri: University of Missouri Press, 2006), 149.

Aletheia has a double meaning of "truth" and "reality." Briefly, truth is "reality becoming luminous for its structure" and "truth does not refer only to a reality outside of man and confronting man, but also to the process of reality in which man himself becomes an event, the event of the carrier of consciousness."[192]

Yet, one is not able to see the reality clearly whenever he or she faces the reality or takes part in it. On January 14, 1965, Voegelin delivered the Ingersoll Lecture entitled "Immortality: Experience and Symbol" at Harvard Divinity School. As a philosopher, Voegelin told his audience, "a philosophy of consciousness is not a substitute for revelation. For the philosopher is a man in search of truth; he is not God revealing truth." However, at the same time Voegelin said, "the philosopher can help to make revelation intelligible, but no more than that."[193] Here, one might see the difference between the philosophy in Voegelin's eyes and that in popular culture. For Voegelin, "philosophy by definition has its center in the experiences of transcendence."[194] In a New Year's Day letter of 1953 to a friend, Voegelin wrote, "Philosophizing seems to me to be in essence the interpretation of experiences of transcendence."[195] God's revelation is the source of "transcendence." In this regard, Voegelin borrowed from Plato a word to help make sense of the reality in which human beings live. It is μεταξύ (metaxy), literally meaning "in-between." This word appeared in Plato's *Symposium and Philebus*.[196] In

192 Eric Voegelin, *The Collected Works of Eric Voegelin: Volume 33, The Drama of Humanity and other Miscellaneous Papers, 1939–1985* (Columbia, Missouri: University of Missouri Press, 2004), 357.

193 Eric Voegelin, *The Collected Works of Eric Voegelin: Volume 12, Published Essays, 1966–1985* (Baton Rouge: Louisiana State University Press, 1990), 79.

194 Eric Voegelin, *The Collected Works of Eric Voegelin: Volume 15, Order and History: Volume 2, The World of the Polis* (Columbia, Missouri: University of Missouri Press, 2000), 349.

195 Eric Voegelin, *The Collected Works of Eric Voegelin: Volume 30, Selected Correspondence, 1950–1984* (Columbia, Missouri: University of Missouri Press, 2007), 122–23.

196 Eric Voegelin, *The Collected Works of Eric Voegelin: Volume 12, Published Essays, 1966–1985* (Baton Rouge: Louisiana State University Press, 1990), 279–81.

the Chinese translation of *Autobiographical Reflections* and *The Voege-linian Revolution*, Daniel Hsu rendered *metaxy* into "间际" and "兼际" respectively, both pronounced as "jianji" but with different Chinese characters.[197]

In this lecture about immortality, Voegelin drew his audience's gaze not only to "in-between" but also further to God's revelation in Jesus Christ. If "in-between" captures the reality of human existence from the direction of a human being seeking God, the full divinity and full humanity of Jesus Christ is God's revelation to human beings about the reality of human existence from the direction of the Incarnation. Voegelin did this by quoting Chalcedon Definition in A.D. 451, "Our Lord Jesus Christ ... truly God and truly man ... recognized in two natures ... the distinction of natures being in no way annulled by the union, but rather the characteristics of each nature being preserved and coming together to form one person and subsistence." In this sense of the Incarnation, Voegelin said: "History is Christ written large." It is just as from the direction of human beings, Plato's Republic considered the republic "man written large."[198]

In a 1970 article, "Equivalences of Experience and Symbolization in History," Voegelin elaborated on this state of "in-between" by penetrating the tension in it: "The question of constants in the history of mankind, it will have become clear, cannot be answered through propositions concerning right order, or through a catalog of permanent values, for the flux of existence does not have the structure of order or, for that matter, of disorder, but the structure of a tension between truth and deformation of reality. Not the possession of his humanity but the concern about its full realization is the lot of man. Existence has the structure of the In-Between, of the Platonic *metaxy*, and if anything is constant in the history of mankind it is the language of tension between

---

197 Eric Voegelin, Ellis Sandoz ed., Xu Zhiyue trans., *Autobiographical Reflections* (Beijing: Huaxia Press, 2009), 73 Ellis Sandoz, Xu Zhiyue trans., *The Voegelinian Revolution: A Biographical Introduction (Second Edition)*, (Shanghai: Shanghai Joint Publishing Company, 2012), 183.

198 Eric Voegelin, *The Collected Works of Eric Voegelin: Volume 12, Published Essays, 1966–1985* (Baton Rouge: Louisiana State University Press, 1990), 78–79.

life and death, immortality and mortality, perfection and imperfection, time and timelessness; between order and disorder, truth and untruth, sense and senselessness of existence; between *amor Dei* and *amor sui*, *l'âme ouverte* and *l'âme close*; between the virtues of openness toward the ground of being such as faith, love, and hope, and the vices of enfolding closure such as hubris and revolt; between the moods of joy and despair; and between alienation in its double meaning of alienation from the world and alienation from God."[199]

Voegelin went on to caution that "if we split these pairs of symbols, and hypostatize the poles of the tension as independent entities, we destroy the reality of existence as it has been experienced by the creators of the tensional symbolisms."[200] The metastatic apocalypse Voegelin often spoke of is one of the examples manifesting such splitting. Even facing God's revelation in Jesus Christ, one could not help turning a blind eye to the tension of the full divinity and full humanity in Jesus Christ by focusing on either pole of the tension. Various kinds of such splitting would result in a misunderstanding of God's reality and hence the deformation of the reality of humanity and the wider world.[201]

All this might bring to mind a letter that played a foundational role in helping establish Chalcedon Definition. It was written by the bishop of Rome, Leo I (c. 391/400–461), to the bishop of Constantinople, Flavian (?–449) on June 13, A.D. 449.[202] One paragraph of the letter is especially relevant to the tension Voegelin highlighted: "Since ... the characteristic properties of both (divine and human) natures and

---

199 Eric Voegelin, *The Collected Works of Eric Voegelin: Volume 12, Published Essays, 1966–1985* (Baton Rouge: Louisiana State University Press, 1990), 119–120.

200 *Ibid.*, 120.

201 Eric Voegelin, *The Collected Works of Eric Voegelin: Volume 34, Autobiographical Reflections: Revised Edition, with a Voegelin Glossary and Cumulative Index* (Columbia, Missouri: University of Missouri Press, 2006), 167–68.

202 Mark A. Noll, *Turning Points: Decisive Moments in the History of Christianity* (Grand Rapids: Baker Academic, 2003), 75; This letter is historically called *The Tome*, with one of its English translations:http://www. ccel.org/ccel/schaff/npnf212.ii.iv.xxviii.html .

substances are kept intact and come together in one person, lowliness is taken on by majesty, weakness by power, mortality by eternity, and the nature which cannot be harmed is united to the nature which suffers, in order that the debt which our condition involves may be discharged. In this way, as our salvation requires, one and the same mediator between God and human beings, the human being who is Jesus Christ, can at one and the same time die in virtue of the one nature and, in virtue of the other, be incapable of death. That is why true God was born in the integral and complete nature of a true human being, entire in what belongs to him and entire in what belongs to us."[203]

If "History is Christ written large," then one might see how God has revealed his creation, redemption and governance through Christ in the history of one's life, the humanity and the wider world. One might see how God has helped his human beings who were created in his image to see his image through Christ. One might see how God has helped his human beings, finite creatures by nature, to enjoy the immortality of being with the infinite creator through Christ. In this history, human beings live not just in this world nor out of the world but between the eternity of God and the transience of humanity through Christ. In this sense, it is no surprise to see Voegelin telling Sandoz about the philosophy of history in the final chapter of *Autobiographical Reflections*, "Eschatology and Philosophy: The Practice of Dying," this way: "Hence, every philosophy of history must take cognizance of the fact that the process of history is not immanent but moves in the In-Between of this worldly and other-worldly reality. Moreover, this In-Between character of the process is experienced, not as a structure in infinite time, but as a movement that will eschatologically end in a state beyond the In-Between and beyond time. No philosophy of history can be considered to be seriously dealing with the problems of history unless it acknowledges the fundamental eschatological character of the process."[204]

203 Mark A. Noll, *Turning Points: Decisive Moments in the History of Christianity* (Grand Rapids: Baker Academic, 2003), 78; Richard A. Norris Jr., trans. and ed., *The Christological Controversy* (Philadelphia: Fortress, 1980), 148.

204 Eric Voegelin, Ellis Sandoz ed., Xu Zhiyue trans., *Autobiographical Reflections* (Beijing: Huaxia Press, 2009), 123. There is some change to the

Jesus told human beings nearly two thousand years ago: "Repent, for the kingdom of heaven is near."[205] Since then, various names have been given to the age in which human beings live. For Voegelin, the end of this world seems to be the most accurate description. As a human being who considered the center of philosophy to be the experiences of transcendence, Voegelin thought what a philosopher did was "the practice of dying." In his view, "the practice of dying" is in fact "the practice of immortalizing." In the eschatological tension, the understanding of the reality of human existence would "become luminous." But this "does not mean that the nature of man can be transfigured within history." In other words, the "consciousness of the eschatological expectation is an ordering factor in existence; and it makes possible the understanding of man's existence as that of the viator in the Christian sense—the wanderer, the pilgrim toward eschatological perfection—but this pilgrimage still is a pilgrim's progress in this world."[206]

The "metaxy" first appeared in Voegelin's published works in 1964.[207] That was in a German article, "Ewiges Sein in der Zeit." It was translated into English as "Eternal Being in Time" by Gerhart Niemeyer (1907-1997), a political philosopher who left his native Germany after Hitler came to power in 1933 and later became a professor at the University of Notre Dame. In that article, Voegelin said metaxy was an experience of "a meeting of time with eternity, and of man and God." Like his Harvard lecture on immortality, Voegelin in that article differentiated

Chinese translation in the Chinese version of this writing; Eric Voegelin, *The Collected Works of Eric Voegelin: Volume 34, Autobiographical Reflections: Revised Edition, with a Voegelin Glossary and Cumulative Index* (Columbia, Missouri: University of Missouri Press, 2006), 147.

205 Matthew 4: 17.

206 Eric Voegelin, Ellis Sandoz ed., Xu Zhiyue trans., *Autobiographical Reflections* (Beijing: Huaxia Press, 2009), 123. There is some change to the Chinese translation in the Chinese version of this writing; Eric Voegelin, *The Collected Works of Eric Voegelin: Volume 34, Autobiographical Reflections: Revised Edition, with a Voegelin Glossary and Cumulative Index* (Columbia, Missouri: University of Missouri Press, 2006), 147.

207 Eric Voegelin, *The Collected Works of Eric Voegelin, Volume 17, Order and History: Volume IV, The Ecumenic Age* (Columbia, Missouri: University of Missouri Press, 2000), 24.

between philosophy and revelation with the former from the direction of "the human seeking-and-receiving pole" and the latter from the direction of "the divine giving-and-commanding pole."[208]

From 1964 on, "metaxy" was frequently used in Voegelin's late life. Other than "Eternal Being in Time," "Immortality: Experience and Symbol" and "Equivalences of Experience and Symbolization in History," many of Voegelin's essays had "metaxy" as a crucial viewpoint in exploring politics and history. They include "The Gospel and Culture" in 1971, "On Hegel: A History in Sorcery" in the same year, "Reason: The Classic Experience" in 1974, "Response to Professor Altizer's 'A New History and a New but Ancient God?'" in 1975, "Wisdom and the Magic of the Extreme: A Meditation" in 1983, and his swan-song, "Quod Deus Dicitur."[209] Of course, in the last two volumes of *Order and History*— *The Ecumenic Age* and *In Search of Order*—"metaxy" also figured prominently.[210]

It is true that Voegelin did not borrow "metaxy" from Plato until late in his life. Yet, he had already expressed his understanding of this situation when he was young. In 1933, 32-year-old Voegelin published his third book, *The History of the Race Idea: From Ray to Carus*. He pointed out in its introduction that man "stands between God and the subhuman world" and this "intermediate status" is not "a self-contained existence" but participates in "both the higher and the lower world." He said "By virtue of his soul, man is united with the divine *pneuma*; his *sarx*, he partakes of transitoriness; his existence is 'inauthentic' [*uneigentlich*]. The condition of his existence is that of being lost, an existence from

---

208 Eric Voegelin, *The Collected Works of Eric Voegelin, Volume 6, Anamnesis: On the Theory of History and Politics* (Columbia, Missouri: University of Missouri Press, 2002), 312, 324, 329, 332, 335.

209 For these essays, see: Eric Voegelin, *The Collected Works of Eric Voegelin: Volume 12, Published Essays, 1966–1985* (Baton Rouge: Louisiana State University Press, 1990).

210 Eric Voegelin, *The Collected Works of Eric Voegelin, Volume 17, Order and History: Volume IV, The Ecumenic Age* (Columbia, Missouri: University of Missouri Press, 2000); Eric Voegelin, *The Collected Works of Eric Voegelin, Volume 18, Order and History: Volume V, In Search of Order* (Columbia, Missouri: University of Missouri Press, 1999).

which he must be freed in order to ascend to the realm of his true existence with his 'authentic' nature."[211]

Then, the words of Voegelin mingled with the quotes from *Imitation of Christ* of Thomas à Kempis (c. 1380–1471), a German monk: "Man must live according to the example of Christ and follow Him," " 'Take care therefore to withdraw your heart from love of what is visible, allowing it to center on things unseen,'" "The most important event in man's life is death; he must arrange his days with death in mind," "Every day is to be lived as if it were the last, and the soul should always be anxious for the world beyond the senses. Perfect calm of the soul can be found only in the eternal gaze upon God—'sed non est hoc possible, durante me in hac mortalitate' [but this is not possible while I am in this mortal state]." Immediately after this, Voegelin explained why earthly existence is to be called "mortal"—"not because life ends in death but because the quality of *mortalitas* makes the whole duration of life something contemptible, unreal, from which the soul is liberated into a higher life, a higher reality" which is manifested in "heavenly glory" in life after death. Only there can humans look upon God's glory face to face and "taste the Word of God made flesh."[212]

It might be puzzling to see the author of a book exploring the history of the race idea begin his writing by outlining his thoughts about life and death. But if reading just a little further, one would find that Voegelin wanted to sketch out his idea concerning "the image of man" or rather, what on earth man is, through sharing his comments about life and death. Voegelin went on to use the angle of German philosopher Immanuel Kant (1724–1804) to express astonishment that "philosophers could ever have come up with the idea that so imperfect and transitory a creature as man could ever fulfill the meaning of his life in his earthly existence and not need the hope of a life after death to perfect his faculties." Voegelin then sighed, "the Christian idea of the coming of the Kingdom of God is so secularized that the kingdom of perfected man is envisioned as attainable

---

211 Eric Voegelin, *The Collected Works of Eric Voegelin, Volume 3, The History of the Race Idea: From Ray to Carus* (Baton Rouge: Louisiana State University Press, 1990), 4.
212 *Ibid.*, 4–5.

on earth in an unending historical process; on the infinitely distant temporal horizon the kingdom evolved on earth and the one effected by God come together." After this, Voegelin returned to Kant. He said the thought of the German philosopher himself was vacillating and conflicting and it constituted "the first step on the way to a reworking of an image of man increasingly distant from the Christian one." For Kant "sees the kingdom of heaven as a remote, earthly one," though "life in this world is imperfect, a perfect existence in turn can only be conceived as an earthly existence—an otherworldly life, after careful reflection, seems to Kant to be only an imperfect substitute for life on this earth."[213]

One might see from here that the young Voegelin had already reflected on the deformation of the worldview brought by the Enlightenment. A key point lies in how to capture the reality of human beings through life and death. Obviously, such a Christian idea as "not of the world" nor "out of the world" had a lifelong impact on Voegelin.[214] In a book published in 2006, *Republicanism, Religion, and the Soul of America*, Sandoz recalled how Voegelin arranged his Lutheran form of funeral. Voegelin asked that two New Testament passages be read for his interment service. One was "Verily, verily, I say unto you, except a grain of wheat fall into the ground and die, it abides alone: but if it die, it brings forth much fruit. He that loves his life shall lose it; and he that hates his life in this world shall keep it unto life eternal"; The other, "Love not the world, neither the things that are in the world. If any man love the world, the love of the Father is not in him. For all that is in the world, the lust of the flesh, and the lust of the eyes, and the pride of life, is not of the Father, but is of the world. And the world passes away, and the lust thereof: but he that does the will of God abides forever." Sandoz's recollection continued: "When Eric's wife, Lissy, asked him why he would want that second passage read, he is said to have replied, 'for repentance.'" The one who witnessed this scene was not Sandoz, but Paul Caringella.[215] In the

213 *Ibid.*, 5–6.
214 John 17: 14–15.
215 Ellis Sandoz, *Republicanism, Religion, and the Soul of America* (Columbia, Missouri: University of Missouri Press, 2006), 116. The former passage is John 12: 24–25; the latter, 1 John 2: 15–17.

last six years of Voegelin's life in this world, Caringella was his assistant. It was due to Caringella, a visiting fellow at Hoover Institution, who "took down the dictation from an almost inaudible voice" of Voegelin that "Quod Deus Dicitur," Voegelin's last work, reached paper.[216] Caringella is also one of the four members of the editorial board of *The Collected Works of Eric Voegelin.*

Since 2006 when I first came to read Voegelin and Sandoz, I have seen this account of Voegelin's funeral arrangement a number of times. But it was when I began this piece of writing in late 2012 and early 2013 that it impressed me most. Over this period of time, a passage of 1 Corinthians 15 often came to my mind—"What you sow does not come to life unless it dies. When you sow, you do not plant the body that will be, but just a seed, perhaps of wheat or of something else. But God gives it a body as he has determined, and to each kind of seed he gives its own body. All flesh is not the same: Men have one kind of flesh, animals have another, birds another and fish another. There are also heavenly bodies and there are earthly bodies; but the splendor of the heavenly bodies is one kind, and the splendor of the earthly bodies is another. The sun has one kind of splendor, the moon another and the stars another; and star differs from star in splendor. So will it be with the resurrection of the dead. The body that is sown is perishable, it is raised imperishable; it is sown in dishonor, it is raised in glory; it is sown in weakness, it is raised in power; it is sown a natural body, it is raised a spiritual body. If there is a natural body, there is also a spiritual body. So it is written: 'The first Adam became a living being'; the last Adam, a life-giving spirit. The spiritual did not come first, but the natural, and after that the spiritual. The first man was of the dust of the earth, the second man from heaven. As was the earthly man, so are those who are of the earth; and as is the man from heaven, so also are those who are of heaven. And just as we have borne the likeness of the earthly man, so shall we bear the likeness of the man from heaven. I declare to you, brothers, that flesh and blood cannot inherit the kingdom of God, nor does the perishable

---

216 Eric Voegelin, *The Collected Works of Eric Voegelin: Volume 12, Published Essays, 1966–1985* (Baton Rouge: Louisiana State University Press, 1990), 376.

inherit the imperishable. Listen, I tell you a mystery: We will not all sleep, but we will all be changed—in a flash, in the twinkling of an eye, at the last trumpet. For the trumpet will sound, the dead will be raised imperishable, and we will be changed. For the perishable must clothe itself with the imperishable, and the mortal with immortality. When the perishable has been clothed with the imperishable, and the mortal with immortality, then the saying that is written will come true: 'Death has been swallowed up in victory.' 'Where, O death, is your victory? Where, O death, is your sting?' The sting of death is sin, and the power of sin is the law. But thanks be to God! He gives us the victory through our Lord Jesus Christ. Therefore, my dear brothers, stand firm. Let nothing move you. Always give yourselves fully to the work of the Lord, because you know that your labor in the Lord is not in vain."[217]

That I quoted this long passage here is not just because Voegelin mentioned the death of "a grain of wheat" and eternal life before he died, nor just because he said in *The Ecumenic Age* that when "reading the First Letter to the Corinthians, I have always the feeling of traveling with Paul, from *phthora* to *aphtharsia* in a homogeneous medium of reality,"[218] but also because reading this long passage as well as the works of Voegelin and Sandoz has made an impact on my own understanding of life, death, and the reality of human existence. When I sent my first email to Professor Sandoz consulting him about the history of freedom at about eight o'clock in the morning of February 19, 2006, I did not expect I would receive his reply less than four hours later. Even far beyond my expectation, our correspondence would still continue seven years after that and I would be baptized in a church after getting to know Professor Sandoz and later Daniel Hsu who unexpectedly helped me find this church. Without all these surprises, I could not imagine I would

217 1 Corinthians 15: 36–58.
218 Eric Voegelin, *The Collected Works of Eric Voegelin, Volume 17, Order and History: Volume IV, The Ecumenic Age* (Columbia, Missouri: University of Missouri Press, 2000), 312; Ellis Sandoz, Xu Zhiyue trans., *The Voegelinian Revolution: A Biographical Introduction (Second Edition)*, (Shanghai: Shanghai Joint Publishing Company, 2012), 247; Ellis Sandoz, *The Voegelinian Revolution: A Biographical Introduction* (New Brunswick, New Jersey: Transaction Publishers, 2000), 237.

somewhat get to understand what the books Professor Sandoz gave me were all about. Without these surprises, I could not imagine I would be able to begin writing down what I have learned from my initial reading of these books. Without these surprises, I could not imagine these books, 1 Corinthians and many other books of the Bible would make me begin to know afresh about myself and the wider world.

When I read Sandoz's preface to the Chinese edition of *The Voegelinian Revolution*, "the shadow" it mentioned brought to mind "the reality" that often appeared in the works of Voegelin. When I saw "the reality," I would think of "the shadow." If it were just a few years ago, I would not have been sensitive to the contrast between these two words. Only over the recent couple of years did the contrast start taking shape in my mind. It all began towards the end of 2010. That was when my English Bible study group was reading Colossians. Before that, we had spent about one year and a half finishing Genesis. We met every Monday evening. We used the New International Version. During the weeks on Colossians, one verse caught my eyes. It was, "These are a shadow of the things that were to come; the reality, however, is found in Christ."[219] In other popular versions like the King James Version, the translation would read, "Which are a shadow of things to come; but the body is of Christ." What makes the two versions different here lies in the verse's latter half. If turning to the original Greek version, one would see the King James Version might be closer to the literal meaning.[220] In Greek, "the body" is σῶμα (soma), which also means "the substance." But "the reality" in the New International Version unexpectedly helped bring "a shadow" to my attention. Since then, the contrast between "the reality" and "the shadow" has seemed to become ever alive in my life. If using my own words to express what I have learned, is that only in Christ could one see the reality of the world, or more straightforwardly, only Christ is the reality.

And yet then, I did not expect this impression would be made even deeper in the following two years. After Colossians, my English Bible study fellowship took more than a year to do Exodus. After that, it was

---

219 Colossians 2:17.
220 See the Greek: http://www.scripture4all.org/OnlineInterlinear/NTpdf/col2.pdf .

Galatians, and Matthew. In the first half of 2012, we came to the last 15 chapters of Exodus. The contrast between "the shadow" and "the reality" resurfaced when we studied how the LORD told Moses to make a sanctuary for the LORD himself to dwell in. The copy of the Bible I have been using has a cross-reference system. It pointed to Hebrews 8:5 when I took a closer look at Exodus 25:9, 40. After turning to Hebrews 8:5, I found this verse just explained what the two verses in Exodus mean—"They serve at a sanctuary that is a copy and shadow of what is in heaven. This is why Moses was warned when he was about to build the tabernacle: 'See to it that you make everything according to the pattern shown you on the mountain.'"[221] Previously, the chapters about building the tabernacle in Exodus read like a pedestrian account concerning architectural engineering. But in the context of the Hebrews response, all this took on a different look. The history in Exodus appears in a far wider dimension. Though it was made exactly according to the pattern God showed Moses, the tabernacle was not the real one but "a copy and shadow of what is in heaven."[222] And what is the real tabernacle? The first two verses of Hebrews have made it clear, "The point of what we are saying is this: We do have such a high priest, who sat down at the right hand of the throne of the Majesty in heaven, and who serves in the sanctuary, the true tabernacle set up by the Lord, not by man."[223] The contrast between "the reality" and "the shadow" not only resurfaced before my eyes but also the tension between them was striking.

If the tabernacle in Exodus is but "a copy and shadow of what is in heaven," then the things that are not made according to the pattern God shows cannot even be counted as "a shadow" of "the reality." They might be counted as among "the shadow" Sandoz pointed out in his preface to the Chinese edition of *The Voegelinian Revolution*. If it could be expressed in the Voegelinian way, what makes the things among "the shadow" that is not of "the reality" is that they are not projected from "theophany" but "egophany." If one does not know "the reality" and its

---

221 Hebrews 8:5; Exodus 25:9, 40.

222 See the Greek: http://www.scripture4all.org/OnlineInterlinear/NTpdf/heb8.pdf.

223 Hebrews 8:1–2.

"shadow," he or she would not recognize "the shadow" that is not of "the reality" but would count it as "the shadow" of "the reality" or even "the reality" itself. For anyone who lives in the shadow but wants to know the reality, the life of Voegelin might be a heartening encouragement. Like many of his contemporaries, Voegelin lived in the shadow that is not of the reality. But unlike many of them, he bore a unique witness to a life-long journey in recapturing the reality. In Voegelin, the difference lies not just in "God is the measure of all things" instead of "Man is the measure of all things," but the image of God in his mind is much less from the human imagination than from God's revelation through Christ.

The difference was shown in the older Voegelin's asking for the two passages of the Bible to be read at his funeral "for repentance." It was also reflected in young Voegelin's particular attachment to *Imitation of Christ*. For Voegelin, "History is Christ written large," and the gospel is "the truth of reality."[224] For him, the message of "For in Christ all the fullness of the Deity lives in bodily form"[225] is about the "divine reality," which is only manifested fully in Christ since Christ is "the image of the invisible God, the firstborn over all creation" and "the head over every power and authority."[226] The "divine reality" revealed only in Christ is the ground upon which the reality of all the things created is based, and hence ultimately real.[227] The "divine reality" has a two-fold meaning for human beings: on the one hand, human beings "have been given fullness in Christ";[228] on the other hand, God is "beyond the In-Between of existence."[229]

---

224 Eric Voegelin, *The Collected Works of Eric Voegelin: Volume 12, Published Essays, 1966–1985* (Baton Rouge: Louisiana State University Press, 1990), 211.
225 Colossians 2:9.
226 Eric Voegelin, *The Collected Works of Eric Voegelin: Volume 12, Published Essays, 1966–1985* (Baton Rouge: Louisiana State University Press, 1990), 192–93. Colossians 1:15; 2:10.
227 Eric Voegelin, *The Collected Works of Eric Voegelin: Volume 34, Autobiographical Reflections: Revised Edition, with a Voegelin Glossary and Cumulative Index* (Columbia, Missouri: University of Missouri Press, 2006), 177.
228 Colossians 2:10.
229 Eric Voegelin, *The Collected Works of Eric Voegelin: Volume 12, Published Essays, 1966–1985* (Baton Rouge: Louisiana State University Press, 1990), 193.

To a considerable extent, what led Voegelin to prefer such words as "reality" and "divine reality" to more popular ones like "truth" and "God" is because the latter were so abused that they have lost its original meanings in the world Voegelin lived in. In *Autographical Reflections*, Voegelin took a whole chapter to discuss this problem with Sandoz. It is entitled, "Why Philosophize? To Recapture Reality!" From the question mark and the exclamation mark here, one might be able to feel the emotional way Voegelin spoke about the matter.[230]

For Voegelin, linguistic corruption is not unique to the modern age that is inundated by various ideologies. Similar ages include the time when Plato confronted the Sophists. Voegelin called the corrupted language "idols" by borrowing the classification from British philosopher Francis Bacon (1561–1626). He also mentioned Russian writer Alexander Solzhenitsyn (1918–2008) who, in his 1967 novel *Cancer Ward*, "had to fall back on Bacon and his conception of idols in order to defend the reality of Reason in his own existence against the impact of Communist dogma." In comparison, linguistic corruption in America is not reflected in the situation like that in the then Soviet Union where the authorities controlled scholars, but in what Voegelin said "the intellectual terrorism of institutions." The institutions here include "the mass media, university departments, foundations, and commercial publishing houses." Despite this, Voegelin pointed out that "science can continue, and even flourish" in America where "our Soviet Writer's Union cannot enlist governmental power for the purpose of suppressing scholars," and hence, "there are always enclaves in the West."[231]

---

230 Eric Voegelin, Ellis Sandoz ed., Xu Zhiyue trans., *Autobiographical Reflections* (Beijing: Huaxia Press, 2009), 94–108; Eric Voegelin, *The Collected Works of Eric Voegelin: Volume 34, Autobiographical Reflections: Revised Edition, with a Voegelin Glossary and Cumulative Index* (Columbia, Missouri: University of Missouri Press, 2006), 118–126.

231 Eric Voegelin, Ellis Sandoz ed., Xu Zhiyue trans., *Autobiographical Reflections* (Beijing: Huaxia Press, 2009), 94–95. There is some change to the Chinese translation in the Chinese version of this writing; Eric Voegelin, *The Collected Works of Eric Voegelin: Volume 34, Autobiographical Reflections: Revised Edition, with a Voegelin Glossary and Cumulative Index* (Columbia, Missouri: University of Missouri Press, 2006), 118–19.

When I got to know Professor Sandoz in 2006, a major question I asked him was relevant to why "there are always enclaves in the West." The West here mainly refers to North America and West Europe. Professor Sandoz gave me his first reply by attaching a draft of his John Witherspoon Lecture delivered in Washington D.C. in 2004. John Witherspoon (1723–1794) was president of the College of New Jersey, later Princeton University. Among the 56 signatories of the Declaration of Independence, Witherspoon was the only active clergyman and the only college president. Sandoz's lecture, "Republicanism and Religion: Some Contextual Considerations," is also a part of his book published later in 2006, *Republicanism, Religion, and the Soul of America*. Around 2006, I consulted hundreds of experts and scholars in various fields across the world about how and why individual liberty under the rule of law was first institutionalized in the West and why it has survived there as nowhere else. Among the responses I have received, Professor Sandoz's is rare. Even among those who value Christianity or the Christian faith, his analysis is somewhat different.

In his John Witherspoon Lecture, Sandoz pointed out: "It is this ever-present balanced living tension with the divine Ground above all else, perhaps, that has made the United States so nearly immune politically to the ideological and eschatological maladies that have ravaged the modern world, such as fascism and Marxism and now Islamism."[232] Here, Sandoz apparently borrowed from the way Voegelin analyzed the world to interpret the characteristics of American politics. The "divine Ground" is similar to "divine reality" but the "Ground" with a capital G places emphasis on a point that this reality is the supreme reality for all the created reality to be grounded upon.[233] And "the ideological and eschatological maladies" belong to the symptoms of what Voegelin called "egophany" that deforms and eclipses the reality. The "eschatological" here is not of the biblical eschatology but of "the metastatic apocalypse."

232 Ellis Sandoz, *Republicanism, Religion, and the Soul of America* (Columbia, Missouri: University of Missouri Press, 2006), 49.
233 Eric Voegelin, *The Collected Works of Eric Voegelin: Volume 34, Autobiographical Reflections: Revised Edition, with a Voegelin Glossary and Cumulative Index* (Columbia, Missouri: University of Missouri Press, 2006), 161.

A little more specifically, "this ever-present balanced living tension with the divine Ground" Sandoz pointed out is shown in two aspects. In the American political environment, "the historically affirmed vocation of a special people under God still could be pursued through active devotion to public good, liberty, and justice solidly grounded in Judaeo-Christian transcendentalism. Citizens were at the same time self-consciously also pilgrims aware that this world is not their home, that they were merely sojourners passing through this mysterious process of historical existence in the attitude of *homo viator*, since nothing better than hope through faith avails them."[234] In the tension between the two aspects, America nearly avoided being drawn into radicalism. Radicalism here includes all kinds of ideologies based upon "egophany" since the Enlightenment,[235] and such sentiments as considering America "the new Israel or chosen people and even the site of the inauguration of the thousand-year reign of God's saints on earth."[236]

Sandoz enumerated the factors that make America different. He wrote, "Advocates of republicanism in the Anglo-American Whig tradition (to be distinguished firmly from French Jacobinism, which was both atheistic and anti-property) assert liberty and justice in resistance against tyranny and arbitrary government and do so in the name of highest truth." He stressed that the former had "a religious and specifically Protestant Christian root."[237] British writer John Milton (1608–1674) and British politician Algernon Sidney (1623–1683) were mentioned as two main examples who were significant in the spread of the Whig Republicanism.[238] Then Sandoz portrayed a larger historical scene by

---

234 Ellis Sandoz, *Republicanism, Religion, and the Soul of America* (Columbia, Missouri: University of Missouri Press, 2006), 49.

235 *Ibid.*, 2–3.

236 Ellis Sandoz, *Republicanism, Religion, and the Soul of America* (Columbia, Missouri: University of Missouri Press, 2006), 42–46. Revelation 20: 1–6.

237 Ellis Sandoz, *Republicanism, Religion, and the Soul of America* (Columbia, Missouri: University of Missouri Press, 2006), 4. Protestant derives from "protestantem" meaning "one who publicly declares or protests" that refers to Christians protesting Roman Catholic orthodoxy.

238 *Ibid.*, 4–6.

quoting a point of British historian George Trevelyan (1876–1962) that the Bible played the most important role in shaping the British spiritual world since the sixteenth century. In this regard, Sandoz particularly referred to the pioneering work of John Wycliffe (1320–1384) and William Tyndale (1492–1536) in the translation of Scripture into English.[239]

John Wycliffe was an early proponent of reform in the Roman Catholic Church and William Tyndale a leading figure during the Protestant Reformation. Both paid a heavy price for the English Bible translation. Tyndale even was executed as a heretic. Both the Popes and European governments then almost forbade any vernacular Bible translation without permission. Only the authorized Latin version, the Vulgate, was legal. They thought any unauthorized translation would misrepresent the original meaning. Tyndale's translation from the original Hebrew and Greek turned out to be a major source of the King James Version published in 1611. Apart from the unfinished part in the Old Testament owing to his execution, the majority of the popular KJV is out of Tyndale's single-handed work.[240] For Sandoz, the translations of Scripture and their spread show the formation of Christian egalitarianism in Britain.[241] This conviction further led to the rise of democracy in America. Sandoz traced Christian egalitarianism to a time earlier than Wycliffe and Tyndale. Around 1000, an author known as "Anglo-Norman Anonymous" elaborated on the idea of "the priesthood of all (baptized) believers" in *York Tractates*.[242]

Against all this backdrop, Sandoz went on to highlight a foundational role the Great Awakening starting in 1730 played in moulding the American spirituality. He explained how the theology and sermons of

---

239 *Ibid.*, 12–13.
240 David Daniell, *The Bible in English: Its History and Influence* (New Haven: Yale University Press, 2003), 448.
241 Sandoz here referred to 1 Peter 2:9, "But you are a chosen people, a royal priesthood, a holy nation, a people belonging to God, that you may declare the praises of him who called you out of darkness into his wonderful light."
242 Ellis Sandoz, *Republicanism, Religion, and the Soul of America* (Columbia, Missouri: University of Missouri Press, 2006), 13. For *York Tractates*, see http://normananonymous.org/ENAP/ToC.jsp , especially 24c.

such theologians as John Wesley (1703–1791) and Jonathan Edwards (1703–1758) helped strengthen the personal intimacy with God among Christians in America. Sandoz emphasized that the rich experience of God—rather than doctrines and just one side of experience—constituted the common ground of the two theologians. "Knowledge of, obedience to, and delight in God all presuppose, reinforce, and interpenetrate one another," forming "a creative and dynamic equipoise." Sandoz quoted a study of Wesley and Edwards by Richard B. Steele, a theologian saying, "One who claims to know God without obeying him is an antinomian ... to know God without loving him, a rationalist...to obey God without loving him, a Pharisee ... to love God without obeying him, a hypocrite ... to love or obey God without knowing the Scriptures in which he is revealed, an illuminist."[243] Sandoz also mentioned George Whitefield (1714–1770), a well-known evangelist whose view about free will and predestination was different from Wesley's. Yet it is this difference that shows the richness in experiencing God and any side of experience in anyone's life would not represent the whole experience. But that does not mean there are no fundamentals, as Whitefield said, "Let a man go to the grammar school of faith and repentance, before he goes to the university of election and predestination. A bare head-knowledge of sound words availeth nothing. I am quite tired of Christless talkers."[244]

Seeing such a religious richness before the founding of the United States, Sandoz did not just focus on a few personalities. In 1991, he published *Political Sermons of the American Founding Era, 1730–1805*. With more than 1600 pages, it includes fifty-five sermons of fifty-five preachers, their brief biographies and introductions to the sermons. It would help today's readers to know about what those Christians of diverse backgrounds thought of politics in that turbulent time. But however different they were, they shared at least one common ground. In the book's foreword, Sandoz wrote, "all our writers agree that political liberty and religious truth are vitally intertwined." Sandoz elaborated on this point by not just borrowing from French sociologist Alexis de Tocqueville (1805–1859), it was religion that "gave birth to America," but

243 *Ibid.*, 30.
244 *Ibid.*, 39–40.

also quoting US historian Carl Bridenbaugh (1903–1992), for the Americans before the Revolution, "the very core of existence was their relation to God."[245]

In today's America, it appears not common for a political philosopher like Sandoz to look at politics from human's relation to God. It is just like what Voegelin said in his late life that an important problem facing America was "the intellectual terrorism of institutions." In Voegelin's philosophized language, a typical manifestation of this problem is like this, "The realities excluded can vary widely, but the one item that always has to be excluded is the experience of man's tension toward the divine ground of his existence."[246]

Sandoz recalled that his interest in this dimension went back to at least his undergraduate years. In *A Government of Laws: Political Theory, Religion, and the American Founding* published in 1990, Sandoz said he "was struck by the coincidence of concerns and insights of chief spokesmen of the American order and of the great classical philosophers of antiquity." He also found that "the In God We Trust imprinted on the coins in our pockets represented in laconic American fashion the report of a cultural consensus." It would be more difficult to understand the existence of the Americans if this consensus is ignored. But Sandoz wrote, "that contextual and existential dimension is routinely ignored in typical secularizing accounts of the American mind and culture, once the Puritan epoch of the seventeenth century is left behind."[247]

It was in such a secularizing intellectual environment that Sandoz ran across not only those authors who valued human's relation to God but also a professor on campus who would help him go even further in

245 Ellis Sandoz, *Political Sermons of the American Founding Era, 1730–1805* (Indianapolis, Indiana: Liberty Fund, 1991), xiv.

246 Eric Voegelin, Ellis Sandoz ed., Xu Zhiyue trans., *Autobiographical Reflections* (Beijing: Huaxia Press, 2009), 99; Eric Voegelin, *The Collected Works of Eric Voegelin: Volume 34, Autobiographical Reflections: Revised Edition, with a Voegelin Glossary and Cumulative Index* (Columbia, Missouri: University of Missouri Press, 2006), 123.

247 Ellis Sandoz, *A Government of Laws: Political Theory, Religion, and the American Founding* (Columbia, Missouri: University of Missouri Press, 2001), xi–xii.

this dimension. Sandoz cannot forget his first encounter with Voegelin—
"From the time I first heard him lecture, when I was a young undergraduate student in 1949, I never doubted that Voegelin was profoundly
Christian, whatever the ambiguities of his formal church affiliation."[248]
Interestingly, one of Sandoz's students also mentioned Sandoz's church
affiliation. In a letter to Sandoz in 2008, this student wrote: "When I was
in college I did not attend church regularly, but one Sunday I attended
First Baptist Church in Commerce[249] and you were there. I don't know
anything about your religious beliefs then or now, but your presence at
church said a great deal to me. It said that if a man with a mind and an
education like Dr. Sandoz can have a place for God in his life, then I,
too, can have a healthy life of both the mind and the spirit."[250]

This letter from one of Sandoz's students gives a glimpse of the
place of faith among the intellectuals in contemporary America. At least
some people would think that faith and intellect cannot coexist in a single person. A person of faith seems to be without intellect and a person
of intellect appears not to need faith. Most of the scholars I have contacted work at universities or research institutes in North America or Europe. Many hold a similar view about faith and intellect with those in
Europe seeming more notable. I once sent an early draft of my manuscript exploring the history of freedom to an influential political historian
whom I had gotten to know in 2006. This professor gave me a prompt
and kind reply as he had before. He said the book "would I feel sure be

---

248 Ellis Sandoz, *Republicanism, Religion, and the Soul of America* (Columbia, Missouri: University of Missouri Press, 2006), 114.

249 Commerce is a city in southern US state of Texas. It is home to Texas
A&M University–Commerce. From 1968 to 1978, Sandoz was a professor
and head of Department of Political Science at East Texas State University,
which later became Texas A&M University–Commerce. For Prof. Sandoz's   webpage,   see   http://www.lsu.edu/artsci/groups/voegelin/
sandoz.shtml .

250 Charles R. Embry, "Ellis Sandoz as Master Teacher: Consistent in Belief,
Steadfast in Purpose," in John von Heyking and Lee Trepanier, eds.,
Teaching in an Age of Ideology (Lanham, Maryland: Lexington Books,
2012), 156. Other than Prof. Embry's essay about Prof. Sandoz, this book
that was published in October 2012 also included articles regarding such
philosophers as Voegelin, Strauss, Niemeyer, Arendt.

of wide interest" and suggested I try to get it published, "but I'm afraid I am not in any way a religious person, so your Christian message passes me by."

All this reminds me of a scene in my undergraduate days. I often went to the university's library where among the section of politics *A History of Political Theory* by American political philosopher George Holland Sabine (1880–1961) was one of the books that impressed me most. Compared to the official Chinese books on the history of political ideas, Sabine's was quite different in the way he wrote. I do not remember how many pages I read at that time. But his work was among the earlier ones that helped me begin learning to know the Western political history.

Another scene is about reading *Tradition*, written by American sociologist Edward Shils (1910–1995). I bought a copy of its Chinese edition on July 15, 1994, a few days after finishing the high school study and attending the National College Entrance Examination. This copy remains on my shelf. On the title page is a passage I transcribed after reading this book. Its English translation reads as follows, "Men make their own history, but they do not make it as they please; they do not make it under self-selected circumstances, but under circumstances existing already, given and transmitted from the past. The tradition of all dead generations weighs like a nightmare on the brains of the living. And just as they seem to be occupied with revolutionizing themselves and things, creating something that did not exist before, precisely in such epochs of revolutionary crisis they anxiously conjure up the spirits of the past to their service, borrowing from them names, battle slogans, and costumes in order to present this new scene in world history in time-honored disguise and borrowed language." It does not come from Edward Shils, but Karl Marx. During the period of December 1851–March 1852, Marx wrote an essay, "Der 18te Brumaire des Louis Napoleon" or "The Eighteenth Brumaire of Louis Bonaparte," which appeared in 1852 in the first issue of a New York-based German monthly magazine, *Die Revolution*.[251]

---

251 For its Chinese edition: http://marxists.anu.edu.au/chinese/PDF/Marx-Engels/me08.pdf ; for its English translation: http://www.marxists.org/archive/marx/works/1852/18th-brumaire/index.htm .

Though Marxism has been China's state ideology since 1949, not many readers in China seem to have taken a closer look at Marx's books. I finally got more time to read some books with interest instead of being under pressure to pass an exam upon wrapping up the high school years. The passage of Marx was what I stumbled upon after reading *Tradition*. A feeling at that time and afterwards was that Marx's own words were not the same as the Marxism propaganda prevalent across China that has been much more empty and hollow and meaningless. And if the passage Marx wrote somewhat makes sense, it seems to apply in Marx himself and his followers as well.

However, be they Shils or Marx or Sabine or such thinkers I read later as Austrian-British economist and political philosopher Friedrich Hayek (1899–1992) who penned *The Constitution of Liberty* and was a friend of Voegelin's when they were at the University of Vienna,[252] these intellectuals are quite different from Voegelin and Sandoz in terms of their world views. That is despite the differences between the former ones are not much less significant. Voegelin and Sandoz are not the same as Alexis de Tocqueville and Max Weber either, though the latter two attach great importance to Christianity. Compared to all these thinkers, the uniqueness of Voegelin and Sandoz may lie in the way they see the world: they do not treat human beings as the leading role in the drama of history. In their eyes, both the rebellion of human beings against God, their quest for God, and God's grace upon human beings as well as his judgment constitute a multi-dimensional panorama of history.

In *Autobiographical Reflections*, Voegelin told Sandoz about a brief career at Harvard where he taught the history of political ideas after his life in America just began. An editor approached Voegelin about enlisting him to write "a textbook of moderate size—I believe 200 to 250

252 Eric Voegelin, *The Collected Works of Eric Voegelin, Volume 4, The Authoritarian State: An Essay on the Problem of the Austrian State* (Columbia, Missouri: University of Missouri Press, 1999), 23; Eric Voegelin, *The Collected Works of Eric Voegelin: Volume 34, Autobiographical Reflections: Revised Edition, with a Voegelin Glossary and Cumulative Index* (Columbia, Missouri: University of Missouri Press, 2006), 34–35; Eric Voegelin, Ellis Sandoz ed., Xu Zhiyue trans., *Autobiographical Reflections* (Beijing: Huaxia Press, 2009), 6–7.

pages were envisaged—for this series." In the field of political science at America's institutions of higher learning, "the standard work" at that time was Sabine's *A History of Political Theory* that was first published in 1937. Voegelin planned to use it "as a model of what had to be included or excluded." However, as he "began working more deeply into the materials," Voegelin found that all the previous treatment he had read was inadequate and what he had known was insufficient. Therefore, he did not finish the book on time. Meanwhile, Voegelin discovered that the conventional writing then about the history of political ideas started with the ancient Greek philosophers and ended up with modern ideologies. He said this limitation was untenable. While later teaching in the University of Alabama, Voegelin realized that he would not be able to grasp the medieval politics well without knowing further about the origins of Christianity. And that would require "going into the Jewish background." Then Voegelin began to study Hebrew with a local rabbi. Owing to both Voegelin's linguistic talent and the growing interest in China after the Second World War, the university's political science department elected Voegelin to teach China's politics. Voegelin started learning Chinese and studying ancient China, especially the thoughts of Confucius and Lao-tse. He said this helped him a lot because he could "recognize in the revolutionary operas propagated by Madame Mao Tse-tung the pattern of the ballet libretti of the Chou period, with the slight difference that the Chou authors celebrated the victory of the Chou Dynasty, whereas the modern revolutionary operas celebrate the victory of the revolutionary armies." For Voegelin, the 1945–1950 years were "a period of indecision" or "a period of theoretical paralysis." And yet it was just this seemingly unending quest for reality that bore fruit in the latter half of Voegelin's life.[253]

Sabine's *A History of Political Theory* in Voegelin's experience reminded me not just of my own encounter with the same book but also

253 Eric Voegelin, Ellis Sandoz ed., Xu Zhiyue trans., *Autobiographical Reflections* (Beijing: Huaxia Press, 2009), 63–65. There is some change to the Chinese translation in the Chinese version of this writing; Eric Voegelin, *The Collected Works of Eric Voegelin: Volume 34, Autobiographical Reflections: Revised Edition, with a Voegelin Glossary and Cumulative Index* (Columbia, Missouri: University of Missouri Press, 2006), 89–91.

of how one could easily live in the shadows of oneself and other selves without knowing the eclipse of the realty. But how to walk out of all these shadows? I thought of a passage of words that was quoted in Voegelin and Sandoz more than once. It is, "So you, son of man, I have made a watchman for the house of Israel; whenever you hear a word from my mouth, you shall give them warning from me. If I say to the wicked, O wicked man, you shall surely die, and you do not speak to warn the wicked to turn from his way, that wicked man shall die in his iniquity, but his blood I will require at your hand. But if you warn the wicked to turn from his way, and he does not turn from his way; he shall die in his iniquity, but you will have saved your life."[254] Voegelin read this passage to his audiences when he delivered the lecture of *Hitler and the Germans* in 1964 in the University of Munich. However, Voegelin did not address it to those present alone but the clergy and theologians of the church in Germany. Along with nine other points, Voegelin wanted all these people to learn this passage by heart, "Lower clergy, copy it out daily ten times; bishops and theologians, daily a hundred times; theologians who have received a Cross of Merit from the Federal Republic, daily two hundred times, until they have got it."[255]

Before my correspondence with Professor Sandoz began in February 2006, I had gotten to know about him and Voegelin by running across a book he edited through the searching system of China's National Library. It is *The Roots of Liberty: Magna Carta, Ancient Constitution, and the Anglo-American Tradition of Rule of Law*.[256] During 2004–2005, I translated a book with a similar title: *Roots of Freedom: A Primer on Modern Liberty*, and the author is Professor John W. Danford at Loyola University in Chicago.[257] What I did not expect then is that from the two books

---

254 Ezekiel 33:7–9. Revised Standard Version (RSV).

255 Eric Voegelin, *The Collected Works of Eric Voegelin: Volume 31, Hitler and the Germans* (Columbia, Missouri: University of Missouri Press, 1999), 200–201.

256 Ellis Sandoz, *The Roots of Liberty: Magna Carta, Ancient Constitution, and the Anglo-American Tradition of Rule of Law* (Columbia, Missouri: University of Missouri Press, 1993).

257 John W. Danford, *Roots of Freedom: A Primer on Modern Liberty* (Wilmington, Delaware: ISI Books, 2000).

uncovering the roots of liberty and freedom I would get to know more about the thoughts of Sandoz and his teacher and friend Voegelin, and some of his American and international colleagues as well as Professor Danford and his friends like Joseph Cropsey and Thomas Pangle, a political science professor at University of Texas at Austin. What I did not expect in a deeper sense is that because of the appeal of the roots of liberty and freedom I would be attracted to know about those who have been drawn to not just the roots of liberty and freedom but also the "divine reality" and have done the work of "a watchman" to diverse extent. Ezekiel did not claim to be a watchman but "the word of the LORD came to Ezekiel."[258] However, human's response is not unimportant. In this regard, different responses have different outcomes. As the LORD said to Ezekiel, "Son of man, say to the house of Israel, 'This is what you are saying: "Our offenses and sins weigh us down, and we are wasting away because of them. How then can we live?"' Say to them, 'As surely as I live, declares the Sovereign LORD, I take no pleasure in the death of the wicked, but rather that they turn from their ways and live. Turn! Turn from your evil ways! Why will you die, O house of Israel?'"[259]

In "The Gospel and Culture" published in 1971, Voegelin talked about God's drawing and human's responding in the viewpoint of the Voegelinian philosophy that is, "the experiences of transcendence." Voegelin drew his audience's attention to how the incarnate God has drawn individuals across the globe through his death on the cross and his resurrection. He stressed that it was after a group of Greeks requested to see Jesus that Jesus made these remarks: "The hour has come for the Son of Man to be glorified. Very truly I tell you, unless a kernel of wheat falls to the ground and dies, it remains only a single seed. But if it dies, it produces many seeds ... Now is the time for judgment on this world; now the prince of this world will be driven out. And I, when I am lifted up from the earth, will draw all people to myself."[260] It was similar when

---

258 Ezekiel 1: 3.
259 Ezekiel 33: 10–11.
260 Eric Voegelin, *The Collected Works of Eric Voegelin: Volume 12, Published Essays, 1966-1985* (Baton Rouge: Louisiana State University Press, 1990), 180–81. John 12: 23–32.

Jesus said earlier, "No one can come to me unless the Father who sent me draws him, and I will raise him up at the last day."[261] For Voegelin, humans' seeking and God's drawing "do not denote two different movements but symbolize the dynamics in the tension of existence between its human and divine poles."[262] Of course, a human being could still seek oneself rather than God. However, all this would ultimately not be in the hands of humans. Voegelin quoted what God said in Jeremiah, "Behold! What I have built, I will pull down; and what I have planted, I will tear up—and you see great things for yourself? Seek them not! For behold! I will bring evil upon all flesh—says Yahweh—But your life will I give you, as a prize of war, in every place where you go."[263]

In this existential panorama where God interacts with humans, one could see the history recorded in the Bible refers not just to persons, countries, and time in the Old and New Testaments. The Scripture is not only about the past but also the present, the future and the eternity. It is like the sample or the epitome of history. As Voegelin laid it bare, "History is Christ written large."[264] In this multi-dimensional scene, one could see not just "nothing new under the sun,"[265] but also something new above the sun. But the new and the old are intertwined. The fallen human remains standing in this fallen and temporary world. Even a human being who has responded to God's drawing by repentance and return and thus has been "set apart"[266] remains a sinner. This is what the apostle Paul sighed, "We know that the whole creation has been groaning as in the pains of childbirth right up to the present time"[267] and "What a wretched man I am! Who will rescue me from this body of death?

---

261 John 6:44.

262 Eric Voegelin, *The Collected Works of Eric Voegelin: Volume 12, Published Essays, 1966–1985* (Baton Rouge: Louisiana State University Press, 1990), 183.

263 *Ibid.*, 186. Jeremiah, 45:4–5.

264 Eric Voegelin, *The Collected Works of Eric Voegelin: Volume 12, Published Essays, 1966–1985* (Baton Rouge: Louisiana State University Press, 1990), 78.

265 Ecclesiastes 1:9.

266 Exodus 28: 3, 41; John 10: 36, 17:19.

267 Romans 8: 22.

Thanks be to God—through Jesus Christ our Lord! So then, I myself in my mind am a slave to God's law, but in the sinful nature a slave to the law of sin."[268] It is also what Paul saw about the present and the prospect, "Now we see but a poor reflection as in a mirror; then we shall see face to face. Now I know in part; then I shall know fully, even as I am fully known."[269] And it is like what Sandoz quoted from British poet Alexander Pope (1688–1744) about the human existence of in-between, "… He hangs between; in doubt to act or rest; In doubt to deem himself a god or beast; In doubt his Mind or Body to prefer; Born but to die, and reas'ning but to err; …. Created half to rise, and half to fall, Great lord of all things, yet a prey to all; Sole judge of Truth, in endless error hurl'd; The glory, jest and riddle of the world."[270]

Seeing the humans and the wider world in this way, one would find prevalent the co-existence of both the simple and the complex and both the temporary and the eternal. In this light, it would be perhaps less difficult to make sense of the tension in the world of political ideas of Europeans and Americans both Voegelin and Sandoz mainly examined. On the one hand, the Christian faith and the Christian church have played a shaping role in the West's spiritual world over the past more than ten centuries. On the other hand, individuals and different groups of people in the West have been under the influence of diverse ideas and patterns of behavior. This means even the same Christianity could mean something different among different persons. So it is no surprise at all to witness so many denominations and schools of ideas in Western history. Apart from the Christian faith, the Greek philosophy, the Roman politics, the British common law, the Continental European law, local customs and traditions, the Islam philosophy, the Enlightenment and many phenomena that cannot be suitably categorized may have exerted impacts to various extent over the West.

On the level of political operations, things could be more complicated. Sandoz wrote, "Politics is itself a sort of mediocre thing, neither

---

268 Romans 7: 24–25.
269 1 Corinthians 13: 12.
270 Ellis Sandoz, *A Government of Laws: Political Theory, Religion, and the American Founding* (Columbia, Missouri: University of Missouri Press, 2001), 223–25.

the noblest nor meanest realm but an in-between sphere; it is not the way to salvation, either in the beyond or in the world." Sandoz referred to John Locke's view, which was, "we being, in degrees of perfection, much more remote from the infinite being of God than we are from the lowest state of being, and that which approaches nearest to nothing."[271] For Sandoz, Locke's political idea itself reflects this mediocre state. Locke offered an effective solution to the political crisis of his time by, for example, appealing to natural law based on human reason, contract theory, private property, toleration, and liberty of conscience. But at the same time, Locke brought about "the incipient formulation of a radically immanentist conception of human existence." As a reduction of the human reality, "this doctrine stimulated the rise of totalitarian democracy as the malformed brother of liberal democracy" after the Enlightenment and the French Revolution. Sandoz borrowed from the comparison in Genesis between Cain and Abel, the first two sons of Adam and Eve.[272] It might be reminiscent of the contrast between East and West Germany, North and South Korea, Chinese mainland and Hong Kong, Macau and Taiwan, or in a wider sense, between East and West Europe, Soviet Union and the United States.

Yet, the comparison Sandoz put forward is not confined to this world alone. He pinpointed a crisis facing "liberal democracy." In *The Politics of Truth and Other Untimely Essays: The Crisis of Civic Consciousness* published in 1999, Sandoz quoted the first president of Czechoslovakia, Tomáš Garrigue Masaryk (1850–1937), "our vulgar liberalism fears the ultimate questions of life as the devil fears holy water." Then, Sandoz went further by pointing out this, "In a time when liberal democracy appears to be the only practicable alternative to authoritarianism or worse, it is precisely requisite that the ultimate questions of human existence be explored and, so far as possible, that the truth of reality be recovered as a living possession. Only thus can it be woven into the fabric of

271 *Ibid.*, 223. From Locke's *An Essay Concerning Human Understanding*, Book III, Chapter VI, 12: http://www.gutenberg.org/cache/epub/10616/pg10616.html .

272 Ellis Sandoz, *A Government of Laws: Political Theory, Religion, and the American Founding* (Columbia, Missouri: University of Missouri Press, 2001), 81–82. Genesis 4:1–24.

representative free government as the texture of political order, civic consciousness, and institutionalized statecraft in service of the good life. This, it appears to me at least, is the world-historic task of an authentic politics of truth—if a plunge into the abyss is to be averted."[273]

That was part of the speech Sandoz gave on May 17, 1995, when he was awarded the degree *Philosophiae doctorem, Honoris causa* at Palacky University. *The Politics of Truth and Other Untimely Essays* also included an article based on an address Sandoz delivered at the Federal Parliament of Czechoslovakia in May 1991. Again, Sandoz said that politics was not the way to salvation, and as "fallible and sinful human beings" no one "possesses a monopoly on truth." In this respect, he held that "'My kingdom is not of the world'[274] is the Gospel's lodestar." And the maxim of British statesman Winston Churchill (1874–1965) was borrowed to emphasize Sandoz's view on politics in this world: "Democracy is the worst form of government except for all the others." He talked about a range of specific issues concerning "creating democratic free government in Czechoslovakia after forty-odd years of communist Russian tyranny," such as neutrality of lawyers, constitution as fundamental law, free press, secret police, the worldwide impact of ideologies in American universities, private property, federalism, personal liberties, the independence of the universities, local autonomy, elections. From these points, readers would find that Sandoz's ideas about liberal democracy were not based upon what Masaryk described as "vulgar liberalism." Instead, what Sandoz has been doing is to recover the reality of politics from both this world and beyond.[275]

Which reminded me of a letter I received from Professor Sandoz in the evening of March 9, 2012. Since February 2006, the emails between Sandoz and I may have amounted to hundreds. But this note is among what has impressed me most. I was then writing an article entitled "How

273 Ellis Sandoz, *The Politics of Truth and Other Untimely Essays: The Crisis of Civic Consciousness* (Columbia, Missouri: University of Missouri Press, 1999), 41–42.

274 John 18: 36.

275 Ellis Sandoz, *The Politics of Truth and Other Untimely Essays: The Crisis of Civic Consciousness* (Columbia, Missouri: University of Missouri Press, 1999), 13–34.

to live in the two worlds at once." Sandoz told me, "Don't Neglect St. Augustine's CITY OF GOD on the subject! Start w/ Bk 14 last chap. then Bk 15 etc. His theme is the 2 cities, earthly and divine, so close to your subject but a bit harsh. The tension is not easy to resolve. I've been working on related matter reading GALATIANS, esp. chap. 4:26-5:1. Very powerful. See also my discussion in REPUBLICANISM pp. 17ff. on Wesley and the Second Reformation so influential in America." The "Second Reformation" is the Great Awakening discussed in Sandoz's *Republicanism, Religion, and the Soul of America.* I had read part of Augustine's *City of God* and Paul's Galatians. But only with Sandoz's reminder have I become much more conscious of the tension between the two cities or two worlds visible in Galatians and *City of God* when I continued to read the history in the Bible, the history of the church and the society in the West, and daily life.

In *City of God*, Augustine said Cain and Abel were of the two different cities with the former being the first-born and of the city of humans, and the latter being born later and of the city of God.[276] For Augustine, the process of being born first as a natural life and born later as a spiritual life would happen in an individual person God predestined and the human race as a whole. It is just like what Paul wrote in 1 Corinthians: "The spiritual did not come first, but the natural, and after that the spiritual."[277] It is similar in Galatians: "For it is written that Abraham had two sons, one by the slave woman and the other by the free woman. His son by the slave woman was born according to the flesh, but his son by the free woman was born as the result of a promise. These things are being taken figuratively: The women represent two covenants. One covenant is from Mount Sinai and bears children who are to be slaves: This is Hagar. Now Hagar stands for Mount Sinai in Arabia and corresponds to the present city of Jerusalem, because she is in slavery with her children. But the Jerusalem that is above is free, and she is our mother ... At that time the son born according to the flesh persecuted the son born by the power of the Spirit. It is the same now. But what does Scripture

---

276 *City of God*, Book 15, Chapter 1: http://www.ccel.org/ccel/schaff/npnf102. iv.XV.1.html .

277 1 Corinthians 15: 46.

say? 'Get rid of the slave woman and her son, for the slave woman's son will never share in the inheritance with the free woman's son.' Therefore, brothers, we are not children of the slave woman, but of the free woman."[278] Immediately afterwards, Paul wrote: "It is for freedom that Christ has set us free. Stand firm, then, and do not let yourselves be burdened again by a yoke of slavery."[279] In the past, I found this sentence had been widely quoted. But only with Sandoz's reminder did I begin to ponder more deeply about its meaning by reading these verses together. In the spiritual dimension of daily life, freedom and slavery may happen more in the same person than in different persons. Therefore, freedom in this world alone is not freedom in a genuine sense; and yet while living in this temporal and unfree world, one could also exist at once—and thus not wholly—in the eternal and free world. What connects these two worlds is God's redemption of his humans through Christ and human's response through faith in Christ.

This is what Voegelin meant in his late life by following Christ, "To follow Christ means to continue the event of divine presence in society and history: 'As you have sent me into the world, so I have sent them into the world' (John 17:18)."[280] Following Christ in this sense is a far cry from following a great person or a model citizen in a moralistic sense. It is but a witness to God's creation, redemption and governance because of God's drawing. Only in the "divine reality"—Christ—that God on his own initiative revealed to his humans, would the human reality be shown. It is not just about the human reality in this world or in eternity, but in both. So, the human reality in this world is not completely meaningless. But one should not be content with the reality in this world alone, for that would prevent him or her from seeing the reality of this world. It is like Jesus using the metaphor of things in this world to illustrate things in heaven, "he did not say anything to them without using a parable. So was fulfilled what was spoken through the prophet: 'I will

---

278 Galatians 4: 22–31.
279 Galatians 5:1.
280 Eric Voegelin, *The Collected Works of Eric Voegelin: Volume 12, Published Essays, 1966–1985* (Baton Rouge: Louisiana State University Press, 1990), 190.

open my mouth in parables, I will utter things hidden since the creation of the world.'"[281] And before being arrested, Jesus told his followers: "Though I have been speaking figuratively, a time is coming when I will no longer use this kind of language but will tell you plainly about my Father ... I have told you these things, so that in me you may have peace. In this world you will have trouble. But take heart! I have overcome the world."[282] Between the created and the creator, the finite and the infinite, the sinful and the sinless, the powerless and the powerful, the mortal and the immortal, the dishonor and the glory, the natural and the spiritual, the earthly and the heavenly, it is Christ who connects the two worlds that would otherwise be incompatible and it is in the tension of Christ's connection that provides the human existence with dynamics and vitality.

This scene brought me back to sometime in 2004 when I worked at China's state television. During the supper break, I would find a somewhat quiet place to read a book that was not very relevant to my work. I was then already beginning my quest in the history of liberty. One book was about European medieval history. Written by American historian Brian Tierney, it was entitled, *The Crisis of Church and State: 1050-1300*. Its Introduction impressed me much, "To maintain order and unity in groups larger and less homogeneous than extended family systems is a complex and difficult task. Mere force is seldom sufficient in the long run. The most common solution has been to endow the ruler who controls the physical apparatus of state coercion with a sacral role also as head and symbol of the people's religion. Primitive societies commonly attribute magical powers to their chieftains; the Pharaohs of Egypt, the Incas of Peru, the emperors of Japan were all revered as divine beings; the Roman Caesars bore the title *Pontifex Maximus*. In modern totalitarian despotisms, where the party structure provides a travesty of a church, the simultaneous control of party and state is the very essence of a dictator's authority. We need not be surprised, then, that in the Middle Ages also there were rulers who aspired to supreme spiritual and temporal power. The truly exceptional thing is that in medieval times

---

281 Matthew 13: 34–35.
282 John 16: 25–33.

there were always at least two claimants to the role, each commanding a formidable apparatus of government, and that for century after century neither was able to dominate the other completely, so that the duality persisted, was eventually rationalized in works of political theory and ultimately built into the structure of European society. This situation profoundly influenced the development of Western constitutionalism. The very existence of two power structures competing for men's allegiance instead of only one compelling obedience greatly enhanced the possibilities for human freedom. In practical life over and over again in the Middle Ages men found themselves having to make genuine choices according to conscience or self-interest between conflicting appeals to their loyalty. On the theoretical level, intellectuals were led to formulate detailed arguments about the deposition of tyrannical kings or popes and to define with more and more precision the due limits of their respective powers."[283]

Also I was reminded of a letter I received on January 24, 2006 from Harold Berman (1918-2007). That was a year before Berman passed away. Berman has been best known perhaps for his *Law and Revolution.* In his letter, Berman's opinions are similar to Tierney's. He pointed out that "plural political and plural spiritual jurisdictions—in one word, 'pluralism'—that was the chief source of freedom." The reason that Berman identified the situation as "pluralism" instead of the "duality" Tierney referred to is that Berman held that within the duality of church and state more separations were developed in the European history. That is, there have been separate churches within the church and separate governments within the government. In the years 2004–2006 and several years before, scholars like Tierney and Berman presented me an image of the tension between the spiritual and the temporal in European political history. Looking back, I now consider this tension to be a shadow of the deeper tension. It does not just show the tension between the two worlds or cities, but the tension originated with the incarnation of Christ and the subsequent rise and growth of the Christian church in the European political history.

---

283 Brian Tierney, *The Crisis of Church and State: 1050–1300* (Medieval Academy of America, 1988), 1–2.

If this tension was only manifested in European history, it would be unique to Europe. But world history shows that this tension has been found in both the personal and social lives of many places around the globe, though not as prominently as it was in Europe and North America. What Voegelin and Sandoz have witnessed in their lives and their books are testimony to the rise and fall of this tension in Europe and North America. During the years since I have gotten to know Professor Sandoz, I have begun to take note of this tension at work in many lives including mine in China and the wider world. All this has gone beyond my expectations. When I started my quest for liberty, there was some curiosity about the unknown world and some respect for and pursuit of something eternal. And yet, all this looked dim and I did not know what on earth it would be. When the reality was unfolding with the passage of time, it seemed it was what I had met before but was in fact much more than what I could imagine.

It is like what one of the first words I saw in Voegelin's books describes, "In the study of creature one should not exercise a vain and perishing curiosity, but ascend toward what is immortal and everlasting."[284] As epigraph of the five-volume *Order and History*, it is from *De Vera Religione or On True Religion*, a book Augustine wrote when he was about thirty-six years old.[285] The context of this sentence is to help its readers know "how far reason can advance from visible to invisible things in its ascent from temporal to eternal things."[286] The reason Augustine said here differs significantly from the reason the Enlightenment advocated. It is not the reason whose measure is human but the grace God gave humans to know God and his creation.[287] Such is also the

---

284 Ellis Sandoz, Xu Zhiyue trans., *The Voegelinian Revolution: A Biographical Introduction (Second Edition)* (Shanghai: Shanghai Joint Publishing Company, 2012), 130. There is some change to the Chinese translation in the Chinese version of this writing; Ellis Sandoz, *The Voegelinian Revolution: A Biographical Introduction* (New Brunswick, New Jersey: Transaction Publishers, 2000), 116.

285 John H. S. Burleigh ed., Augustine: *Earlier writings* (Louisville, Kentucky: Westminster John Knox Press, 2006), 222.

286 *Ibid.*, 251.

287 *Ibid.*, 251, 247.

reason in Voegelin. He noted, "Reason itself isn't natural," "The 'natural reason' is due to God's grace,"[288] and "The Life of Reason in the classic sense is existence in tension between Life and Death."[289] Of course, Voegelin's quote from Augustine itself also explains what they mean by reason.

If further exploring the meaning of reason in ancient Greece and the early church, one would find out the relation of the reason in Augustine and Voegelin with God's grace from another perspective. Reason in modern European languages, such as "reason" in English and "raison" in French, derives from "ratio" in Latin, which originates in "λόγος" (logos) in Greek. Interestingly, "ideology" that was mentioned earlier derives from "logos" as well. Logos has multiple layers of meaning. Literally, it means word. It also means idea, reason. For ancient Greek philosophers like Heraclitus (535–475), logos refers to both the description of the existence and its explanation, both the word that can be heard and the word that reveals the reality and cause, both human's ideas and the laws at work in the universe, both the form in spirit and the manifestation in material.[290] Perhaps more interestingly, logos also appears in John of the Bible. In the popular Chinese Union Version, it was translated as "道" (dao, or tao), which likewise has such multiple layers of meaning in the Chinese language context as both word and way. According to John, God revealed himself through his incarnation in Jesus Christ who is the logos or tao human beings have pursued. However, the logos or tao revealed in God's incarnation is not the same as the one humans as limited and sinful creatures pursue. The logos or tao in humans' description could be no more than dim. Only in God's incarnation, in the way humans could understand, will human

288 R. Eric O'Connor ed., *Conversations with Eric Voegelin* (Montreal: Thomas More Institute, 1980), 138; Ellis Sandoz, *Republicanism, Religion, and the Soul of America* (Columbia, Missouri: University of Missouri Press, 2006), 118–119.

289 Eric Voegelin, *The Collected Works of Eric Voegelin: Volume 12, Published Essays, 1966–1985* (Baton Rouge: Louisiana State University Press, 1990), 279.

290 W. K. C. Guthrie, *A History of Greek Philosophy: Volume 1, The Earlier Presocratics and the Pythagoreans* (Cambridge University Press, 1979), 38, 414–33.

beings really see the logos or tao in the sense of "the Word was with God" and "the Word was God."[291] The logos or tao is both God's word and God himself. It is like what Jesus said, "I am the way and the truth and the life. No one comes to the Father except through me. If you really knew me, you would know my Father as well. From now on, you do know him and have seen him,"[292] for "No one has ever seen God, but God the One and Only, who is at the Father's side, has made him known."[293]

In the history where God interacts with humans, knowledge of the reality has become clearer from very dim.[294] And according to Genesis, the process wherein God created all things itself appears to be from dim to clear. Or it is from "formless and empty" to "separated." "In the beginning God created the heavens and the earth. Now the earth was formless and empty, darkness was over the surface of the deep, and the Spirit of God was hovering over the waters. And God said, 'Let there be light,' and there was light. God saw that the light was good, and he separated the light from the darkness."[295] Facing the earth that "was formless and empty" and darkness that "was over the surface of the deep," God created light and thus "separated the light from the darkness," and hence the separation of day and night. After creating the expanse, God separated water from water. He then separated ground from water. And there was the separation of plants bearing seeds and trees "according to their

291 John 1:1.
292 John 14:6–7.
293 John 1:18.
294 In Voegelin, this experience is from "compact" to "differentiation." Eric Voegelin, *The Collected Works of Eric Voegelin: Volume 34, Autobiographical Reflections: Revised Edition, with a Voegelin Glossary and Cumulative Index* (Columbia, Missouri: University of Missouri Press, 2006), 153, 155, 274; Eric Voegelin, *The Collected Works of Eric Voegelin, Volume 5, Modernity without Restraint: The Political Religions; The New Science of Politics; and Science, Politics, and Gnosticism* (Columbia, Missouri: University of Missouri Press, 2000), 151–52; Ellis Sandoz, *The Voegelinian Revolution: A Biographical Introduction* (New Brunswick, New Jersey: Transaction Publishers, 2000), 105; Ellis Sandoz, Xu Zhiyue trans., *The Voegelinian Revolution: A Biographical Introduction (Second Edition)* (Shanghai: Shanghai Joint Publishing Company, 2012), 120.
295 Genesis 1: 1–4.

various kinds,"[296] and the separation of stars, of creatures "according to their kinds,"[297] of man and woman, of the seventh day and six other days.[298] The separation here is consistent with "sanctification"[299] in the Bible. In the Old Testament, God set Noah, Abraham, the Israelites apart from other people. In the New Testament, God set those who believed in him apart from the world. In his redemption of humans, God seemed to continue his way in creation. What the incarnate God said for his followers before his arrest might be viewed as both explanation and summary of this separation and sanctification—"For them I sanctify myself, that they too may be truly sanctified."[300] However, he added immediately, "My prayer is not for them alone. I pray also for those who will believe in me through their message, that all of them may be one, Father, just as you are in me and I am in you. May they also be in us so that the world may believe that you have sent me. I have given them the glory that you gave me, that they may be one as we are one."[301] Though separation and sanctification are two characteristics in God's creation and redemption, they are not in contradiction to being one. Neither separation nor sanctification would mean alienation from God. Instead, it is God's self-revelation so that his created beings may participate in him,[302] and "have been given fullness in Christ."[303]

Furthermore, in this process of being separated and being one at the same time, God's self-revelation enables humans to see not just the reality of their relationship with God, but also the reality of God's inner relationship. Father and Son are different but are one. Father and Son are one

---

296 Genesis 1: 11.

297 Genesis 1: 21.

298 In *Orthodoxy*, British writer G. K. Chesterton (1874-1936) wrote, "All creation is separation. Birth is as solemn a parting as death." See http://www.gutenberg.org/cache/epub/130/pg130.html .

299 Sanctify, in Greek, "ἁγιάζω"(hagiazó) and in Hebrew "קָדַשׁ"(qadash), literally means "to (be) set ... apart from ..." See https://biblehub.com/greek/37.htm, https://biblehub.com/hebrew/6942.htm.

300 John 17: 19.

301 John 17: 20–22.

302 Lamentations 3: 24; Hebrews 12: 10; 2 Peter 1: 4; Revelation 1: 9, 20–6.

303 Colossians 2: 10.

but different. This kind of relationship might let people think of the one between humans. Anyone could not help treating others from one's own self. It is no surprise at all that human history has not been short of dictatorships. Unlike humans, the Son as "the King of Kings and Lord of lords"[304] is no dictator.[305] He is "the King of Kings and Lord of lords" but was sent by the Father,[306] and is in the Father always,[307] obeying the Father's commands,[308] doing what the Father does,[309] spreading the Father's words.[310] The Father is no dictator either. "For as the Father has life in himself, so he has granted the Son to have life in himself."[311] And, "For the Father loves the Son and shows him all he does. Yes, to your amazement he will show him even greater things than these."[312] Meanwhile, "the Father judges no one, but has entrusted all judgment to the Son."[313] Yet, it is not just the relationship between Father and Son. Theirs with the Spirit is striking as well. Mary, the mother of Jesus, "was found to be with child through the Holy Spirit."[314] "Jesus was led by the Spirit into the desert to be tempted by the devil."[315] After being baptized, "he saw heaven being torn open and the Spirit descending on him like dove. And a voice came from heaven: 'You are my Son, whom I love; with you I am well pleased.'"[316] Jesus even used this word to let humans know the status of the Spirit—"Anyone who speaks a word against the Son of Man will be forgiven, but anyone who speaks against the Holy Spirit will not be forgiven, either in this age or in the age to come."[317] His words give a clear picture about the relationship between Father, Son, and Spirit—

304 1 Timothy 6: 15; Revelation 17: 14, 19: 16.
305 John 5: 19, 30.
306 John 5: 37.
307 John 17: 21.
308 John 15: 10.
309 John 10: 37.
310 John 14: 24.
311 John 5: 26.
312 John 5: 20.
313 John 5: 22.
314 Matthew 1: 18.
315 Matthew 4: 1.
316 Mark 1: 10–11.
317 Matthew 12: 32.

"But the Counselor, the Holy Spirit, whom the Father will send in my name, will teach you all things and will remind you of everything I have said to you."[318] Just as Jesus said, "The words I say to you are not just my own. Rather, it is the Father, living in me, who is doing his work,"[319] "the Son can do nothing by himself; he can do only what he sees his Father doing, because whatever the Father does the Son also does,"[320] "By myself I can do nothing, I judge only as I hear, and my judgment is just, for I seek not to please myself but him who sent me,"[321] the Spirit "will not speak on his own; he will speak only what he hears, and he will tell you what is yet to come."[322] In this sense, it would be very reasonable for Jesus to say this when he sent his followers—"Therefore go and make disciples of all nations, baptizing them in the name of the Father and of the Son and of the Holy Spirit."[323]

In stark contrast with the reality of God's relationship with humans through incarnation and that of God's inner relationship, the human's attitude towards the coming of God is not receptive. "He was in the world, and though the world was made through him, the world did not recognize him. He came to that which was his own, but his own did not receive him."[324] After being born, Jesus was wrapped in cloths by Mary and placed in a manger, "because there was no room for them in the inn."[325] Facing the divine reality, the reality of the human and the world becomes visible.[326] Although human beings may have pursued God to various extents, the God in the eyes of humans would be a far cry from the divine reality God revealed. It is likewise when the truth, justice and love in the sight of humans are compared with those in God's revelation. Otherwise, humans "would not have crucified the Lord of glory. However, as it is written: 'No eye has seen, no ear has heard, no mind has

---

318 John 14: 26.
319 John 14: 10.
320 John 5: 19.
321 John 5: 30.
322 John 16: 13.
323 Matthew 28: 19.
324 John 1: 10–11.
325 Luke 2: 7.
326 For more details, see Chapter 5, The Politics of Jesus.

conceived what God has prepared for those who love him,'"[327] In reading Voegelin and Sandoz, the contrast between the reality and the shadows is one of the most important things I have learned. This unexpected reward has helped me to read the Bible and all relevant books. It has helped me to learn to know and experience the reality in the world that is simultaneously simple and complex, temporal and eternal. Just because of this, I have begun to find out how deeply I am still stuck in a variety of shadows. And I have to admit that if I had known God I would not have crucified the Lord of glory, and "what God has prepared for those who love him" is indeed that "No eye has seen, no ear has heard, no mind has conceived."

To know and experience the reality is thus far more than a matter of knowledge and experience. It is a matter of life and death. Towards the very end of Voegelin's life in this world, a lady named Hiawatha Moore helped Voegelin's wife to take care of Voegelin. On the morning of January 19, 1985, Moore received a call from Mrs. Voegelin. When she got there, Voegelin was breathing heavily. Moore sat down on the bed, putting her arms around Voegelin and praying for him in her heart. Suddenly, she felt a voice saying, "You know that little Bible, when you cleaned up?"[328] She reached over and got that book and opened it without knowing what it was. It was Psalm 25. She began to read for Voegelin who was still breathing heavily. She read the 17th verse, "The troubles of my heart are enlarged. Oh, bring me out of my distress."[329] Voegelin made his last heavy breath. Moore felt she was not shaking and the bed was not either. Voegelin was not breathing anymore. She got up calling Mrs. Voegelin. That was about 7:30. "That was the way he went. It was like he was waiting for permission to leave, you know?" recalled Moore, "Like his heart was heavy, he was just stressed. But 'How do I give this up?' And when I read it, it was like someone gave him permission. He accepted it and went on."[330]

---

327 1 Corinthians 2: 8–9.
328 Barry Cooper and Jodi Bruhn, eds., *Voegelin Recollected: Conversation on a Life* (Columbia, Missouri: University of Missouri Press, 2008), 12.
329 Psalms 25: 17.
330 Barry Cooper and Jodi Bruhn, eds., *Voegelin Recollected: Conversation on a Life* (Columbia, Missouri: University of Missouri Press, 2008), 13.

Appendix to Chapter 8
Our Stand on Registration

Beijing Shouwang Church
Chief Pastor Jin Tianming
July 18, 2007
Preface

When the new Religious Affairs Provisions were issued in late 2004, we hopefully considered them a significant step forward taken by the government in solving the issue concerning the unregistered churches.[331] To us, they showed that the government was willing to treat both the Three-Self and unregistered churches as equal according to law, and that could pave the way for the possibility of allowing churches outside the Three-Self to be registered. With this hope, we expected that the relationship between church and state in China would finally be on the right track. Yet, in the two years that followed, as indicated by the result of our church's applying to become a registered religious organization according to the new provisions, and the subsequent result of the administrative review, the policy of the relevant government department looked the same as before. In our case, religious organizations are still interpreted only as the Three-Self Patriotic Movement Committee of the Protestant Churches of China. This means any church that wants to register with the government must either join the Three-Self or at least win the approval of the Three-Self. History shows that if house churches in China could be registered with the provision of joining the Three-Self, then they would already have been registered several decades ago without

---

331 It first appeared in the 2008 spring issue of *Almond Flowers* magazine. It was translated into English by Promise Hsu.

having to wait until the new Religious Provisions were issued. So we have two fundamental questions to be answered: According to the Religious Provisions promulgated by the State Council, could the unregistered house churches be registered as religious organizations? Is the religious department's interpretation of the Religious Provisions in keeping with the original intention of the State Council when it drew up the regulation?

Part 1
Our efforts in registration and result

In early 2005, after prayer and discussion, we decided to apply to register with the government as a religious organization.

On May 11 2006, after more than one year of preparation, we formally applied to the Ethnic, Religious and Overseas Chinese Affairs Office of Beijing Haidian District for registration as a religious organization. On May 17, the Office gave a written reply saying "according to Regulations for Registration and Management of Social Organizations ... the issue you presented regarding the registration of religious organizations should be referred to the civil affairs department which you seek advice and apply to on the basis of actual fact."

Then, on June 28 2006, we sent our application for registration to the Social Organization Office of Beijing Haidian Civil Affairs Bureau, which on the same day formally accepted our application. Two days later, the Office gave a written reply which said if anyone wants to apply to establish a religious organization an "approved document by its supervisory department" must be sent. It stated that the Ethnic, Religious and Overseas Chinese Affairs Office of Beijing Haidian District is the supervisory department of religious organizations in Haidian.

Upon this requirement, we sent the Ethnic, Religious and Overseas Chinese Affairs Office of Beijing Haidian District a preliminary application for registration on July 3, 2006. After receiving the application, the Office asked for some supplementary material. We submitted the material later that day and the Office immediately accepted our application. Then the Office consulted its supervisory department and on July 6 it asked for more material. By July 18, we handed in all the material.

Three days later, the Office formally accepted our application and showed us a Notice on Agreeing to Examine and Approve and Receipt of Application Material for Examination and Approval.

On August 11 2006, the Ethnic, Religious and Overseas Chinese Affairs Office of Beijing Haidian District gave its decision saying, "after examining, we find the pastor of the suggested 'Beijing Haidian Shouwang Christian Church' has not been approved by the registered legal religious organization of Beijing, so the organization does not have staff with qualifications appropriate to the professional activities of the organization, which does not accord with Article 10, Clause 4 of Regulations for Registration and Management of Social Organizations, therefore our office won't approve the application."

To gain the pastoral qualification, one must get approval of the Three-Self. We cannot accept this interpretation and reply, from either a legal or theological perspective. On the basis of the Administrative Review Law of the People's Republic of China, we made a request on October 9, 2006, for administrative review to the Beijing Religious Affairs Bureau about the decision of the Ethnic, Religious and Overseas Chinese Affairs Office of Beijing Haidian District.

Upon receiving our Request for Administrative Review (one copy was submitted at the Bureau while the other was sent through Express Mail Service), the Beijing Religious Affairs Bureau tried to decline our request with various excuses, and were not even willing to give us a receipt for the submitted material. It later claimed that it had never received the request through EMS. However on December 5, 2006, we received the Decision After Administrative Review from the Beijing Religious Affairs Bureau with the reply that "upheld the administrative decision made by the Ethnic, Religious and Overseas Chinese Affairs Office of Beijing Haidian District."

Part 2
Our query on government's decision over church registration

Both the Decision After Examination made by the Ethnic, Religious and Overseas Chinese Affairs Office of Beijing Haidian District and the Decision After Administrative Review from the Beijing Religious

Affairs Bureau indicate that any group who wants to register with the government as a Christian organization according to the Religious Affairs Provisions must win approval of the Three-Self. To this, we still would like to use the main contents of our Request for Administrative Review to express our opinion [In the following statement, the request was made by Jin Yongkui (Jin Tianming), the chief pastor of Beijing Shouwang Christian Church, to the Ethnic, Religious and Overseas Chinese Affairs Office of Beijing Haidian District]:

...

I   The Ethnic, Religious and Overseas Chinese Affairs Office of Beijing Haidian District misused the regulation when it made the decision

The reason the Office gave for disapproving our request is that we do not have a pastor who has been approved by the registered legal religious organization of Beijing. The Office said it was based on Article 13 of Beijing Religious Affairs Regulations. But we consider the Office has misused the regulation.

1. Religious professional staff is not a necessity for establishing a religious organization.

Article 6 of the State Council's Religious Affairs Provisions reads: "When religious groups are founded, changed, or disbanded, they shall register such events according to Regulations for Registration and Management of Social Organizations."

Article 10 of Regulations for Registration and Management of Social Organizations stipulates the necessary conditions for establishing a social organization, of which Clause 4 requires that "there be staff with qualifications appropriate to the professional activities of the organization."

As for the detailed requirements, Article 4 of Rules for Implementation on Registration and Management of Religious Organizations co-issued by the State Council's Religious Affairs Bureau and Civil Affairs Ministry states: "The requirements for the registration of a religious organization: (1) The organization must have its name, office address and a person in charge; (2) The organization must have rules that do not run counter to the Constitution, laws and regulations; (3) The organization must have its legal income; (4) The organization must have scriptures, doctrines and rules that are subject to textual criticism, in line with our country's religious tradition and do not go against the rules of the groups; (5) The organization's members must represent wide walks of life."

Which means, if the organization has a person in charge then it has met the requirement in Regulations for Registration and Management of Social Organizations that "there be staff with qualifications appropriate to the professional activities of the organization." In other words, it is unnecessary for the organization to have "religious staff" before the organization is established, since the installment of religious staff is the religious organization's internal affairs, made independently by the organization after it is established for carrying out activities.

2. The installment of religious staff is the religious organization's internal affairs, made after the organization is established.

Article 27 of the State Council's Religious Affairs Provisions states: "After installing its religious staff and sending it for the record to the religious affairs department of the People's Government at county level or above, the religious organization can carry out its religious activities." A prerequisite that applies to this article is that the religious organization has been established. So, the installment of religious staff is what is done after the organization is established. And it is the religious organization's internal affairs. The regulation also stipulates that the authority of the religious affairs department over this issue is confined to putting it on record only, rather than examination and approval.

Likewise, Article 13 of Beijing Religious Affairs Regulations is to regulate the religious organization's internal affairs after it is established. But the Ethnic, Religious and Overseas Chinese Affairs Office of Beijing Haidian District mistakenly applied it to the issue of examination and approval before the religious organization is established, which goes against the law.

3. The installment of religious staff can only be made by the religious organization itself rather than other religious organizations.

Article 5 of Regulations for Registration and Management of Social Organizations states: "The state will protect social organizations and their activities conducted in accordance with the law, regulations and rules; other organizations or persons must not unlawfully interfere with them." As the internal affairs of a religious organization, the installment of religious staff should not be unlawfully interfered with by other organizations or persons. It can't be decided by other religious organizations.

The decision made by the Ethnic, Religious and Overseas Chinese Affairs Office of Beijing Haidian District that the installment of a pastor of Beijing Shouwang Christian Church should be decided by other religious organizations goes against not only Article 5 of Regulations for Registration and Management of Social Organizations, but also the basic principle that social organizations should stand equal with each other.

II. The misuse of the regulation by the Ethnic, Religious and Overseas Chinese Affairs Office of Beijing Haidian District will lead to grave chaos in the church-state relationship.

The decision made by the Ethnic, Religious and Overseas Chinese Affairs Office of Beijing Haidian District concerning the installment of religious staff according to Article 13 of Beijing Religious Affairs Regulations means the non-Three-Self Protestant churches must gain approval of the Three-Self Protestant Patriotic Movement Committee to be registered as religious organizations. To us, this will result in serious chaos in the church-state relationship in China and will also re-intensify the contradictions between the Three-Self and the non-Three-Self churches in faith and history.

1. That the registration of non-Three-Self churches must win approval of the Three-Self Patriotic Movement Committee runs counter to both the Constitution and Religious Affairs Provisions.

First, the Constitution stipulates that citizens of the People's Republic of China enjoy freedom of religious beliefs. This freedom should not only refer to freedom of thought since freedom of thought is a given fact that cannot be stripped of by any person or organization. So, freedom of religious beliefs should much more refer to the right that citizens of religious beliefs can lead a normal life of religious beliefs in line with their religious scriptures and traditions. With regard to religious groups, the government's Religious Affairs Provisions do not list the Three-Self Patriotic Movement Committee as the only religious group that other Protestant organizations must join. Any church should have the right to be registered as a religious organization. No doubt this right is in accordance to the Constitution. We do not deny that the Three-Self Patriotic Movement Committee has the constitutional right to exist as a registered religious organization. Yet, if its exercise of the constitutional right means all the non-Three-Self churches lose their constitutional right, then the constitutional right it exercises is not a constitutional right at all. Therefore, the practice that only by the approval of the Three-Self churches can the non-Three-Self churches apply for registration has gravely violated the Constitution.

Second, the practice that demands the non-Three-Self churches join the Three-Self churches through administrative examination and approval has also gravely violated the principle of the separation of church and state. We believe neither the government nor the Three-Self Patriotic Movement Committee should have or has the right to make such a demand. If it is made by the government then it has gone beyond its limits of power meddling with the internal affairs and belief of the church. (We will show later that the main difference between the Three-Self Patriotic Movement Committee and the non-Three-Self churches does not lie in the form of organization but in stance on belief and theology.) And if it is made by the Three-Self Patriotic Movement Committee, then it shows the Three-Self has become an extension of the government's function of administration. If it is so, what qualification does the Three-Self have for determining the qualification of pastorship in the newly established religious organizations? The paradox this practice has brought about is evident.

We believe a truly down-to-earth approach to the issue of the non-Three-Self churches is this: the right of the non-Three-Self churches to be registered by law should be recognized, they should be seen as religious organizations equal with the Three-Self churches before the law, so that healthy church-state relationship can be formed on the basis of the rule of law, which goes along with the goal of building a harmonious society in China. On the contrary, any practice that cracks down on one side while propping up the other will only bring about the result that goes against the government's wishes. This has been proved by the history of the Chinese churches in recent decades.

2. That the registration of non-Three-Self churches must win approval of the Three-Self Patriotic Movement Committee, which runs counter to both the Constitution and Religious Affairs Provisions, will intensify the contradictions between the Three-Self and the non-Three-Self churches in faith and history. For from both the belief and theology of the Christian tradition and the history of Chinese churches over the past more than five decades, the Three-Self Patriotic Movement Committee has no credentials to determine the pastorship in non-Three-Self churches.

First, the Three-Self Patriotic Movement Committee is a product of a special historical period, created through the political movement at that time. We believe church cannot be united with political power, nor can it participate in political movement. Whenever it is "weak in power" or has "numerical superiority," church's alliance with political power must bring about the secularization of church and church's interference in political power. This has been proved entirely by the church in medieval Europe. The separation of church and state is a principle most churches around the world abide by, which has been proved by history favorable to the social development. The creation of the Three-Self Patriotic Movement Committee itself has violated the principle of separation of church and state. Therefore, it can't be a representative of most churches, nor can it be a leadership organization that liaises churches with the same stance as most churches. It has no credentials to determine the pastorship in non-Three-Self churches, which is a crucial reason why so many Christians and churches did not join the Three-Self Patriotic Movement Committee, either when the Three-Self was established or five decades later.

Second, the history of the Three-Self movement shows it has not brought about the growth of churches, making a great number of churches closed instead (for instance, Beijing had 66 Protestant churches but only 4 remained after the Three-Self movement). What's more, some pastors and believers were sent to prison only because they did not participate in the Three-Self Patriotic Movement Committee. Of course, this has something to do with the general circumstances then. However, as a party concerned, the Three-Self has made no apology for it until now. This is another important reason why the Three-Self Patriotic Movement Committee, though registered as a Christian organization, has not been accepted by many non-Three-Self churches.

Third, there has been an evident distinction between the Three-Self Patriotic Movement Committee and non-Three-Self churches with regard to belief and theology since it was established. What the Three-Self Patriotic Movement Committee holds is what is called "liberal" theology in church history, while non-Three-Self churches are evangelical. It is another important reason why some church leaders did not join the Three-Self Patriotic Movement Committee at the early stage of the movement. More than fifty years later, it's still evident in the Three-Self's theological construction that doubts the inerrancy of the Holy Bible and cripples the fundamental Christian doctrines such as Righteousness through Faith. These practices, which have gone astray from the basic Christian belief, can't be accepted by the evangelical non-Three-Self churches. That the pastorship in non-Three-Self churches is determined by the Three-Self Patriotic Movement Committee means the latter has become the "judge" deciding the legitimacy and orthodoxy of the former. It cannot be accepted by most non-Three-Self churches.

Fourth, to abide by the Three-Self principle does not mean churches must join the Three-Self Patriotic Movement Committee. The Three-Self Patriotic Movement Committee has mistakenly equated the Three-Self principle in church planning with joining the Three-Self Patriotic Movement Committee. If the Three-Self principle (Self-governing, Self-support and Self-propagation) is a must for churches to be registered, we couldn't agree more (Beijing Shouwang Christian Church has long realized the Three-Self—Self-propagation, Self-support and Self-governing—in a truly Three-Self way). The state's Religious Affairs Provisions (Article 4) stipulate that "All religions shall uphold the principle of independence and autonomy." Its essence is the Three-Self principle. Yet, to identify with the Three-Self principle does not mean one must join the Three-Self Patriotic Movement Committee; conversely, that churches do not join the Three-Self Patriotic Movement Committee does not mean they disagree with the Three-Self principle in church planning. Moreover, the Three-Self Patriotic Movement Committee itself was in fact not established in a way of Self-propagation, Self-support and Self-governing. It was set up through obtaining property left behind by foreign ministries and evangelists (in most cases without proper and formal handover). And it brought into its own system those established churches by taking advantage of political movement. So it's not difficult to see that such a Three-Self would be in an untenable position among Christian churches that genuinely uphold the Three-Self principle. And it's apparently unconvincing that the criteria about the realization of the Three-Self principle rests in whether a church has joined such a Three-Self organization or not, and that this even is made as a precondition for registration.

Lastly, the membership of the Three-Self Patriotic Movement Committee can't be used as a standard to judge whether a church is patriotic or not. Since the Three-Self Reform Movement was changed into the Three-Self Patriotic Movement in 1954, the issue of patriotism has been used by the organization as a sharp political weapon to silence anyone who disagrees with it. A logic was formed in the social atmosphere then that not joining the Three-Self Patriotic Movement Committee was against the Three-Self principle, and against the Three-Self principle was against patriotism and against patriotism, was against revolution. Now more than five decades on, when building a harmonious society tops the government's agenda, such logic seems to be no longer mentioned publicly since it has been regarded as an "extreme-left" route. Yet, if the government's religious affairs department does not give up such logic consciously or even uses it as the underlying yardstick for church registration, a likely result will be that a great number of Christians who are patriotic but refuse to join the Three-Self Patriotic Movement Committee will be pushed into opposition artificially, which will definitely do patriotic citizens a great harm and is unfavorable to the social harmony, stability and prosperity.

3. That the registration of non-Three-Self churches must win approval of the Three-Self Patriotic Movement Committee does not conform to the religious policy that the relevant government department has repeatedly asserted including the assertion from the Three-Self Patriotic Movement Committee itself.

In response to the questions of "must the registered Protestant organizations join the 'Three-Self'? Can they not join the 'Three-Self' and become independent organizations?", State Religious Affairs Bureau Director Ye Xiaowen says clearly: "the 'Three-Self' is a non-governmental Christian organization while the registration is a government work. Whether join the 'Three-Self' organization or not does not constitute a requirement for registration." (*Telling the Truth of Religions in China to the American People—A Transcript of Ye Xiaowen's Q&A*, Religion and Culture Press, 1999, pp. 90–91) Since the "Three-Self" is "a non-governmental Christian organization," then what qualification has it to determine the pastorship in other religious organizations? And since registration is "a government work," then why must the registration be approved by the "Three-Self"?

Ding Guangxun, the former Chairman of the Three-Self Patriotic Movement Committee, once gave his comments in an interview about the issue of China's house church registration: "For example, there're some reports abroad that the reason why underground churches don't register is that they are unwilling to register with the 'Three-Self' claiming the 'Three-Self' people have some problems with their belief. In fact it is a big misunderstanding, because the registration is not with the 'Three-Self' but with the government's religious affairs department by law." (Ethnic and Religious Affairs Committee of Zhejiang Province, www.zjsmzw.gov.cn, *Bishop Ding Guangxun on Theological Construction*, Zhang Xiuxiu.) Since the Three-Self itself has made it clear that the registration of house churches has nothing to do with the Three-Self, then the reason given by the Ethnic, Religious and Overseas Chinese Affairs Office of Beijing Haidian District for refusing the registration request of Beijing Shouwang Christian Church is apparently untenable.

•••

The foregoing paragraphs are the main reasons we put forward in our Request for Administrative Review submitted to the Beijing Religious Affairs Bureau. Now, we still believe they conform to both Religious Affairs Provisions and Regulations for Registration and Management of Social Organizations. And we believe they also conform to the current situation of churches in China. So, our query is apparent: what on earth is the stance over the issue of the registration and the interpretation of the relevant regulations of the State Council and the State Religious Affairs Bureau that's responsible for leading the country's religious affairs? We hope the State Religious Affairs Bureau will give its explanation on this issue, which we believe will be the most authoritative and final interpretation.

Part 3
Suggestions for building harmonious church-state relations

As is well-known, since the Three-Self movement in the 1950s, there has been a kind of church in China that doesn't join the Three-Self Patriotic Movement Committee, commonly known as "house churches." House churches have suffered many hardships and even various kinds of persecution over the past fifty years because they did not join the "Three-Self" organization and thus fell into the so-called "illegal" status. (Yet, since no Religious Law has ever been promulgated, it is questionable whether house churches can be judged "illegal.") Despite this, God has kept his churches alive. Over the past fifty years, they have veritably experienced God's providence, presence and blessing and they have grown into an extensive community of Christian believers beyond the Three-Self.

Fifty years on, neither house churches nor the government can neglect the existence of each other. It's high time that both sides faced each other to solve the problem. It would be a blessing for the church, the government and the wider society. In today's China where the construction of a harmonious society has been high on the agenda, we would like to make a few suggestions.

I. House churches should give up old enmity, opening talks with the government.

Over the past half-century, an inappropriate church-state relationship has done harm to Chinese churches. This historical harm in turn has brought two major attitudes to Chinese churches. One is the submission to the governing authorities out of fear. A typical representative of this attitude is the early Three Self Patriotic Movement, which stresses that "Everyone must submit himself to the governing authorities, for there is no authority except that which God has established. The authorities that exist have been established by God. Consequently, he who rebels against the authority is rebelling against what God has instituted." (Romans 13:1–2) Yet, it overlooks an equally important biblical teaching that "rulers hold no terror for those who do right, but for those who do wrong. Do you want to be free from fear of the one in authority? Then do what is right and he will commend you … if you do wrong, be afraid … Therefore, it is necessary to submit to the authorities, not only because of possible punishment but also because of conscience." (Romans 13:3–5) It is impossible to realize the ideal to love God and to love the country with the submission to the government "not out of conscience that comes from the fear of God, but out of fear," since there is no love in the submission out of fear. As it goes in the Bible, "There is no fear in love. But perfect love drives out fear, because fear has to do with punishment. The one who fears is not made perfect in love." (1 John 4:18) The other attitude is to try and avoid facing the government based on the belief that the authorities come from the devil because of the long-standing oppression and persecution the church has experienced. A typical representative of this attitude is the house churches in the past. We understand that this attitude does not go in line with the teachings of the Bible either. The Bible has clearly told us that the government's right to govern the country is given by God and therefore it should be respected. The submission to the authorities comes from the conscience out of the fear of God. (Romans 13:5) If the church always avoids facing the authorities with the feeling of being hurt and goes underground, then it is impossible to do its duty of glorifying God and benefiting people. As it goes in the Bible, "You are the salt of the earth. But if the salt loses its saltiness, how can it be made salty again? It is no longer good for anything, except to be thrown out and trampled by men. You are the light of the world. A city on a hill cannot be hidden. Neither do people light the lamp and put it under a bowl. Instead, they put it on its stand, and it gives light to everyone in the house. In the same way, let your light shine before men, that they may see your good deeds and praise your Father in heaven." (Matthew 5:13–16)

In order to establish an appropriate church-state relationship, the Chinese church must go out of the shadow caused by historical harm, face the government, open dialogue with the government, actively make it known what the church believes and where it stands, let the government know more about the truth of a real church, and shoulder the social responsibility on its own. All this would make a positive impact on the church, the government and the wider society. Of course, the dialogue between the church and the government hasn't gone without difficulty. For our part, we understand such a process needs more time and it's possible for the church to pay the price once again. Although it is not what we would like to see, the church should take its due responsibility.

II.   The realization of the principle of separation of church and state is the key to solving the house church issue.

The realization of the basic principle of separation of church and state constitutes the nucleus of building harmonious church-state relations. In this process, the government has a more important role to play. Especially with regard to improving its relations with the house church, the government should make its due efforts.

First, the government should respect citizens' freedom of religious belief and protect the normal religious activities of house churches. What we mean by saying "freedom of religious belief" does not only refer to freedom of individual mind but also freedom of practice in religious belief, *i.e.*, citizens who have religious belief have the right to lead their life according to their own scriptures and doctrines. Otherwise, freedom of religious belief is but nominal since every belief involves the relevant religious activities. Of course, freedom of religious belief is not unlimited by law. Yet, the aim of the rule of law is to protect public safety or other people's fundamental rights from being infringed upon. As it goes in *International Covenant on Civil and Political Rights*, "Freedom to manifest one's religion or beliefs may be subject only to such limitations as are prescribed by law and are necessary to protect public safety, order, health, or morals or the fundamental rights and freedoms of others." (Article 18) It means that our religious life and activities are free as long as our religious life and activities won't harm "public safety, order, health, or morals or the fundamental rights and freedoms of others." Given this standard, the meetings of house churches are the normal religious activities and should be protected rather than being banned as long as they won't harm "public safety, order, health, or morals or the fundamental rights and freedoms of others." (Religious Affairs Provisions: Article 3) Otherwise, it would be ludicrous that it's legal to get together for studying ancient literature but illegal to get together for studying the Bible, and it's legal to get together for singing but illegal to get together for hymning.

Second, the government should respect the independence of the church and genuinely uphold "the principle of independence and self-governance" of the church. (Religious Affairs Provisions: Article 4) We would like the government to understand that the independence and self-governance of the church is part and parcel of the faith the church has kept. It even determines whether the church belongs to Jesus Christ. In order to safeguard the church's independence and self-governance, the church has suffered many persecutions. Despite this, the church never gives it up. And of course, the church can't give it up. Otherwise, the church would give up the basic principles of its beliefs and would no longer be after God's own heart. The independence and self-governance of the church means the church has the right to elect and remove its leaders, develop ministry and manage finance. The installment of religious staff is a classic example concerning the church's right of self-governance. From the viewpoint of independence and self-governance of the church, the installment of a pastor apparently should be made according to the principles of the Bible. The pastor should be elected by the church members who are led by the Holy Spirit rather than being approved by the government's religious department or the Three-Self organization. And the relevant regulation also stipulates that the authority of the religious affairs department over the church activities is confined to putting on record only rather than examination and approval. If the government would really like to build harmonious church-state relations, it should abide by the principle of the separation of church and state completely letting the church self-govern and self-support. Of course, to defend the sovereignty of the church does not mean the church is immune from other state laws. As a social organization, the church should accept the necessary legal supervision and its staff should be put on record.

Third, the government should view the Three-Self and house church equally and shouldn't try to bring the house church into the Three-Self system through administrative regulations. We have no intention to deny the legality of the Three-Self. Nor do we deny that the church in the Three-Self is the church of Jesus Christ and those who sincerely believe in Jesus Christ are our brothers and sisters. What we cannot accept is that the Three-Self has the authority over the house church. As it is made clear in our Request for Administrative Review, a genuinely positive and down-to-earth attitude the government should have is to acknowledge that the house church is entitled to be registered as a religious organiza-tion that is equal before the law with the Three-Self church. This attitude would help build healthy church-state relations on the basis of law and in accord with the goal of building a harmonious society in China. On the contrary, any approach that favors one party and cracks down on the other would only lead to the other way around. It has been very evident in the history of Chinese church over the past several decades.

III. The registration of house church should be solved by law.

As a faith-based group, the Christian church has been in existence on the earth for two thousand years. The meaning of the church's regis-tration does not lie in the point that an organization becomes a church through registration, but through registration the church becomes a social organization that exercises its legal right and shoulders its due social re-sponsibility. A child is born a human being no matter whether he or she is registered with the authorities for residence. But once he or she is reg-istered, the person can exercise his or her legal right and shoulder his or her due social responsibility.

Over the past fifty years, the government has come from wiping out religion to taking control of religion (the Three-Self movement is a typi-cal example), from taking control of religion to cracking down on reli-gion (it often outlaws house churches in the name of keeping social stability), and from cracking down on religion to beginning to manage religion by law (Religious Affairs Provisions were issued and are in effect). Now, the time is ripe for the government to peacefully face the house church as the citizen's normal life of belief and normalize the church-state relations by law, rather than consider it a sensitive political issue or an issue of public security.

History shows that the government's approach to the house church issue from either political or public security angle has brought damage to both the government and the house church, resulting in the religious citizens' distrust of the government and estrangement between the government and the citizens of religious beliefs, which apparently go against the goal of building a harmonious society and the state stability. Therefore, given that no Religious Law has yet been promulgated, the most wise and down-to-earth approach is to allow the house church to register with the government as a religious organization based on the Religious Affairs Provisions. It is true that the Religious Affairs Provisions are not perfect. But after all, they are the first administrative regulation that aims to solve religious issues within the framework of law. And for now, they are the only possible legal way to normalize the relations between the government and the house church.

Conclusion

For two thousand years, the church of Jesus Christ has never stopped praying before God for each and every country the believers are in, even if they are misunderstood by their compatriots and harmed by their government. For the church believes that praying for the country is the will of God: "I urge, then, first of all, that requests, prayers, intercession and thanksgiving be made for everyone—for kings and all those in authority, that we may live peaceful and quiet lives in all godliness and holiness. This is good, and pleases God our Savior." (1 Timothy 3:3) And this is our wish when writing this report. We sincerely hope the report will be used for paving the way for building harmonious church-state relations, removing the wall between the government and the church and promoting the peace and stable development of the motherland. May God keep His church in China and bless China! Amen.

Finally, with the aim of building harmonious church-state relations and solving the issue of the registration of the house church, we would like to ask the State Bureau of Religious Affairs three questions concerning the registration of the house church. We very much look forward to the explicit answers.

1. As for the articles in the Religious Affairs Provisions regarding religious organizations, is it that they only refer to the Three-Self Patriotic Movement Committee when it comes to the Protestant church in China?

2. According to the Religious Affairs Provisions, can a house church be registered as a religious organization independent of the Three-Self Patriotic Movement Committee?

3. According to the Regulations for Reporting Religious Personnel for Record (approved by the State Bureau of Religious Affairs on December 25, 2006, and in effect since March 1, 2007), if the house church would like to be registered as a religious organization independent of the Three-Self Patriotic Movement Committee, does it mean that the house church can only be registered as a national religious organization?

Appendix to Chapter 13
A Letter from 1851

I did not expect I would really hear from this organization—The Royal Commission for the Exhibition of 1851. But at 10:13 p.m. April 28, 2010, Beijing time, my email inbox did receive a message from one of its people. In her note, Mrs. Angela Kenny told me that they found in their archives a copy of a British press report on March 22, 1850, about Prince Albert's speech the previous day declaring the founding of The Royal Commission for the Exhibition of 1851.

It came just a day after I wrote to the commission inquiring about the speech and the origin of the Exhibition of 1851. From Mrs. Kenny's email, I got a photocopy of the report showing not only the speech but also how the audiences responded to it. What surprised me is that an organization that was established for holding the first World Exposition remains alive. It has a website where I found the contact information. But it wasn't until I got the message from Mrs. Kenny that I came to be well aware of the fact that it is indeed still running. Since 1851, the commission has used the profits of the exhibition to build a number of museums and what would become well-known institutions of learning like the Imperial College and the Royal Colleges of Art and Music. The commission also has been providing scholarships for young people to study in Britain and abroad. Among these scholars, 12 were Nobel Prize laureates.

I knew this fact a couple of days before Shanghai was to host Expo 2010. Then I wrote an article about this discovery for *Vista*, a leading news and general-interest Chinese magazine at which I worked then. The magazine published most of the piece. Apart from what the 1851 commission has done, the article mentioned Prince Albert's speech and went on to explore why the husband of Queen Victoria related the study of science and technology to the image of God.

Below is the main part of the speech the then thirty-year-old Francis Albert Augustus Charles Emmanuel delivered at the Mansion House, London, on March 21, 1850.

... Gentlemen, I conceive it to be the duty of every educated person closely to watch and study the time in which he lives, and as far as in him lies, to add his humble mite of individual exertion to further the accomplishment of what he believes Providence to have ordained. (Cheers.)

Nobody, however, who has paid any attention to the particular features of our present era will doubt for a moment that we are living at a period of most wonderful transition, which tends rapidly to accomplish that great end—to which indeed all history points— the realization of the unity of mankind. (Great cheering.)

Not a unity which breaks down the limits and levels the peculiar characteristics of the different nations of the earth, but rather a unity that is the result and product of those very national varieties and antagonistic qualities.

The distances which separated the different nations and parts of the globe are gradually vanishing before the achievements of modern invention, and we can traverse them with incredible speed; the languages of all nations are known and their acquirements placed within the reach of everybody; thought is communicated with the rapidity, and even by the power of lightning.

On the other hand, the great principle of the division of labour, which may be called the moving power of civilization, is being extended to all branches of science, industry, and art.

Whilst formerly the greatest mental energies strove at universal knowledge, and that knowledge was confined to a few, now they are directed to specialities, and in these again even to the minutest points. But the knowledge acquired becomes at once the property of the community at large; whilst, formerly discovery was wrapt in secresy, it results from the publicity of the present day that no sooner is a discovery or invention made than it is already improved upon and surpassed by competing efforts. (Cheers.) The products of all quarters of the globe are placed at our disposal, and we have only to choose what is the best and the cheapest for our purposes, and the powers of production are entrusted to the stimulus of competition and capital.

So man is approaching a more complete fulfilment of that great and sacred mission which he has to perform in this world. His reason being created after the image of God, he has to use it to discover the laws by which the Almighty governs His creation, and, by making these laws his standard of action, to conquer nature to his use— himself a divine instrument.

Science discovers these laws of power, motion, and transformation; industry applies them to the raw matter which the earth yields us in abundance, but which becomes valuable only by knowledge; art teaches us the immutable laws of beauty and symmetry, and gives to our productions forms in accordance with them. (Cheers.)

Gentlemen, the exhibition of 1851 is to give us a true test and a living picture of the point of development at which the whole of mankind has arrived in this great task, and a new starting point from which all nations will be able to direct their further exertions. (Cheers.)

I confidently hope that the first impression which the view of this vast collection will produce on the spectator will be that of deep thankfulness to the Almighty for the blessings which He has bestowed upon us already here below; and the second, the conviction that they can only be realized in proportion to the help which we are prepared to render each other,—therefore, only by peace, love, and ready assistance, not only between individual, but between the nations of the earth.

Appendix to Chapter 16
A Quest for International Journalism

September 16, 2011

To whom it may concern,

My name is Promise Hsu, an independent journalist based in Beijing, the capital of China.[332] I wish to participate in this fellowship about coaching and leadership based on my professional life as a journalist so far. I want to learn and grow further with my colleagues from around the globe and help my younger colleagues to learn and grow both as a person and as a media practitioner.

I have been a journalist since 1999 when I finished a five-year undergraduate study majoring in International Journalism at Beijing Broadcasting Institute, a leading institution of higher learning in broadcast journalism in China. For six years, I worked at *China Central Television* or *CCTV*, China's state-run broadcaster, as a world affairs reporter covering mainly domestic and international politics. I helped launch the English news channel of *CCTV* in 2000. That was the first ever 24-hour global news television channel in China. My colleagues came from China, America, Canada, Europe, Australia, New Zealand, the Philippines and some other parts of the world. I also have experience of working with radios, magazines, newspapers and websites. I helped set up a weekly newspaper and a monthly magazine. I wrote articles or columns for a number of leading Chinese-language business and news-and-general-interest magazines and websites over the past few years, such as

332 It was originally written as an essay of interest for The Media Project's 2012 Coaching and Leadership Fellowship.

Global Entrepreneur, Vista, Asian Business Leaders, yeeyan.org. And my writings in English appeared in some American magazines and websites like *World Magazine, Christianity Today, Compass Direct News,* and *The Media Project.*

In the meantime, I helped launch and joined in training programs at the university where I studied and the media organizations I worked with. For example, in 1995 Zheng Ye, a university classmate and I invited Carrie Gracie, then a *BBC* correspondent in Beijing and now a *BBC* news presenter in London,[333] to give a lecture at my university about the British public service broadcaster. While working at *CCTV*, I helped younger colleagues learn how to write and read a story and how to produce a program based on the excellent examples from *BBC, CNN, Reuters, The Associated Press, AFP, The Economist* and the like. In April 2008, I took part in inviting John Micklethwait, the Editor-in-Chief of *The Economist*, to share his thoughts regarding the international weekly newspaper with my colleagues in Beijing. That came a year after my colleagues and I did an interview with Daniel Franklin, Executive Editor of *The Economist*. In 2009 and 2010, I gave talks about how *The Economist* could keep growing more than 160 years since its inception at the two magazines' offices where I worked. From 2008 on, I have attended or helped organize seminars and workshops of The Media Project, a non-profit educational and research organization for journalists worldwide, in Australia, America, Indonesia, the Philippines, and China. In 2009 and 2011, I was nominated to attend Stein am Rhein Symposium for Leaders of the Next Generation of stars, a global forum for young professionals from diverse fields, first in Stein am Rhein, Switzerland and then in Penglai, China. And in August 2007, I was invited to address the annual international conference of American Political Science Association in Chicago about my research concerning the history of liberty.

All those experiences have equipped me to begin developing

---

333 The first time I came into contact with Carrie Gracie was in early 1990s when I was a high school student. She wrote back answering my queries regarding some basic facts of *BBC*. In early 2014, Carrie Gracie became *BBC*'s first ever China Editor. See: "Carrie Gracie leaves *BBC News Channel*," January 3, 2014, BBC News, http://www.bbc.co.uk/news/entertainment-arts-25590442 .

personal, local, global, historical and holistic perspectives whether it be politics, business, culture, science and technology. Many of the articles I have written aimed at making myself, my colleagues and the broader audiences cultivate not only independent but also multi-dimensional viewpoints. A series of pieces, first appearing in the *Global Entrepreneur* magazine from 2008 to early 2010 and later in some other media, explored the spiritual and intellectual foundations of a free and responsible citizenry by telling stories behind the headlines and studying institutions as different as companies, churches, universities, foundations, and political parties. During the process, I made field trips to some of the hardest-hit areas of the Sichuan Earthquake in southwest China, rallies of 2008 US presidential elections in northeast America, rising companies and skyscrapers in Abu Dhabi and Dubai in the United Arab Emirates. Some articles intended to shed light on the factors that helped build up such far-reaching figures in shaping freedom and responsibility as John Calvin, a 16th-century French theologian whose thoughts profoundly influenced Western society, and Peter Drucker, himself once a journalist, a columnist for decades and widely considered the founder of modern management, and Marshall McLuhan, a Canadian philosopher known for coining the expressions "the global village" and "the medium is the message."

Of course, neither figures nor institutions should become a cult of personality. They are just part of the far wider world. Numerous stories are to be told. The stories are told to tell the truth. The truth could help both the journalists and the audiences make better sense of the world we live in and how we could live a free and responsible life. For me, both The Media Project and The Poynter Institute stand for supporting and promoting excellent journalism, which is part and parcel of a free and responsible civilization. From the seminars and workshops I have attended, I have been very impressed by the visionary leadership of Dr. Arne Fjeldstad, CEO of The Media Project, and the significance of faith in journalism he has highlighted. I have never been to The Poynter Institute. If granted an opportunity, I believe I will benefit a lot, along with my global colleagues, from the respected tradition to which the institute has held fast for decades—"a journalism that informs citizens and enlightens public discourse" and "independent journalism in the public interest."

The other day, I read what Nelson Poynter, the founder of the institute, said in 1977 about the value of being a journalist: "It's a great privilege to run a newspaper, it's certainly been more rewarding than just having some stocks or bonds and living off the dividends or coupons. I guess I'm rather narrow-minded in that respect. I'd rather be a newspaper editor than the richest man in the world." I really appreciate this rather broad mind and would like to share it with as many colleagues as possible.

Thank you so much for your consideration.

Best regards,

Sincerely,

Promise Hsu

Appendix to Epilogue
Civil Society: Shadow and Reality

It has been exactly six years since I had the honor of attending my first ever annual international meeting of Eric Voegelin Society at the American Political Science Association.[334] Six years later, also in Chicago, though not in the same hotel, I have another privilege for another annual international conference of EVS at APSA. Like the first time, I still can't believe I am here again.

I miss Professor Ellis Sandoz whom I met for the first time in 2007 at this gathering, and who has been helping me since 2006 with my liberty project. Without Professor Sandoz, I would never have read Eric Voegelin and have known the Eric Voegelin Society, let alone come here to see so many who have helped or benefited me in various ways. I plan to visit Professor Sandoz in Baton Rouge in a few days, hoping to learn more from him and to share with him what I have learned here.

In 2007, I delivered a paper entitled "God and the Essence of Liberty: A Preliminary Inquiry into the History of Freedom." That summarized the major things I had learned mainly during the initial two years of research after I started up a project exploring the history of liberty in 2005. The chief point then was, "the single most important thing I would like to share with you here is this. The faith in God as the LORD is the beginning of freedom."

---

334 This appendix was written for the 29th international conference of the American Political Science Association, August 29–September 1, 2013, in Chicago, Illinois. It was planned to be delivered at Eric Voegelin Society's Panel 7: Liberty and Order in China after the 18th Party Congress at 2:00 p.m. August 30, 2013. But the presentation was not made fully at that time.

Now, in 2013, that humble and little paper has grown into a humble and little book tentatively entitled *China's Quest for Liberty: A Personal History of Freedom*. It is expected to be published by St. Augustine's Press in spring 2014. It is, again, Professor Sandoz who helped contact Mr. Bruce Fingerhut, the founder of St. Augustine's Press.

In the epilogue of that small book, I learned to recall some of the most important things I have known from reading Eric Voegelin and Ellis Sandoz over the past several years. A key issue concerns the contrast between shadow and reality. Here, I will not go into detail about how I was led, much beyond my expectation, to become aware of and even sensitive to the distinction between shadow and reality. That can be found in the book's epilogue.[335]

I will explore civil society and its history as an example to indicate how the differentiation of shadow and reality could help show the deeper meaning of and broader perspective on civil society as both an important political idea and an important political institution. This, I think, will help make much more sense of not only liberty and order, or rather still lack of them, after the 18th Party Congress in China but also how liberty and order can still be grown and revealed in China and the wider world now and beyond.

About three months ago, on May 22-24, 2013, the Chinese University of Hong Kong held a workshop named "China's Religious NGO and Civil Society." The night of May 23 saw a debate, "Should the house church get involved in building civil society?"

This debate was of surprise help for me. Whatever thought one would have, he or she was required to follow the moderator's arrangement as being either for or against. It would demand that any participant shelve one's own idea and speak out why one is for or against. A significant help was that I was led to reflect on civil society itself, that is: what on earth is a civil society, what is a citizen?

---

335 Most of the epilogue, "The Reality of Politics: A Preliminary Reading of Eric Voegelin and Ellis Sandoz," was published as an independent essay in *VoegelinView*. It was presented in six parts beginning in late April 2013: http://voegelinview.com/all-Current-Articles/the-reality-of-politics-pt-1.html.

Basically, the Chinese expression of "公民社会" (transliterated as, gongmin shehui) is the translation of "civil society" in English or its equivalents in other European languages. They owe their origin to "societas civilis" in Latin, which first appeared in Cicero's (106 B.C.–43 B.C.) *De re publica* or *On the Commonwealth*. According to Cicero, it was "a common feeling of right" that united a commonwealth that was "a community of interests" where "the law is the bond of civil society." Here, "civil society" was also rendered as "community of citizens" since "community" is closer to the original meaning of "societas" than "society."[336]

An even older origin of "civil society" was found in Aristotle's (384 B.C.–322 B.C.) *Politics*, "koinonia politike" meaning "political community," which refers to polis in Greek or civitas in Latin or city in English. Around 1279, a theologian called Giles of Rome (c.1243–1316) translated "koinonia politike" into "societas civilis." This has come to be used widely from the fifteenth century on.[337]

For Aristotle, "political community"—city—is not merely a combination of families and villages but the highest community of human beings. Compared with families and villages, political community seeks greater and higher interests in both degree and nature.[338] A political community is made up of free citizens under the rule of law for the public interests.

However, there is no significant difference yet between state and society in either "political community" of Aristotle or "community of citizens" of Cicero. This difference is characteristic of what "civil society" means since late medieval and modern times of the West. A civil society, in this sense, is made up of free citizens who volunteer to join together

---

336 Helmut K. Anheier and Stefan Toepler eds., *International Encyclopedia of Civil Society* (Springer Science+Business Media, 2010), 342; Cicero, Francis Barham and C. D. Yonge trans., *On the Commonwealth* (Harper and Brothers, 1877), 444, 383; Cicero, Niall Rudd trans., *The Republic and The Laws* (Oxford University Press, 2008), 22.

337 Dominique Colas, Amy Jacobs trans., *Civil Society and Fanaticism: Conjoined Histories* (Stanford University Press, 1997), 28.

338 Peter L. Phillips Simpson trans, *The Politics of Aristotle* (The University of North Carolina Press, 1997), 8.

for their public interests under the rule of law and free of the state's coercion and interference. In a further differentiation, a civil society would also mean it should be free of commercial interests and thus constitute the third sector outside of state and business.[339]

In the current Chinese context, talk of civil society evidently shows (and is also considerably due to) a lack of civil society in China's mainland. Such insufficiency seems to be in the sense of both ancient Graeco-Roman and late medieval and modern times. In the Chinese mainland, the state is not a political community under the rule of law, and the voluntary association of citizens and their self-governance are subject to the state's coercion and interference. The case of China may illustrate that without a political community in ancient Graeco-Roman sense, it is very hard for a civil society in the sense of late medieval and modern periods to emerge viably.

How the state could be brought under the rule of law is a key issue. In *Politics*, Aristotle pointed out, "it is more proper that law should govern than any one of the citizens."[340] A word of Cicero has been repeatedly quoted indicating his view on human's relation to law, "all of us are servants of the law that we can be free."[341]

Similar expressions not only have appeared often in the history of the West but also have spread further in the wider world.[342] For instance, in China, many persons have heard more or less about the difference between "the rule of law" and "the rule of man." That came no matter whether he or she has read Aristotle or Cicero. They may have not yet

---

339 Peter Wagner ed., *The Languages of Civil Society* (Berghahn Books, 2006), 28; Jean Cohen and Andrew Arato, *Civil Society and Political Theory* (The MIT Press, 1994), 84–85; Virginia Ann Hodgkinson and Michael W. Foley eds., *The Civil Society Reader* (University Press of New England, 2003), 1.

340 Aristotle, William Ellis trans., *Politics: A Treatise on Government* (J M Dent & Sons Ltd., 1912), Book III, Chapter XVI: http://www.gutenberg.org/files/6762/6762-h/6762-h.htm .

341 E. Gillian Clark, Tessa Rajak eds., *Philosophy and Power in the Graeco-Roman World: Essays in Honour of Miriam Griffin* (Oxford University Press, 2002), 64.

342 Brian Z. Tamanaha, *On the Rule of Law: History, Politics, Theory* (Cambridge University Press, 2004).

known of James Harrington (1611–1677) or what he wrote in *The Commonwealth of Oceana*, "in a well-ordered commonwealth, not men should govern, but the laws" or "a commonwealth is an empire of laws and not of men."[343] However, it seems not many persons would agree seriously that any country with "commonwealth" or "republic" being part of its name could be under the rule of law instead of man. In comparison, a country like the United Kingdom rather than the People's Republic might be considered a paragon of the rule of law, albeit far from perfect.

As the idea of the rule of law was echoed in the Western history, it would be accompanied by another idea that could not be neglected. That is, law is not made by humans but humans discover law. It is the point that the American constitutional law scholar, Edward Samuel Corwin (1878–1963), made at the opening of part one of *The "Higher Law" Background of American Constitutional Law*.

Corwin quoted ancient Greek statesman, Demosthenes (384 B.C. – 322 B.C.), "Every law is a discovery, a gift of god,—a precept of wise men," showing this idea had existed from the ancients. He then quoted Calvin Coolidge (1872–1933), then the U.S. president, "Men do not make laws. They do but discover them ... That state is most fortunate in its form of government which has the aptest instruments for the discovery of law," proving "the persistence of the notion."[344]

If law is not what humans make but discover, it would mean the existence of law is independent of human beings. The questions are: where do humans discover law? who makes law? Humans in different times and places would think differently about the origins of law. For Demosthenes,

343 James Harrington, *The Commonwealth of Oceana*, Part I: http://www.gutenberg.org/files/2801/2801-h/2801-h.htm . See a Chinese translation: James Harrington, He Xin trans., *The Commonwealth of Oceana* (The Commercial Press, 1963).

344 Edward Samuel Corwin, "The 'Higher Law' Background of American Constitutional Law," in *Harvard Law Review*, Vol. 42, No. 2 (Dec., 1928), 153:http://www.classicapologetics.com/special/Corwin.HLR.12-1928.pdf. See a Chinese translation: Edward Samuel Corwin, Qiang Shigong trans., *The "Higher Law'" Background of American Constitutional Law* (Joint Publishing, 1996), 1.

law is "a gift of god." In human history, those who consider law "a gift of god" or hold similar views are very few. But, who is god? Or rather, who is the God? What is the thing about God? Are gods in ancient Greek and Roman cultures the makers of law? Are god or gods in other cultures God?

In this regard, the Christian church's impact is impossible not to be seen. The Christian church shaped the emergence of civil society in the sense of late medieval and modern times with the distinction between state and society as a main feature. A point that may be worthy of note is that the Christian church here is not just about its rise beginning in the first century A.D. but also the previous history leading up to it. That refers to the history when God set the Israelites apart from other nations recorded in the Old Testament. Already in the Old Testament, an Israelite king was not both monarch and priest.[345] In the time of the New Testament, the separation between the Christian church and the state is more evident.[346]

---

345 Numbers 16: 39–40: "So Eleazar the priest collected the bronze censers brought by those who had been burned up, and he had them hammered out to overlay the altar, as the LORD directed him through Moses. This was to remind the Israelites that no one except a descendant of Aaron should come to burn incense before the LORD, or he would become like Korah and his followers." 2 Chronicles 26: 18: "They confronted him and said, 'It is not right for you, Uzziah, to burn incense to the LORD. That is for the priests, the descendants of Aaron, who have been consecrated to burn incense. Leave the sanctuary, for you have been unfaithful; and you will not be honored by the LORD God.'"

346 Matthew 22: 21: "... Then he (Jesus) said to them, 'Give to Caesar what is Caesar's, and to God what is God's.'" An historical instance might be worthy of note. Hosius of Cordoba (c. 256 – 359) was a bishop of Cordoba of today's southern Spain. As a chief spiritual adviser to the Roman Emperor Constantine (c. 272 – 337), Hosius played a significant role in shaping the Council of Nicaea in 325 and the Nicene Creed. In a letter to Constantius II (317– 361), a son of Constantine, Hosius made it clear his view about the demarcation between church and state. That was when he was nearly 100 years old, towards the end of his life in this world. He wrote, " ... Cease these proceedings, I beseech you, and remember that you are a mortal man. Be afraid of the day of judgment, and keep yourself pure thereunto. Intrude not yourself into Ecclesiastical matters, neither

Of course, it could be viewed from an angle of culture that Israel's monotheism was passed on through the spread of the Christian church

give commands unto us concerning them; but learn them from us. God has put into your hands the kingdom; to us He has entrusted the affairs of His Church; and as he who would steal the empire from you would resist the ordinance of God, so likewise fear on your part lest by taking upon yourself the government of the Church, you become guilty of a great offence. It is written, 'Render unto Cæsar the things that are Cæsar's, and unto God the things that are God's.' Neither therefore is it permitted unto us to exercise an earthly rule, nor have you, Sire, any authority to burn incense." In the later history of the Roman Empire and that of Europe afterwards, similar ideas would become a recurrent theme and would considerably mould the uniquely spiritual and social framework of West Europe and North America. See: http://www.ccel.org/ccel/schaff/npnf204 .xx.ii.vi.html ; W. H. C. Frend, *The Rise of Christianity* (London: Darton, Longman and Todd, 1984), 535–36. Hosius' whole letter can be found in *Historia Arianorum* by Athanasius (c. 296 – 373). The idea on church and state of the Roman bishop, Gelasius I (? – 496), has also been repeatedly quoted in the Western history. For Gelasius, only Christ is the true priest and true king simultaneously. He wrote, " ... Before Christ's Advent, it may be, there were those who combined the role of kings with that of priests—as a prophetic sign, to be sure, yet in actual practice; the sacred history tells us that holy Melchizedek was such a one (Gen. 14: 18). (This was the pattern which the devil imitated, usurping tyrannically, as always, what belongs to the worship of God, when pagan emperors used to bear the title *pontifex maximus*.) But once the true priest-king entered on the stage of history, there was no ruler who assumed the name of priest, nor any priest who laid claim to the royal scepter. For though the members of Christ, the true priest-king, partake of his nature, and so are said all-encompassingly to have assumed the two aspects of it—generically within the holy people, the 'royal priesthood' (1 Pet. 2: 9)—he has mediated this privilege by an all-encompassing manner of distributing it. Mindful of human weakness, as befits his care for his own, he has made a distinction between the two roles, assigning each its sphere of operation and its due respect. In this way he planned that the medicine of humility should keep his people free from further infection by human pride. Christian emperors were to depend on priests for their eternal life, priests were to profit from imperial government for their historical existence. Spiritual activity must have a distance from routine interruptions; so God's soldier does not involve himself in secular affairs (2 Tim. 2: 4), while those involved in se-

along the coasts of the Mediterranean Sea and came to form an important part of what is called "Western civilization" after integrating with various local cultures.

With a view of the Christian faith, monotheism in the sense of culture is more about its manifestation in form. In substance, it is the true image of God, his governing order and all the relevant reality revealed through the Word becoming flesh to his human beings, not just the Israelites but persons across the world. The protagonist is not any believer, nor the belief, but God himself.[347]

Then, what is even more fundamental is about knowing who the God is and obeying the true God. If not knowing the true God, how can human beings discover and obey the true law God made, let alone talk about civil society or political community under the rule of law? But if stopping short of an idea that knowing the true God and obeying him is favorable to building a country or society under the rule of law, it is still not of the essence. If there is a law higher than a constitution, like the "higher law" Corwin discussed, there should be a higher country.

In the context of the history recorded and interpreted in the Bible,[348] a higher country is God's kingdom or the kingdom of heaven. It is what the God who became flesh began to proclaim on earth, "Repent, for the

cular affairs are seen to have no charge of divine affairs. That way is safeguarded, on the one hand, the modesty of each other, avoiding the pride to which the double responsibility might give rise; on the other, each sphere has a specially qualified and trained profession. Pull all that together, and it is clear that the secular power cannot 'bind and loose' a pontiff." See: Oliver O'Donovan and Joan Lockwood O'Donovan, eds, *From Irenaeus to Grotius: A Sourcebook in Christian Political Thought 100-1625* (William B. Eerdmans Publishing Company, 1999), 178–79. Walter Ullmann, *The Growth of Papal Government in the Middle Ages: A Study in the Ideological Relation of Clerical to Lay Power* (London: Methuen, 1955), 24–28. George E. Demacopoulos, *The Invention of Peter: Apostolic Discourse and Papal Authority in Late Antiquity* (University of Pennsylvania Press, 2013), 73–102.

347 Hebrews 1: 1–4. Colossians 1: 15–20.

348 2 Timothy 3: 16–17: "All Scripture is God-breathed and is useful for teaching, rebuking, correcting and training in righteousness, so that the man of God may be thoroughly equipped for every good work."

kingdom of heaven is near,"[349], or "The time has come. The kingdom of God is near. Repent and believe the good news."[350] On the one hand, that "the kingdom of heaven is near" means the country of earth is passing, including civil society or political community on earth. On the other hand, knowing God and obeying him would not just mean repentance of a person but leading an eternal life as a member of God's kingdom with other persons of repentance.

In an epistle to the church in Ephesus of today's southwest Turkey, the apostle Paul gave a description of a person in Christ, "Consequently, you are no longer foreigners and aliens, but fellow citizens with God's people and members of God's household."[351] In the widely-circulated Chinese Union version, "fellow citizens with God's people" is rendered as "being in the same country with fellow saints." But in the Greek and some popular English versions, it is "fellow citizens with God's people" [sumpolitai ton hagion (fellow citizens with the saints)].[352] The original meaning of "citizens" (politai) is members of a polis (city). In Latin, "civis" originally means lying down and settlement. It could refer to family and love.

Likewise, Paul wrote this in a letter to the church in Philippi of today's northeast Greece, "But our citizenship is in heaven. And we eagerly await a Savior from there, the Lord Jesus Christ, who by the power that enables him to bring everything under his control, will transform our lowly bodies so that they will be like his glorious body."[353] Again, in the popular Chinese Union version, "But our citizenship is in heaven" is translated as "But we are countrymen in heaven." In the Greek and some popular English versions, it is "But our citizenship is in heaven" [Hemon gar to politeuma en ouranois huparchei (literally: Of us for the citizenship in heavens is belonging)].[354] The root of "citizenship" (politeuma) is also [polis (city)].

Right here one may see a very interesting phenomenon. With the

---

349 Matthew 4: 17.
350 Matthew 1: 15.
351 Ephesians 2: 19.
352 See: http://www.scripture4all.org/OnlineInterlinear/NTpdf/eph2.pdf .
353 Philippians 3: 20–21.
354 See: http://www.scripture4all.org/OnlineInterlinear/NTpdf/phi3.pdf .

coming of the kingdom of heaven, countries on earth will be destroyed. Yet, the "kingdom" or "country" itself will remain. So will the "citizenship." In the kingdom that will last forever, a person of God is still a citizen. This means that even at the end of the ages, talking about "citizen," "citizenship" and "country" or "kingdom" is not just still meaningful but even more so because their deeper and everlasting meaning has been revealed. This country or kingdom can still be called polis or civitas. It is "the Jerusalem that is above,"[355] "the new Jerusalem,"[356] or "*City of God*" (De Civitate Dei)[357] Augustine (354–430) highlighted according to the Bible.[358]

355 Galatians 4: 26: "But the Jerusalem that is above is free, and she is our mother." According to the commentaries made by Martin Luther (1483 – 1546) http://www.ccel.org/ccel/luther/galatians.vii.html and John Calvin (1509 – 1564) http://www.ccel.org/ccel/calvin/calcom41.iii.vi.iv.html , "that is above" is not geographically speaking, but spiritually and essentially. It means of heaven.

356 Revelation 3:12: "Him who overcomes I will make a pillar in the temple of my God. Never again will he leave it. I will write on him the name of the city of my God, the new Jerusalem, which is coming down out of heaven from my God; and I will also write on him my new name." Revelation 21: 2: "I saw the Holy City, the new Jerusalem, coming down out of heaven from God, prepared as a bride beautifully dressed for her husband."

357 The whole name of Augustine's book is *De Civitate Dei contra Paganos* or *The City of God Against the Pagans*. In 412–426, Augustine spent thirteen years finishing this twenty-two-book tome in his late life. This came against the background of Rome being sacked by the Visigoths in 410, the first time in nearly 800 years. It was less than a hundred years after the Roman Empire officially recognized the Christian church and just 30 years after Theodosius I (347–395) proclaimed Nicene Christianity the sole authorized religion. With this backdrop, the idea of "two cities" came to be caught and would have far-reaching consequences in the Western world. One is the city on earth being of this world under "the prince of this world"; the other, the heavenly city being of God who is the eternal governor. Rome, though referred to as "The Eternal City," is no heavenly city. The heavenly city consists of the humans God redeemed and the serving angels sent by God with God as the Lord and the King. Augustine has been widely known for his deep insight into the idea of the two cities. The city of God Augustine discussed is neither entirely remote from this world

In another view of the Bible, the country on earth is not the true country but a copy with a slight likeness at most of the true one, or simply a fake, parody, or travesty. So is the citizen or citizenship on earth. This view is reflected in Hebrews: "The point of what we are saying is this: We do have such a high priest, who sat down at the right hand of the throne of the Majesty in heaven, and who serves in the sanctuary, the true tabernacle set up by the Lord, not by man ... If he were on earth, he would not be a priest, for there are already men who offer the gifts prescribed by the law. They serve at a sanctuary that is a

in time and space nor realized in this world. It is a phenomenon both temporarily and eternally. There are the humans God redeemed who are aliens and strangers in this world with the faith in God and waiting for the return of Christ. Many of them have left the visible world and many will be doing so. Since Christ has not returned yet according to his promise, the city of God remains sojourning in the city on earth. Once Christ returns, the city on earth will be gone forever and the city of God will be in eternity entirely. In this present world, the two cities are often mingled. According to Augustine, what differentiates the two cities are the two loves: "two cities have been formed by two loves: the earthly by the love of self, even to the contempt of God; the heavenly by the love of God, even to the contempt of self. The former, in a word, glories in itself, the latter in the Lord." See: Preface http://www.ccel.org/ccel/schaff/npnf102.iv.ii.i.html ; Book 11, Chapter 1 http://www.ccel.org/ccel/schaff/npnf102.iv.XI.1.html; Book 14, Chapter 28 http://www.ccel.org/ccel/schaff/ npnf102.iv.XIV.28.html ; Book 19, Chapter 17, 26 http://www.ccel.org/ ccel/schaff/npnf102.iv.XIX.17.html ,http://www.ccel.org/ccel/schaff/ npnf102.iv.XIX.26.html ; Peter Brown, *Augustine of Hippo: A Biography, Revised Edition with a New Epilogue* (University of California Press, 2000), 323–25; before writing *The City of God*, Augustine had already mentioned the idea of "two cities" in his commentaries on Genesis and expressed a wish to elaborate on this subject in the future. For more details, see: John Hammond Taylor, trans. and anno., *St. Augustine: The Literal Meaning of Genesis, Vol. 2, Books 7–12* (Mahwah, New Jersey: Paulist Press, 1982), 146–48.

358 For example, see Psalm 48: 1: "Great is the LORD, and most worthy of praise, in the city of our God, his holy mountain." Psalm 48: 8: "As we have heard, so have we seen in the city of the LORD Almighty, in the city of our God: God makes her secure forever." Psalm 87: 3: "Glorious things are said of you, O city of God."

copy and shadow of what is in heaven. This is why Moses was warned when he was about to build the tabernacle: 'See to it that you make everything according to the pattern shown you on the mountain.'"[359]

Even though the tabernacle in Exodus was built according to the pattern God told Moses, it was not the true tabernacle but "a copy and shadow of what is in heaven." Then, those things that are built not according to the pattern God commands are much less than "a copy and shadow of what is in heaven." They might be called "shadows" projected not from the true one in heaven but from human beings themselves or "the prince of this world."[360]

In his letter to the church in Colosse of today's southwest Turkey, Paul gave a similar expression, "So then, just as you received Christ Jesus as Lord, continue to live in him, rooted and built up in him, strengthened in the faith as you were taught, and overflowing with thankfulness. See to it that no one takes you captive through hollow and deceptive philosophy, which depends on human tradition and the basic principles of this world rather than on Christ. For in Christ all the fullness of the Deity lives in bodily form, and you have been given fullness in Christ, who is the head over every power and authority. ... And having disarmed the powers and authorities, he made a public spectacle of them, triumphing over them by the cross. Therefore do not let anyone judge you by what you eat or drink, or with regard to a religious festival, a New Moon celebration or a Sabbath day. These are a shadow of the things that were to come; the reality, however, is found in Christ."[361] The "reality" is translated from "soma" in Greek and as "body" in some popular English Bible versions.[362] Either body or reality, it is opposed to shadow.

So, as the body of Christ,[363] the Christian church's relationship with this world is clear. Obviously, the church's existence is not for building

---

359 Hebrews 8:1–5.

360 John 12: 31, 14: 30, 16: 11.

361 Colossians 2: 6–17.

362 See: http://www.scripture4all.org/OnlineInterlinear/NTpdf/col2.pdf .

363 Ephesians 1: 22–23: "And God placed all things under his feet and appointed him to be head over everything for the church, which is his body, the fullness of him who fills everything in every way." Colossians 1:24:

civil society or any ideal society in this world. That comes even though the church's existence has benefited the formation of civil society and seems to continue to do so in the wider world. From the angle of social institution, one may count the Christian church as part of civil society. However, if the Christian church is counted only as a social institution, the Christian church will not be the Christian church at all. The church of Christ does not come into being from the society of this world but is "coming down out of heaven from God."[364] As parts or members of Christ's body, the Christians are "aliens and strangers on earth."[365] In this sense, both the Christian church and the Christians have a double identity: being on earth and of heaven. Being on earth is transient and thus not of the essential identity, but a shadow; being of heaven is eternal, of the essential identity, and the body or reality. Without the body or reality, there will be no shadow. The existence of a shadow is for witness to the body or reality. The body of Christ and his various members on earth is for witness to Christ, who is not just "the head of the body, the church"[366] but "before all things,"[367] "the head over every power and authority."[368]

Then, the existence of the Christian church (the Greek word, "ekklesia," literally meaning called out or summoned forth, is the assembly of citizens in public space; the English word, "church," originating in the Greek "kuriakos," means of the Lord) helps one make sense of citizens and civil society by going beyond this temporary world and seeing the eternal identity of fellow citizens and the eternal country. Of course, there is a phenomenon one cannot ignore: the eternal identity as fellow citizens of heaven is ransomed from mortality by the head of this eternal country through giving his own life.

Just from this act of the head of the eternal country, one can begin

"Now I rejoice in what was suffered for you, and I fill up in my flesh what is still lacking in regard to Christ's afflictions, for the sake of his body, which is the church."

364 Revelation 21:2.
365 Hebrews 11: 13. 1 Peter 2:11.
366 Colossians 1:18.
367 Colossians 1:17.
368 Colossians 2:10.

to see what on earth being a citizen of the eternal country means. For unlike in other countries where "the rulers of the Gentiles lord it over them, and their high officials exercise authority over them," in this country, "whoever wants to become great among you must be your slave— just as the Son of Man did not come to be served, but to serve, and to give his life as a ransom for many."[369]

369 Matthew 20: 25–28.

Acknowledgements

Being able to be thankful is worthy of appreciation. In my quest for liberty, I have benefited from help in various forms from Ellis Sandoz, Erica Cooper, John von Heyking, Lee Trepanier, Bruce Fingerhut, Benjamin Fingerhut, Daniel Hsu, Qiu Hong, Zhang Bin, Sun Yi, Zhao Zhou, Zhang Keli, Roberta Green Ahmanson, Howard Fieldstad Ahmanson, Jr., David Aikman, Charlene L. Fu, Arne H. Fjeldstad, Ian Johnson, Beverly Jarrett, Cathy Bruckbauer, Prabhu Guptara, Thomas A. Hollweck, John W. Danford, Orlando Patterson, Zheng Ye, Huang Yikun, Cao Zhi, Chen Guiwen, Li Jin, Ma Li, Zhou Wei, Jul Medenblik, Sarah Chun, Joel A. Carpenter, John Bolt, Jin Tianming, Li Enping, Zhang Xiaofeng, You Guanhui, Li Xiaobai, Lu Bingxia, Yan Xin'en, Song Jun, Xi Lian, Sun Zexi, Lin Yaotang, Cai Mingwei, Xue Hanqing, Zhang He, Xu Guoyong, Lu Jun, Chi Gengjie, Ding Zupan, Ma Xiaoping, Liu Yao, Zeng Miao, Huang Youchang, Li Hua, Shen Jiajin, Hu Jian, Li Yinghua, Zhao Jie, Long Xueqing, He Pengyu, Caroline Comport, Brent Fulton, Narci Herr, Joann Pittman, Baby Lyn Cacho Resulta, Kris Mauren, Todd Huizinga, Fritz Wagner, Ben Cal, Vishal Arora, Paul Glader, Cristi Tepes, Richard A. Potts, Kristanto Hartadi, Bill Cross, Ken Hopper, Will Hopper, Neal Fuller, Angela Lu, Pan Fang, Li Ji, Zhang Butian, Zhao Yuebei, Wybe Bylsma, Li Yingqiang, Sun Pengfei, Sun Xinwei, Li Daosheng, Samuel Lamb, Stephen Tong, Xu Youfa, Liu Yang, Shen Ying, Ling Fenglei, Ma Huanli, Wang Ruohan, Yang Fu, Dai Jinbo, Peng Qiang, Joshua Wang, Sheng Yilai, Jiang Heping, Liu Cong, Rui Chenggang, Zhang Beifu, Fang Yun, Cai Guofen, Cai Wenmei, Xu Qinyuan, Min Huiquan, Li Xinyu, Yu Jie, David Walsh, Jim Dai, Mark Noll, George Marsden, John Wilson, Thomas S. Kidd, Glen G. Scorgie, Kevin Kelly, James Stoner, Sarah Beth Vosburg, Richard Wright, Natasha Percy, Dominic Steele, Donald Bishop, Jemma Bishop, Si Zhanjie,

Zhang Xinmei, John Yang, Lee Yih, Miltinnie Yih, Michael Bouterse, Shaun Bao, Harold Berman, John Witte, Jr., John Micklethwait, Miroslav Volf, Daniel Johnson, Eric McLuhan, Andy Crouch, Matthew Lee Anderson, Daniel Dreisbach, Eamonn Butler, D. Michael Lindsay, Gary Hopwood, Keith Stonehocker, Cliff Johnson, Rob Moll, Jeremy Weber, Tim Morgan, Tang Keyang, Jill Geisler, Martin Ostwald, Rodney Stark, Richard John Neuhaus, R. R. Reno, Richard Pipes, Anthony J. Blasi, Vincent Ostrom, Quentin Skinner, Otto Vervaart, G. R. Evans, Yuan Tseh Lee, Yang Xiaokai, James M. Buchanan, Kenneth J. Arrow, Yuri Pines, Charles Fornara, Robert Metcalf, Geoffrey Lloyd, Katharine Simms, Oscar Handlin, George Kateb, George McLean, Hu Yeping, Fenggang Yang, Wenyu Xie, Larry Iannaccone, Nathan Tarcov, Bruce Lincoln, Li Meng, Wolfgang P. Müeller, Joerg Müeller, Michael Zank, Daniel Bell, Lee Ward, Mark Henrie, John Vella, Jeremy Beer, Alan Boegehold, Hui Xie, Michael Gagarin, Edward Harris, Peter Landau, Roger Collins, John A. Eidsmoe, I. H. Palmier, Stephen B. Presser, Herwig Wolfram, Rachel Fulton, Michael A. Gillespie, Christopher Cullen, David Hart, Ben Sikma, Jon Roland, Eric Foner, Josiah Ober, Claudio Katz, W. V. Harris, Donald Kagan, Leonard Liggio, Philip Pettit, Glen W. Bowersock, Paul H. Rubin, Robert E. Somerville, Leila Choukroune, Randy Peerenboom, Eugenio F. Biagini, Raphael Sealey, Neil MacCormick, Brian Tamanaha, Margaret M. Mitchell, Robert Munro, Rocco Pezzimenti, Malcolm Schofield, Peter Linehan, Linda Woodhead, Shadia Drury, Robert Dahl, Bertell Ollman, W. Wesley McDonald, Eric W. Robinson, Jeff Hart, Andrew Lintott, Julia Crick, Constantin Fasolt, Ian Moxon, P. J. Rhodes, Fergus Millar, Martial Staub, Ramsay MacMullen, John A. Taylor, Blaise Nagy, Richard Kaeuper, Bruce H. Mann, Tony Judt, Anthony Reid, Edward Friedman, Richard Seaford, Lisi Oliver, Chris Bellitto, Timothy D. Barnes, Lester L. Field, Jr., Richard J. Ross, Stephen Morillo, Kanishka Jayasuriya, William Aird, Paul Gottfried, Laurence Claus, Arend Lijphart, Uta-Renate Blumenthal, Shadi Bartsch, William Scheuerman, J. M. Hobson, Tom Bethell, Graeme Lang, Walter Prevenier, David Schaberg, Robert D. Putnam, Charles Tilly, Jules Lobel, Bernard S. Jackson, Lamin Sanneh, Mario Liverani, Jeff Goldsworthy, Joseph Blenkinsopp, Shaye Cohen, Randy E. Barnett, Roger Trigg, Tibor Machan, Thomas Pangle, Richard Elliott Friedman, Adam

J. Kosto, L. W. Hurtado, Robert Parker, Moulakis Athanasios, Robert Swanson, Joseph Levine, Carlo Ginzburg, R.C. van Caenegem, Binkley Woods, Michael Cook, Harry R. Lewis, John Jirik, Paul Kennedy, Shashi Tharoor, Deepak Lal, Jonathan Anderson, Wang Gungwu, Choyun Hsu, Michael Backman, Ezra F. Vogel, Chenggang Xu, Alan Macfarlane, Daniel Franklin, Joseph S. Nye, Jr., Wayne A. Grudem, Jeff Sellers, Terry Mattingly, Paul Marshall, James Rhodes, Glen Stassen, Stephen B. Presser, Carrie Gracie, Nik Gowing, Leslie Hook, Marie-Eve Reny, Peng Dingding, Zhang Heng, Yang Shuang, Li Shushan, Zeng Zhuokun, Nie Yiting, Xu Kaiha, Xu Xinhua, Cui Xueyun, Xu Sa, Huang Jini, Huang Rongguo, Nie Weizhang, Li Wanhua, and some other unique souls I regretfully fail to remember here. My heartfelt gratitude goes to them all. Without them, my history of freedom would have been not only different but also impossible.